The Cambridge Companion to the Saxophone

The Cambridge Companion to the Saxophone tells the story of the
saxophone, its history and technical development from its invention
by Adolphe Sax *c.* 1840 to the end of the twentieth century. It
includes extensive accounts of the instrument's history in jazz, rock
and classical music as well as providing performance guides.
Discussion of the repertoire and soloists from 1850 to the present
day includes accessible descriptions of contemporary techniques and
trends, and moves into the electronic age with midi wind
instruments. There is a dicussion of the function of the saxophone in
the orchestra, in 'light music', and in rock and pop studios, as well as
of the saxophone quartet as an important chamber music medium.
The contributors to this volume are some of the finest performers
and experts on the saxophone.

Richard Ingham is a lecturer at Leeds College of Music and is a
member of the Northern Saxophone Quartet.

Cambridge Companions to Music

The Cambridge Companion to the

SAXOPHONE

EDITED BY
Richard Ingham

CAMBRIDGE
UNIVERSITY PRESS

PUBLISHED BY THE PRESS SYNDICATE OF THE UNIVERSITY OF CAMBRIDGE
The Pitt Building, Trumpington Street, Cambridge CB2 1RP, United Kingdom

CAMBRIDGE UNIVERSITY PRESS
The Edinburgh Building, Cambridge CB2 2RU, United Kingdom   http://www.cup.cam.ac.uk
40 West 20th Street, New York, NY 10011–4211, USA   http://www.cup.org
10 Stamford Road, Oakleigh, Melbourne 3166, Australia

First published 1998

Printed in the United Kingdom at the University Press, Cambridge

Typeset in Adobe Minion 10.75/14 pt, in QuarkXPress™   [SE]

A catalogue record for this book is available from the British Library

Library of Congress cataloguing in publication data

The Cambridge companion to the saxophone / edited by Richard Ingham.
        p.   cm. – (Cambridge companions to music)
Includes bibliographical references (p.   ) and index.
ISBN 0 521 59348 4
1. Saxophone.   I. Ingham, Richard.   II. Series.
ML975.C36   1998
788.7–dc21   98-17404   CIP   MN

ISBN 0 521 59348 4 hardback
ISBN 0 521 59666 1 paperback

From saxophone quartets by Strauss
On days off from the Opera House,
Or works by Milhaud and Ravel
Or Villa-Lobos in Brazil,
To Lester leaping in possessed
By his brass-belled iconoclast,
The sound we hear is yours, Adolphe,
Posterity, its howling wolf,
Time salivating on a reed
And fingering at breakneck speed.

from Douglas Dunn, *An Address to Adolphe
Sax in Heaven* (*Northlight*, 1988)

Contents

Illustrations

Notes on the contributors

Don Ashton, MIMIT, a lifelong champion of the saxophone, author, writer and
arranger, is involved in teaching as varied in level as in scope. Players and
groups of all standards discover his music to reflect an intimate understanding of the saxophone, its sounds and its capabilities in both experienced
and less practised hands. This intimacy extends to the saxophone's mechanics
– with over forty years of experience he is a partner of Woodwind &
Company, repairers well-respected in the UK music industry.

Chris 'Snake' Davis studied at Leeds College of Music and began playing soul and
Motown as the front man for The Alligator Shoes. Following a period of study
on cruise liners and in New York, he formed the band Snake Davis and the
Charmers which toured Europe to great success. Wider exposure for his
talents has come via many performances for television, and many of today's
major recording artists have also appreciated Chris's ability, including Swing
Out Sister, Lisa Stansfield, Paul McCartney, Pet Shop Boys and M-People.

Claude Delangle won first prizes in saxophone and chamber music at the Paris
Conservatoire (CNSM) before beginning his career as an international
soloist. In 1986 Pierre Boulez invited him to join the Ensemble
InterContemporain; he has made twenty recordings and has been Professor of
Saxophone at the Paris Conservatoire since 1988 (following Adolphe Sax,
Marcel Mule and Daniel Deffayet). He is President of the International
Association for the Development of the Saxophone and of the International
Saxophone Committee. Numerous works have been dedicated to him, and his
first performances include works by Berio, Ligeti, Takemitsu, Denisov and
Stockhausen.

Thomas Dryer-Beers received his B.Mus. from Indiana University under Dr
Eugene Rousseau and M.Mus. at North Texas State University under James
Riggs. Since coming to England in 1988 he has taught as a peripatetic music
teacher, lecturer, orchestral and chamber music coach, and private instructor.
He has performed at several World Saxophone Congresses and was a recitalist
at the first and second British Saxophone Congresses. With the Texas
Saxophone Quartet he was an award winner in the Fischoff Chamber Music
Competition and was a member of Saxtet. Thomas is Retail Manager for
Wood, Wind and Reed of Cambridge.

John Helliwell worked as a computer programmer for two years before touring
with the Alan Bown Set in the 1960s. In 1973 he joined the band Supertramp
on saxophone and clarinet, moving to California in 1975, and recording and
touring extensively until 1988, during which time the band's great international success included the albums *Crime of the Century* and *Breakfast in
America*. They have sold fifty million albums to date. Session work in
California and a period of study at the Royal Northern College of Music in

Manchester occupied John before Supertramp began their 'It's About Time' world tour in 1997.

Kyle Horch is a free-lance saxophonist based in London, and has given recital and chamber music performances at the Purcell Room, Queen Elizabeth Hall, British and World Saxophone Congresses, and at many other venues in Britain and abroad. He is a member of the Mistral Saxophone Quartet; other work includes concerts and recordings with symphony orchestras, contemporary and chamber music groups, dance bands and theatrical ensembles. He has given masterclasses at many institutions in Britain, Ireland, Switzerland, Australia, Norway and the USA. He teaches at the Royal College of Music in London.

Richard Ingham is a member of the Northern Saxophone Quartet, with whom he has performed in Britain, Europe, the USA and Japan. He has broadcast and recorded many items of the solo saxophone repertoire and has presented masterclasses in conservatoires in the UK and abroad. He is Visiting Professor of Jazz at the University of St Andrews and lectures at Leeds College of Music. He was chairman of the Clarinet and Saxophone Society of Great Britain (1989–92) and co-directed the first British Saxophone Congresses from 1990 to 1996. He has premièred several new works for midi wind controller.

Gordon Lewin studied at the Royal Manchester College of Music and has had extensive experience in the light music genre as a free-lance player with the orchestras of George Melachrino, Frank Cordell, Philip Greene, Peter Yorke, Robert Farnon, the BBC Television Orchestra, and as a long-term member of the Krein Saxophone Quartet. Radio, television, recording and film sessions were combined with twenty years in the music department of Middlesex University as visiting tutor of clarinet, saxophone and arranging. A prolific writer for woodwind, he has had many arrangements and compositions published.

Thomas Liley has performed throughout the United States in solo and chamber music recitals and as a concerto soloist, and has long been involved with the North American Saxophone Alliance, serving as State Chairman and as Editor of the *Saxophone Symposium*, the quarterly journal of the Alliance. A former member of the United States Navy Band in Washington DC, he has been Professor of Saxophone at the University of Florida and at the University of Kansas, and is currently a member of the music faculties of Joliet Junior College and Olivet Nazarene University in Kankakee, Illinois.

Jean-Denis Michat was a prize-winner at the Paris Conservatoire (CNSM). He is Professor of Saxophone at the Conservatoire in Lyons, Assistant Professor at the Paris Conservatoire, and teaches at the European Summer University in Gap. He is a founder member of the Quatuor Argan and conducts Les Temps Modernes and the saxophone ensemble L'artisinat furieux. As a composer, he writes mainly chamber and vocal works. He is president of the Rhones-Alpes regional Association Pour l'Essor du Saxophone.

David Roach was a founder member of the Myrha Saxophone Quartet with John Harle, Andy Findon and Irita Kutchmy. He has been a member of the Michael Nyman Band since 1983 and the London Saxophonic since 1994, and has made many recordings. He is Professor of Saxophone and Chamber Music at the Guildhall School of Music and Drama in London. David has played for, among others, the Philharmonia Orchestra, the London Symphony Orchestra, the London Sinfonietta, the Royal National Theatre, Frank Sinatra, Elton John and composers Dominic Muldowney, Rachel Portman and Jennie Muskett.

Stephen Trier studied with Frederick Thurston and Walter Lear at the Royal College of Music in London. He was a member of the Royal Philharmonic Orchestra (1950–6), Sadler's Wells Opera (1953–6), the London Symphony Orchestra (1955–68) and the London Philharmonic (1964–95), as well as playing with many chamber groups. He was Professor of Saxophone at the Guildhall School of Music from 1966 to 1988, and Professor of Bass Clarinet and Saxophone at the Royal College of Music from 1970 to 1997. He edited the English-language version of *Le Saxophone en Jouant* by Jean-Marie Londeix.

Nick Turner is a founder member of the Northern Saxophone Quartet, and has performed extensively in Britain as well as giving masterclasses and recitals in the USA, Japan and Europe. Since graduating from the University of Leeds he has combined a busy free-lance career with a very successful teaching practice, also giving concerto and recital performances on both clarinet and saxophone. He is a visiting tutor in saxophone at the University of Leeds, and is a clinician and adviser on woodwind performance and pedagogy.

Preface

The story of the saxophone is one of frustration, despair and discovery in the nine-teenth century, and one of limitless horizons in the twentieth century. By persuad-ing my fellow contributors to tell this story, incorporating a historical overview with authentic technical and performance guidelines, I hope that this book goes some way towards capturing in print the multi-faceted nature of an instrument which, on the brink of the twenty-first century, enjoys a popularity far beyond the imagination of M. Sax, the eponymous hero.

I am grateful to all the authors, who are outstanding performers and experts in their respective fields, first of all for their writing, which I have been privileged to read and study at length during the editing process, and also for their time and patience in answering queries and providing much additional information beyond their original tasks. The history of the saxophone is not extensively docu-mented, and indeed in some areas is documented for the first time in this volume; consequently much patient but rewarding detective work has been necessary. Of existing writing it soon became clear that the books by Harry Gee, Frederick Hemke, Wally Horwood and Jean-Marie Londeix have had an enormous impact on our subject, making this text a slightly easier proposition than it might other-wise have been. Wally Horwood, who sadly died in 1996 and who was to have contributed to this volume, will long be remembered for his scholarship and enthusiasm.

The subject area, encompassing classical music, jazz and rock, is most certainly a wide one, and I am particularly pleased that the authors represent an equally wide cross-section of the international saxophone fraternity. I hope that the content will be attractive to both the casual reader and the saxophile, both of whom will find that the book contains much scientific and academic rigour, yet never loses its aim of telling a story. A book of this length cannot hope to be com-prehensive in every area; information, lists and tables are offered where it is felt that the publication of this material will be beneficial to the future development of the instrument.

My thanks are due to many people who have helped to bring this book to frui-tion. It would not be possible to catalogue here the full extent of Don Ashton's assistance; I will just mention his tireless efforts in producing all the diagrams and charts, music type setting and provision of computer hardware, in conjunction with his scientific knowledge of the subject, kind hospitality and unfailing encour-agement. My colleague Peter Nichols was kind enough to provide an excellent translation of the text by Claude Delangle and Jean-Denis Michat, and I am very glad that I wandered into John Brown's office at Leeds College of Music one after-noon, a meeting which led to John offering his considerable artistic skills in the service of the book.

My wife Julia has tolerated the closed study door for longer than she ought, and has at the same time prevented two very small puzzled children from playing games with pieces of paper and photographs which their father might not have appreciated. I would like to thank Penny Souster at Cambridge University Press for initiating this exciting project, and for her gentle but readily available guidance at all stages of its conception and writing. Many colleagues have provided information and assistance, a small number of whom are mentioned in the Acknowledgements; in particular I am indebted to Eugene Rousseau and Dennis Langfield for their continued help and inspiration.

Acknowledgements

Illustrations

Acknowledgements for kind permission to reproduce illustrations are due to the following:

Association Internationale Adolphe Sax: Figs. 1.1, 1.2

John Robert Brown, pencil drawings: Figs. 8.1–8.7

Lamplight Photography: jacket cover and Figs. 10.1, 10.5

Bruce Ronkin: Fig. 4.1

Photography by S. R. H. Spicer, The Shrine to Music Museum, Vermillion, South Dakota: Figs. 1.3, 1.4.

Eugene Rousseau: Figs. 3.2, 4.2, 4.4, 4.5, 5.1

The Shrine to Music Museum Archives: Fig. 3.1

Sousa Archive, University of Illinois, Champaign Urbana: Fig. 2.2

Yamaha Company: Fig. 2.9

Yanagisawa Company: Fig. 2.8

The extract from *An Address to Adolphe Sax in Heaven* is reproduced by kind permission of the author Douglas Dunn and publishers Faber and Faber (poem from *Northlight* collection, 1988).

Music examples

Reproduced by permission of Editions Alphonse Leduc, Paris/United Music Publishers Ltd: Fig. 10.4; Intersong Music Ltd: Ex. 9.1; Jobete Music UK Ltd: Ex. 9.2.

Musical instruments: All Brass and Woodwind (Leeds).

Research assistance: David Cook, Phyllis Danner, Susan McKenzie, Sarah Markham, Julia Mills, Debra Richtmeyer, Peter Nichols, Bruce Ronkin, John Sampen, William Street, Caryl Sutcliffe, Alec Sykes and many others.

Secretarial assistance: Nicky Croft, Katherine Ingham.

Abbreviations

CASS   Clarinet & Saxophone Society of Great Britain

NASA   North American Saxophone Alliance

Pitch registers are indicated using the Helmholtz scheme:

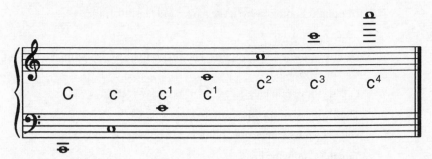

1 Invention and development

THOMAS LILEY

Introduction

The word 'saxophone' means 'the sound of Sax' – specifically that of Adolphe Sax. The Greek word 'phone', according to the *Oxford English Dictionary*, relates in particular to vocal sounds, so we should not be surprised that the saxophone is often described as a 'singing' instrument. In fact, the saxophone is the most flexible and expressive of musical instruments, exceeded, perhaps, only by the human voice. The human voice, of course, is capable of sounds as varied as cheerleading and Schubert lieder; it is capable of producing guttural sounds and fine-spun eloquence, of rabble-rousing and of inspiring. The saxophone is similar in its potential to move people, both viscerally and emotionally.

As a 'singing' instrument, the saxophone is unmatched by its mechanical counterparts. This is often reflected in its classical repertoire, but there can be little doubt that the saxophone is the pre-eminent jazz instrument. If jazz first came from the work-shouts and the blues sung in the nineteenth century, then it is natural that a 'singing' instrument such as the saxophone should be well suited to jazz and popular music. What is remarkable is that the instrument took so long to be adopted by jazz musicians.

The saxophone is the invention of a single man, Adolphe Sax. Both a thinker and a doer, he had the genius to conceive a new and versatile instrument, the practical background to bring his theories to fruition and the foresight to create the mechanisms necessary to ensure that it would become an important part of the musical world.

Adolphe Sax

Born in Dinant, Belgium, on 6 November 1814, Adolphe Sax was the first child of Charles and Maria Sax (christened Antoine Joseph, he was called Adolphe from childhood). Shortly afterwards the family moved to Brussels and Charles began a new and successful career which was to profoundly influence his son – he turned from the manufacture of cabinets and tables to the manufacture of clarinets and brass instruments.

[1]

Fig. 1.1 Dinant, Belgium, birthplace of Adolphe Sax

Charles was appointed Instrument Maker to the Court of the Netherlands, and is perhaps best remembered for his version of the *cor omnitonique*. The instrument was intended as a solution to the numerous and cumbersome crooks of the hand horn, but lost out to the lighter-weight and more efficient valved horn.

Adolphe was often to be found in his father's workshop and at an early age learned the skills necessary to the profession. In addition to the instruction he received from his father, he also received a formal education and music instruction at the Brussels Conservatory. He studied voice and flute; later he also studied clarinet. It is said that Sax could have pursued a successful career as a clarinettist, but his interest in overcoming the instrument's acoustical shortcomings kept returning him to the workshop to seek solutions.

Sax's skill as an instrument maker grew rapidly, and his work soon began to attract favourable comment. Horwood suggests that Charles was principally concerned with the production of instruments for sale and that he left various experimental projects to Adolphe. These experiments included the development of valved bugle-horns – the saxhorns – and the combination of a conical metal tube with a single-reed mouthpiece – the saxophone.[1]

Another important success of this period was the construction of a vastly improved bass clarinet. It was the bass clarinet which first brought Adolphe Sax to Paris in 1839, where he sought out Isaac Dacosta, solo clarinet at the Paris Academy of Music and creator of his own improved bass clarinet. Sax persuaded Dacosta to listen to him perform the solo from Meyerbeer's *Les Huguenots* and to acknowledge the superiority of Sax's instrument. During the course of this first visit Sax met many prominent musicians, including Berlioz, Halévy, Kastner and Meyerbeer. These influential contacts were to prove crucial to Sax when, in 1842, he returned to Paris for good.

Sax's decision to leave Brussels was sealed by officials of the Brussels Exhibition of 1841. Among the items which Sax prepared for the Exhibition were several clarinets and, Sax's friend Georges Kastner tells us, a saxophone. This would have been the first public presentation of the saxophone except that, Kastner continues, the instrument 'was sent flying with a kick by an unknown person at a time when the inventor, Adolphe Sax, was away'.[2] The examining committee recommended the young craftsman's display for the Premier Gold Medal, the Exhibition's highest award. The recommendation, however, was rejected by the Central Jury, which declared against his youth: if Sax were to receive the first prize this year, there would be nothing to give him the next year. Sax's response was typical of the man: 'If I am too young for the gold medal, I am too old for the silver'. Paris beckoned.[3]

Shortly after this incident Sax was visited by an influential aide to the French king Louis-Philippe. Lieutenant General Comte de Rumigny spoke to Sax of ambitious plans to revitalise French military bands, and saw the Belgian's work as a means to that end. Sax was further encouraged by a letter from composer Jacques Halévy, whom he had met in Paris. The self-confident instrument maker left Brussels behind and moved to Paris with his ideas, his creations and his hopes in the spring of 1842.

Successes and opposition

Sax's arrival was heralded by Hector Berlioz in the 12 June 1842 issue of the highly regarded *Journal des débats*. In a column entitled 'Adolphe Sax's Musical Instruments' Berlioz introduced the young inventor to the French public. After a few paragraphs in which Berlioz describes the development of musical instruments, he presents:

> M. Adolphe Sax of Brussels, whose work we have just examined. . . . He is a man of penetrating mind; lucid, tenacious, with a perseverance against all trials, and great skill. . . . He is at the same time a calculator, acoustician, and as necessary also a smelter, turner and engraver. He can think and act. He invents and accomplishes.[4]

Fig. 1.2 Bust of Adolphe Sax

There follows a description of several of Sax's instruments, including the first detailed account of the saxophone. Berlioz closes with the prediction that 'Composers will be much indebted to M. Sax when his instruments come into general use. May he persevere; he will not lack support from friends of art.'[5]

One of the results of this announcement was a public concert that same month at the Paris Conservatoire, at which Sax played proficiently and talked eloquently about his instruments. Sax met and was befriended by many of the most distinguished musicians in Paris, including Auber, Habeneck, Spontini and Donizetti. Funds were gathered for the establishment of the Adolphe Sax Musical Instrument Factory at No. 10 Rue Saint Georges.

He also aroused the beginnings of a bitter enmity between himself and the established instrument makers of Paris. They had been put on notice that the young Belgian would undoubtedly challenge their businesses, and his close association with so many prominent musicians clearly threatened their success. Thus began a round of threats, thefts and legal battles (and, possibly, even an attempt on his life) that would pursue him for decades. Berlioz, in a letter dated 8 October 1843, wrote:

> It is scarcely to be believed that this gifted young artist should be finding it
> difficult to maintain his position and make a career in Paris. The
> persecutions he suffers are worthy of the Middle Ages and recall the antics of
> the enemies of Benvenuto, the Florentine sculptor. They lure away his
> workmen, steal his designs, accuse him of insanity, and bring legal
> proceedings against him. Such is the hatred inventors inspire in rivals who
> are incapable of inventing anything themselves.[6]

Among the tactics employed by these adversaries was an engineered opposition to the general acceptance of Sax's instruments in orchestras. Many important performers served as consultants to instrument manufacturers and refused to play on an instrument by a rival maker. One such incident occurred in 1843, when, while writing his opera *Dom Sébastien*, Gaetano Donizetti prepared a part for the Sax bass clarinet. The principal clarinettist of the Opera orchestra threatened that, if the instrument were to be used, the orchestra would walk out. Donizetti, despite his high regard for Sax, was forced to bow to the musicians' demands.

The animosity between Sax and his rivals intensified when the French government made an announcement that would affect every wind instrument maker in France: the reform of the French military bands. The abysmal state of French military music was an embarrassment to French patriotism and prestige. To address the situation a commission consisting of musical, military and acoustical representatives, and headed by General de Rumigny, met on 25 February 1845. Manufacturers were requested to submit instruments for consideration by the commission; only Sax gave a full response to the invitation.

Perhaps the most auspicious event of the commission's activities occurred on 22 April of that year when two bands performed in competition before an audience, estimated at 20,000, gathered on the Champ du Mars in Paris. One band, under Michele Carafa, director of the *Gymnase de musique militaire* and a member of the commission, represented a conservative reorganisation of the existing ensembles. The other band, directed by M. Fessy, demonstrated fully Sax's comprehensive reforms and his instruments – the saxophone and, especially, the saxhorn.

Each band was to consist of forty-five players and would perform arrangements of music by Adolphe Adam and a work selected by their conductor. The audience declared Sax's ensemble the clear winner, and the commission took the results under advisement as part of the process. The final report, submitted to the Minister of War on 9 August 1845, was a distinct victory for the Belgian – the government had declared a near monopoly mandating the use of his instruments.

Rival instrument makers had been placed in an untenable position. Faced with financial destruction, they consolidated against the common enemy from Dinant. *L'Association générale des ouvriers en instruments de musique* (the United Association of Instrument Makers) was established to protect their interests.

One of the Association's first lawsuits opposed Sax's application to patent the saxophone. Various contradictory lines of attack were made: the instrument does not exist; if it does exist, it is a completely unmusical invention; and, in any event, it is not original because it already exists in other forms. Among the presumed antecedents were the 'English tenoroon', a bass clarinet by Desfontenelles, and the German bathyphone by Wieprecht. In another tactic several saxophones were purchased and sent to other countries; Sax's identification was removed and the instruments were then re-engraved to indicate foreign manufacture. These forgeries were poorly executed and quickly revealed as a ruse.

Of greater legal consequence was the contention that, because the saxophone had been performed before a large public audience during the contest on the Champ du Mars, it was invalid for patent. Here the Association could cite a legal precedent. Sax's response was direct and dramatic: he challenged his opponents to create the instrument (which did or did not exist) known as the saxophone and he withdrew his patent request for a year to give them ample time to do so. The plaintiffs were unable to create a rival instrument.

To respond in the form of a challenge was typical of Sax. Also typical was the impatience that led him to reapply for the patent shortly before the year's respite had elapsed. Sax was granted a patent for the saxophone family on 22 June 1846, sometimes referred to as the birth date of the saxophone. The Association, however, was not through.

The Revolution of 1848 provided the Association with a new opportunity when King Louis-Philippe was forced to abdicate. Louis-Philippe's staff, which included many of Sax's most influential supporters, fled with him. Sax's lengthy relationship with the king was now a serious liability, and the 1845 reforms of military bands were revoked by the new government in a bill introduced by the Association. Orders for new Sax instruments were cancelled and deliveries were returned. The closure of the factory seemed inevitable until an anonymous benefactor stepped forward; his generosity unintentionally led the impulsive Sax to bankruptcy.

The anonymous business associate, concerned by rising unemployment in Paris during the turbulent period, gave Sax 30,000 francs to pay his workmen. Because no receipt was requested, Sax understood the sum to be a gift rather than a loan. The benefactor died in 1852, with the money unaccounted for in his estate. Sax rashly acknowledged in writing that he had received the money as a loan and was immediately ordered to repay the debt within twenty-four hours. He fled to London and pleaded his case by mail. His pleas were ignored and he returned to Paris and financial ruin.

Battles and bankruptcy

The series of lawsuits and appeals begun in 1846 would consume Sax's physical and financial resources throughout the remainder of his life. Although there seems to be no evidence that the Association was involved in the circumstances which led to Sax's bankruptcy, they were undoubtedly pleased by the turn of events. Sax's ability as an inventor was not matched by his acumen as a businessman nor as a litigant.

The Revolution of 1848 greatly affected Sax's legal status. Whereas in late 1847 his patents had been upheld by the courts, by 1849 an appeal by the Association rendered the patents for *bugles-à-cylindres* and saxotrombas void. The saxophone patent, however, was sustained. Appeals and counter-appeals by both Sax and the Association led to an eventual conclusion at the Imperial Court at Rouen in 1854. Eight years after the original lawsuit was filed the high court ruled completely in favour of Sax, declaring that his patents were valid and that he was entitled to damages and reimbursements from the Association. None the less, damage had been done. Time and money which could have been spent creatively and productively had been expended on seemingly endless legal procedures.

Undoubtedly Sax had several reasons to be optimistic at the apparent conclusion of his legal battles. In April 1854 he was appointed Musical Instrument Maker to the Household Troops of Emperor Napoleon III. The emperor further showed his favour by assisting Sax in his bankruptcy. Arrangements were made with Sax's numerous creditors, allowing him to reopen his factory on the Rue Saint Georges, now at No. 50.

Despite his vindication in the courts and the renewed support from the emperor, Sax was adversely affected by his years of legal battles. Perhaps his natural contentiousness was intensified by the slanderous misrepresentations to which he was subjected, or perhaps he felt that he now understood the legal system and could use it to his advantage. Whatever the cause, there can be little doubt that his health was also an important factor.

Since 1853 Sax had been concerned about a dark spot on his lip which had blackened and grown in size. The tumour was diagnosed as malignant; surgical removal of the tumour, including lip and part of the jaw, seemed inevitable. The cancer obstructed Sax's throat to the extent that it became necessary for him to be fed by means of a tube. The recommended operation was delayed by the lawsuits, and Sax cast about for a cure that would avoid disfiguring surgery. He was introduced to Dr Vries, an Indian doctor in Paris, who had achieved some success in treating incurable ailments, and in 1859 the black spot began to decrease until it had completely and miraculously disappeared.

It was during this troubled period that Sax made the decision to return to the courts, but now as a plaintiff. In 1859 Sax sued Pierre Louis Gautrot for a perceived infringement of his saxophone patent. In 1856 Gautrot had patented a family of instruments by M. Sarrus. The instruments, called sarrusophones, were too similar to the saxophone in Sax's judgement. Like the saxophone, the sarrusophone is conical in shape, has the same written range from b to f^3,[7] and is grouped in similar keys and registers. The sounds produced by the two instrument families, however, are markedly different, and the court ruled against Sax, deeming the instruments to be completely different.

Sax again returned to the courtroom as a plaintiff in 1866, and this time was successful in a suit which did him no good. A well-known opera singer, Marie-Constance Sass, had grown dissatisfied with her name and had changed it to 'Sax'. The inventor's objections, upheld by the court, led her to suggest 'Saxe' as an alternative. This was also unacceptable to Sax and to the court, whose ruling gave Sax a victory of doubtful significance.

Other events were of more value to Sax. In 1847 he was appointed Musical Director of the stage brass band at the Opera, a position he would hold until his death, and which would become his sole reliable source of income.[8] On 7 June 1857, Sax was asked to institute a saxophone class at the Paris Conservatoire; he remained in that position until the catastrophic war of 1870 between France and Prussia. He received medals and awards from the emperor and around this time became the father of two sons and a daughter. Charles, born in October 1856, died in infancy in 1858. Adele, born 29 November 1858, lived until 1938, and his son Adolphe Edouard, born 29 September 1859, lived until 1945. Adolphe Edouard continued the family business until it was sold to the Henri Selmer Company in 1928.[9]

Sax continued to present his instruments at various exhibitions and in 1867, at the Paris International Exhibition, was awarded the Grand Prize. Horwood reports that the display included an example of every musical instrument Sax had invented or improved. The centrepiece was an exquisite gold-plated alto saxophone.[10]

This distinction may have been the apex of Sax's life. Because Sax had regained solvency since his bankruptcy of 1852, he was astonished to learn that because the recovery had not been officially recorded by the Commerce Court, he was dismissed from the Legion of Honour. The decoration, bestowed by the emperor in 1849, was one of Sax's most distinguished awards and he wore the cross with justifiable pride. Its loss in 1860 because of an administrative omission humiliated him.

The emperor himself was deposed after the French surrender at Sedan to the Prussians in September of 1870, costing Sax his most influential ally. Many of Sax's close colleagues passed away in the years between 1867 and 1871 – Kastner in 1867, Rossini in 1868, Berlioz in 1869, and Auber and Fétis in 1871. Their counsel and support would be sorely missed in the years ahead.

By this time he was estranged from his brother Alphonse, also an inventor and instrument maker, with whom he had quarrelled at the 1862 Exhibition in London. His father, Charles, had died in 1865, and in 1871 his brother Charles-Joseph passed away; both had provided important assistance at the factory on the Rue Saint Georges.

Sax had been unable to take full benefit of the opportunities his exclusive patents had afforded him. When his patents ceased in the mid-1860s, other instrument manufacturers moved quickly on the expired patents, and orders to the Sax factory diminished. As his financial situation worsened, he was struck another blow.

The French defeat at Sedan caused a number of financial rescissions, including the close of the saxophone class at the Conservatoire in 1870; it would not be reinstated until 1942. Not only was Sax deprived of an important source of income, the future of the saxophone was endangered. Realising that without teachers there could not be students for the new instrument, Sax offered to continue to teach without fee; his proposal was rejected. In 1873 Sax, for the second time, was declared bankrupt.

The Rue Saint Georges factory was shut down, its contents sold to appease creditors. Sax's acclaimed collection of 467 musical instruments was sold in December 1877; many examples are still in museums in Brussels and Paris.[11]

All that remained were the lawsuits and the position of Musical Director at the Opera. The Association had continued to contest the judgement of 1854; throughout the 1880s Sax persevered in his battle for the compensation due him but was never to receive the reparations he had been awarded.

A poignant final petition came from Sax in 1887 in the journal *La Musique des Familles*. In his 'Appeal to the Public' the seventy-two-year-old Sax asks once again for justice in his attempts to gain restitution from the Association after twenty-six years of waiting. This remarkable document brought no response from the legal system.[12] It did succeed, however, in motivating several musicians, led by composer Paul Lacôme,

Fig. 1.3 Alto saxophone by Adolphe Sax, *c.* 1857

in their own appeal on Sax's behalf. The request resulted in a modest pension for the aged inventor.

In keeping with the turbulence of his life, there is also controversy about the date of Sax's death. Several sources, including *Grove*, Horwood, and Ronkin, cite 4 February 1894 as the date of his death. Gee gives, simply, 1894, while Kochnitzky says that 'Sax lived to the age of eighty'.[13] Because Sax was born 6 November 1814, this implies that he lived past 6 November in 1894. The correct date, found in *Baker's*, Deans, and Haine, is 7 February 1894.

The saxophone: theories of invention

Various theories surround the creation of the saxophone, many of which are as complex and confusing as the lawsuits which plagued its creator. Several of these theories seem to have derived some credibility from their mention in the lawsuit of 1846 in which Sax's patent of the saxophone was challenged and, ultimately, upheld. There are, in fact, precedents for Sax's creation, of which his challengers seem to have been unaware.

Frederick Hemke mentions an Argentine instrument cited by Bessaraboff. The instrument is made of a cow's horn whose tip is shaped to resemble a single-reed mouthpiece with a thin reed of bone bound by a silk thread. It is said to have been derived from a similar and even older instrument.[14]

Another presumed ancestor of the saxophone is the alto fagotto. This instrument, invented by William Meikle of Strathaven, in Lanarkshire, and made by George Wood of London in 1830, is 'a conical wooden tube shaped like a bassoon, but sounded by means of a single-reed attached to the end of a bassoon-like crook'.[15] Referred to by Sax's rivals in their suits, the instrument has received several names, including caledonica, tenoroon and dolciano. There is a photograph in Bessaraboff.[16]

An instrument created in 1807 by Desfontenelles, a clock maker in Liseux, was also presented as a predecessor to the saxophone. The joining of a wooden conical tube with a clarinet mouthpiece was untested until Jaap Kool played the instrument in about 1930. He discovered that, unlike the saxophone which overblows an octave, the Desfontenelles instrument produces twelfths, as does the clarinet, and therefore is not a prototype of the saxophone. The instrument is in the collection at the Paris Conservatoire[17] and is pictured in Horwood.[18]

A still-less likely challenger was the bathyphone. Its creator, Friedrich Wilhelm Wieprecht, is credited with the invention of the tuba in 1835 and an improved contrabassoon. The bathyphone is described by Carse as a contrabass clarinet with a 'wide tube doubled like a bassoon, and the eighteen note-holes were all covered by keys working on rod-axles, and arranged in two groups. The metal bell pointed upwards, and at the upper end the bore was continued in a metal tube or crook bent over towards the player.'[19] The instrument, therefore, has no similarity to the saxophone, but the antagonism between the two inventors provided fuel for the legal fires. Baines provides a photograph.[20]

One other candidate proposed as a predecessor to the saxophone is the Hungarian *tárogató*. This primitive instrument has a conical wooden bore and may be seen in Baines.[21] It produced its sound with a double reed until it was modernised by W. J. Schunda of Budapest around 1900, long after the saxophone's invention. In addition to providing the instrument with a single-reed mouthpiece, Schunda also gave it a complete key system.[22]

Opinions of how Sax invented the saxophone fall into three categories according to Hemke: (1) Sax was searching for a clarinet that could play octaves rather than twelfths; (2) he substituted the cup mouthpiece of the ophicleide with a single-reed mouthpiece; and (3) he experimented with a single-reed mouthpiece on a rudimentary bassoon. Still others say that the invention happened by accident or by mistake.[23] Sax's son, Adolphe Edouard, said in 1925 that his father's work was intentional and well thought out, the 'construction of a brass instrument equipped with a vibrating reed and adapted to a parabolic cone'.[24]

Similar confusion exists concerning the exact date of the saxophone's invention. The suggested year of invention varies from sometime around 1840 to 1846, the year of the saxophone patent. Sax himself did not indicate the date, but Maurice Hamel wrote that his father, Henry, a very close friend of the inventor, had said that Sax created the saxophone in 1838. Hamel states that the saxophone came into existence soon after Sax's new bass clarinet, which was presented at the Belgian Exposition of 1835. Hamel's handwritten recollections give the most credible date for the invention of the saxophone.[25]

Early uses

While one may not be surprised that Sax and his supporters found many opportunities to present the new instrument in the fertile musical life of Paris, it is interesting to note how quickly the saxophone spread to other countries. Frederick Hemke and Harry Gee provide us with the names of several saxophone pioneers who travelled to a remarkable number of countries and who laid the foundation for today's performers. Adolphe Sax, of course, was the first to play his creation, but the future of the instrument depended on its being heard by large audiences in a variety of venues. Only names remain for many of these saxophonists – Auroux, Beeckman, Cordier, Demange, Hernandez, Lecerf and Printz – but three individuals should continue to be remembered for their exploits and their artistry.

Louis-Adolphe Mayeur was born in Belgium in 1837, studied clarinet with Klosé at the Paris Conservatoire and saxophone with both Klosé and Sax; he died in 1894. He was regarded as the most brilliant saxophone performer of his era, appearing as soloist with the Brussels Opera and, from 1871, the Paris Opera. He wrote a large number of transcriptions, original works and study material, some of which remain in print.[26]

Mayeur was one of several renowned musicians hired by Sax in 1864 to travel throughout France, Holland and Belgium demonstrating Sax's instruments in concert. We can judge his ability from a review by Johannes Weber in *Le Temps* (4 April 1867), in which Mayeur is described as an excellent artist, '. . . joining a remarkable beauty of sound to a style equally able to present large and expressive melodies as well as executing the most brilliant and most difficult passages'.[27]

A more shadowy and altogether fascinating performer is the saxophonist known only as Souallé. Born in the north of France, his birth and death dates are unknown. He is credited with the first solo appearance of the saxophone in London in 1850, where he performed with the conductor and impresario Louis Antoine Jullien.[28] He is also undoubtedly the first saxophonist to appear in such distant lands as India, Australia, Java and China, performing as 'Ali-Ben-Sou-Alle' on a saxophone he called the 'turcophone'. He also toured throughout Europe. Souallé wrote several works for saxophone that recall his world travels (such as *Souvenirs de Java*, *Souvenirs de Shanghai*) and a few other works; none is currently in print.

There can also be little doubt that he was an artist as well as a world traveller. Souallé is the subject of a laudatory review by Berlioz in the 13 April 1851 issue of *Journal des débats*:

> Mr Souallé, who recently returned from London, produced a great sensation by performing on Sax's masterpiece, the saxophone. *This was the first time the saxophone, with all its advantages, has been heard in Paris* [emphasis added]. This instrument possesses incomparable and expressive qualities; the trueness and beauty of sound which can be produced when one really masters the technique are such that it can, in slow pieces, challenge the finest singers.[29]

Henri Wuille was also hired by Jullien, who took him to England in 1852, and with whom he performed until 1856. While with Jullien he toured the United States as first clarinettist and saxophone soloist. He is credited with the first saxophone solo performance in the United States in a concert presented in New York on 19 December 1853.[30] Born in Belgium in 1822, Wuille studied clarinet with Valentin Bender, who also taught Sax. After his tours with Jullien, Wuille eventually settled in Strasbourg, where he taught at the Conservatoire. He died in Baden, Germany, in 1871.

In the *Revue et Gazette musicale* (11 July 1858), Kastner made the following comments about Wuille's abilities after hearing him perform a *Fantasy on Themes from 'Martha'* with the orchestra in Baden in 1858:

> Adding perfect taste to a marvellous ability and brilliant execution to the solid qualities of a good musician, Mr Wuille enjoys a justly acquired universal reputation. Probably in order to add something to his fame and to show his talent in another way, he selected an instrument [the saxophone] completely capable of showing off his ability as a virtuoso . . . Mr Wuille, moreover, produced marvellous effects on the saxophone and possesses the true sound of that instrument, an advantage often denied to clarinettists.[31]

Development

> All other instruments have come under notable modifications through time
> and migration. And last, all have been perfected by slow progress. The
> saxophone, on the other hand, was born yesterday. It is the fruit of a single
> conception, and from its first day it has been the same instrument it will be
> in the future.[32]

This was the opinion of François-Joseph Fétis, Belgian musicologist
and friend of Sax, writing in his *Biographie universelle des musiciens et
bibliographie général de la musique* of 1844. While it may be true that in
1864 the saxophone had indeed changed little since it was first constructed by Sax, there have been a surprisingly large number of modifications since.[33]

One of the most obvious changes was the decline nearly to extinction
of the orchestral group of saxophones by the end of the nineteenth
century. Sax originally conceived the family of saxophones in two groups,
each extending from sopranino to contrabass: the original orchestral
group in F and C, and the military group alternating in E♭ and B♭. Related
to this decline is a second change, as noted by Albert Lavignac: the
increasing popularity of the alto saxophone.[34] All accounts of the first
saxophone indicate that it was of low register; according to Berlioz in
1843, 'the most beautiful low voice known to this day'. Berlioz more
specifically described the earliest saxophone as 'a transposing B♭ instrument, its range is this: contra B♮ to C², including the chromatic tones'.[35]
Note that Berlioz gives a range of more than three octaves. This alerts us
to a third change: by 1855 Berlioz, in his *Treatise upon Modern
Instrumentation and Orchestration*, had reduced the range to its more
'normal' two-and-a-half octaves.[36]

Why did these changes occur? The first, the decline of the orchestral
group, probably has many related reasons: the pre-existing establishment
of the orchestra as found in the symphonic works of Haydn, Mozart and
Beethoven; the German animosity (perhaps led by Wieprecht) towards
Sax which precluded the saxophone from the advances in orchestration
made by Wagner; and the steadily increasing use of the saxophone in military bands, which favoured the E♭ and B♭ instruments. The second
change, the movement away from the bass and baritone saxophones and
towards the alto, may have been inevitable: if the future of the instrument
depended on public awareness and a growing number of performers, the
virtuosity possible on the smaller instrument makes the alto a more
logical choice rather than the larger, more expensive and relatively
cumbersome bass. The bass saxophone was intended, in part, to fill a void
which was not adequately filled by such instruments as the ophicleide and

the serpent, but was ably filled by two other new instruments – the tuba and, ironically, Sax's bass clarinet.

The question of a decrease in range is more problematic. We have no reason to doubt that Berlioz (and others) heard a three-octave compass from Sax, but apparently the upper range was infrequently used, and remained so for several decades. Sax assisted Kastner in creating his *Méthode complète et raisonnée de saxophone*, the first saxophone method book, published in 1845. 'Kastner's method book probably contains the truest picture of Sax's conception of saxophone performance practices, since the two men worked out many of the book's details together.'[37] The book, 142 pages in length, presents fingerings for a written range of b to f^3. Not until the third decade of the twentieth century did the topic reappear in method books and pamphlets by writers such as Bolduc, Eby, Lyon and Winn.

In addition, to further promote the instrument Sax published at least thirty-five compositions by such composers as Arban, Demersseman, Klosé and Singelée. Nineteen of these works have been obtained by Ronkin, who notes that the written range for the saxophone corresponds to the range in the method book – two-and-a-half octaves from b to f^3, with an optional lower alternative often provided for some of the higher passages.

> Sax was obviously aware that the saxophone was capable of producing tones above high F. . . . Although these high notes are not notated in any of the Sax publications, it is possible that Sax taught altissimo notes to his more advanced students. It would therefore not be unreasonable to assume that these talented students might have employed some high notes in the endings of the Sax publications. However, this is all conjecture. It should be remembered that early reviews of saxophone performance concentrated on the instrument's fluid tone colour and rarely mentioned feats of technical calisthenics or high-note acrobatics.[38]

Technical changes

In 1860 Sax conceived an extraordinary legal manoeuvre. The impending expiration dates of his patents on the saxotromba and the saxophone, and the enormous costs associated with the lawsuits against them, led Sax to petition for an extension of patent. The petition cited Sax's remarkable innovations and the exceptional circumstances which had prevented him from realising any profit from those patents. For only the second time in French history since 1791, such a request was granted. Patents for the saxotromba and the saxophone each received a five-year extension, giving

Sax exclusive rights to the saxophone until 11 May 1866.[39] It is a sure indication of the instrument's popularity that other companies presented their own saxophones immediately after the patent came into the public domain.

It was not until 1887, however, that the Evette and Schaeffer Society filed for a patent that included several modifications of lasting significance. Among these modifications were the addition of a connecting bar to permit a trill from F or F♯ to G♯, a right-hand chromatic side key for F♯, the *bis* key to play B♭ using the first finger of the left hand alone, and the extension of the saxophone range to low B♭.[40]

A patent granted to A. Lecomte and Company in 1888 provided for a single octave key and rollers for the low E♭ and C keys. At about the same time the Fontaine-Besson Company made a saxophone with a right-hand side C trill key.[41]

Legacy

One is constantly fascinated by the impression which the saxophone made on those of Sax's contemporaries who heard the instrument for the first time. The finest musicians in Paris were unanimous in their praise of the sheer beauty of the saxophone's sound. Sax gave a demonstration of the saxophone at the Paris Conservatoire in early June of 1842, soon after his arrival in the French capital. Escudier wrote in *La France musicale* of the 'remarkable . . . intensity and quality of sound. . . . You cannot imagine the beauty of sound and the quality of the notes'.[42] In a *Journal des débats* article which Kochnitzky called the birth certificate of the saxophone,[43] Berlioz proclaimed the sound to be incomparable: 'It is full, mellow, vibrant, extremely powerful and [yet] capable of being soft'.[44]

Kastner, in his *Traité général d'instrumentation* of 1844, spoke of 'the nobility and beauty of its timbre. . . . I cannot say enough times, the saxophone is called to the highest destiny by the beauty of its timbre and that opinion is common with several notable musicians, among others Meyerbeer and Halévy, who have heard it the same time as myself'.[45] In *L'Illustration* of February 1848, we read that 'On hearing it for the first time, Rossini wrote: "This is the most beautiful kind of sound that I have ever heard!" And Meyerbeer said: "It is the beautiful ideal of sound"'.[46] Liszt declared that 'the ensemble has a really magnificent effect',[47] an effect which he did not employ but which was used by Charpentier, Halévy, d'Indy, Massenet and Thomas in their orchestral scores before 1894.

Although at the time of Sax's death in 1894 the saxophone had still

Fig. 1.4 Quartet of Adolphe Sax saxophones: soprano, *c.* 1859; alto, *c.* 1857; tenor, *c.* 1861; baritone, *c.* 1858

secured only a tenuous position in the musical world, in just fifty years it had made remarkable progress towards its eventual acceptance. It took the clarinet perhaps a full century from the improvements by Denner to find its way into the Clarinet Concerto and the symphonies of Mozart.[48] The valved horn was resisted in many quarters and was accepted by the Paris Conservatoire only in 1900, some eighty years after it was first patented by Blühmel and Stölzel in 1818.[49]

As we have seen, several soloists had achieved recognition on numerous concert stages. In addition, the saxophone had been utilised by many symphonic composers, the vast majority of them French, by 1894. The first such use was by Georges Kastner in *Le Dernier Roi de Juda*. The opera, which included the bass saxophone, received a single performance on 1 December 1844.

Only a pair of works from this fifty-year period have entered the mainstream repertoire: Bizet's well-known *L'Arlésienne Suite No. 1* of 1872 and his *Suite No. 2*, arranged by Ernest Guiraud in 1879. Three operas –

Hamlet by Ambroise Thomas (1868), and *Hérodiade* (1881) and *Werther* (1892), both by Jules Massenet – should also be mentioned, along with the ballet *Sylvia* by Léo Delibes (1876). Each of these compositions uses the alto saxophone; for *Hérodiade*, Massenet added the tenor and contrabass saxophones. The foundation had been prepared for orchestral works now numbering in the thousands, including those by composers as varied as Béla Bartók, Paul Hindemith, Charles Ives, Zoltán Kodály, Maurice Ravel, Sergei Rachmaninoff, Dmitri Shostakovich, William Walton and Anton von Webern.[50]

To those who associate the saxophone primarily with jazz it is often a surprise to learn that the instrument is a late addition. It is impossible to say when jazz began, but it is clear that the saxophone had gained only an insignificant role at least two decades after jazz began to crystallise.[51] In those first decades of jazz, the typical ensemble consisted of five or six players – trumpet, clarinet, trombone, and a rhythm section of piano, bass and drums.[52] Very few photographs of jazz musicians before about 1915 include a saxophone, and there is little other evidence to suggest that this eminently well-suited instrument began to exert its extraordinary influence until after World War I.

It was to the band that the saxophone was most enthusiastically welcomed in the nineteenth century. Hemke tells us that the saxophone was accepted in Spanish and English bands in the 1850s, but it was not until 1872 that audiences in the United States were made aware of the effectiveness of the saxophone.[53]

Patrick Gilmore organised an International Peace Jubilee in Boston and invited the finest bands in Europe to perform between 17 June and 6 July 1872. Among those who accepted the invitation was the French Garde Républicaine Band, who had been sent in a bid to regain some of the prestige lost by France in the disastrous Franco-Prussian War. The band's fifty-three members included six saxophonists. After the Jubilee, the ensemble performed thirty-two concerts throughout the United States, receiving enthusiastic reviews.[54] The reviews, in judgements which hold true today, frequently commented on the similarity of the band's sound to that of the orchestra. The saxophones were often cited as one of the principal reasons for this extraordinary sonority.[55]

Shortly thereafter, Gilmore organised the Twenty-Second Regiment Band of New York City. The band's first concert on 18 November 1873 presented saxophone soloist Edouard A. Lefèbre, who remained with the band for nineteen years until Gilmore's death in 1892. Lefèbre headed a section of three saxophones when the band toured Europe in 1878, and a quartet of saxophones for a series of winter concerts in New York that same year. By 1892, Gilmore's band of a hundred musicians included eight saxophonists on soprano, alto, tenor, baritone and contrabass.[56] After Gilmore's death, Lefèbre joined John Philip Sousa's Band to lead a section of three saxophones (alto, tenor and baritone). Sousa had used such a trio during his years conducting the United States Marine Band between 1880 and 1892.[57]

A later member of the Garde Républicaine Band, already a renowned soloist and creator of the *Quatuor de Saxophones de Paris*, would establish a system of teaching the concert saxophone. Marcel Mule was named Professor of Saxophone at the Paris Conservatoire in 1942, seventy-two years after the previous incumbent – Adolphe Sax. Sax's legacy – the sound of Sax – would make remarkable progress in the twentieth century in the hands of such diverse and gifted musicians as Marcel Mule, Sigurd Rascher, Charlie Parker and John Coltrane.

2 In the twentieth century

DON ASHTON

Progressive popularity

By the time of his death in 1894, Adolphe Sax had already achieved the near-impossible, though like many great inventors he would neither recognise this nor profit from it; to introduce a new musical instrument and gain acceptance of typically conservative musicians and public is a feat probably partially paralleled in the last 300 years only by Arnold Dolmetsch's *re-introduction* of the now common recorder. Sax's early liaison with the Garde Républicaine had assured the saxophone of a continuing presence in the French army bands, and it was this strength which eventually fed the instrument into other musical areas as the twentieth century dawned. His efforts in the classical field reaped little reward, and this was to remain a much less active arena for many years.

It is to Sax's credit that most of the acoustical and mechanical improvements to the saxophone constitute refinements which do not significantly depart from the original patents or render the early instruments unplayable today: most are developments appropriate to more modern manufacturing techniques, greater performer agility, or the optimisation of the tonal requirements of players. Since Sax's original patent rightly includes the mouthpiece, it is necessary to record a parallel development here also.

At the beginning of the twentieth century there was a firm and continuing role for the saxophone in the military bands of France, Germany and elsewhere in Europe, with a rather recalcitrant England soon to follow. In America the Gilmore and Sousa showbands did much to extend the exposure of the instrument to the general public. However, in classical music the saxophone made only an occasional appearance, due in large part to the lack of substantial repertoire and the disinterest of orchestral musicians. Indeed the tenuous thread spun by Adolphe's early teaching at the Paris Conservatoire seems barely discernible until reinforced by Marcel Mule and Sigurd Rascher some fifty years later.

Whilst recognising the importance of Sax's own early teaching in the promotion of the saxophone, the lack of any other influential teacher until Mule's appointment at the Paris Conservatoire in 1942 might suggest that the saxophone was generally played badly. However, there

Fig. 2.1 A Hawkes & Son
tenor saxophone, from an
early 1900s catalogue
exhorting English bandsmen
to explore its sonority,
exhibits a mechanical
simplicity alongside its
current Yamaha YTS 62
counterpart

were a few brilliant musicians who, for diverse reasons, decided to apply
their inherent talents to the instrument. General popularity does not necessarily produce excellence, particularly on an instrument which appears
deceptively easy to master. It is therefore important that in all types of
music there have been exponents of the highest calibre.

Edouard Lefèbre, through the bands of Patrick Gilmore and John
Philip Sousa, delighted American audiences with fine quality playing for
nearly forty years. Shortly afterwards the masterful Rudy Wiedoeft was
recording, composing and promoting the saxophone to the public in a
manner allying the instrument with high-class control, nuance and first-
rate entertainment. Wiedoeft's choice of instrument was a happy one for
champions of the saxophone, and fortunately coincided with early
growth in the recording industry and the public's post-war appetite for
novel entertainment. So unfolded the unprecedented saxophone 'craze' of
the 1920s in America, directly responsible not only for the spawning of so
many good quality performers and a large listening public, but also for
tremendous amateur interest. C. G. Conn's manufactory was, from 1921,
encouraged to increase its production threefold until the Wall Street crash
signalled an end to this phenomenal boost to the saxophone's popularity.

Although this 'craze' was not matched outside America, the events
of those years contributed so much to the technical development of the
saxophone, the demands and abilities of its exponents, and the launching

Fig. 2.2 Saxophone section of the John Philip Sousa Band, 1926

of the saxophone into the jazz and dance bands, that it begs appraisal. Despite the original patent specification for a bass instrument, it is the alto in E♭ and the tenor in B♭ which dominate history. But post-war elation demanded excitement and novelty; during the 1920s the soprano and C-melody saxophones were to join the bass in providing that novelty, before all three members of the family slipped into near obscurity for the best part of forty years. Wiedoeft delighted everyone with his witty and sensitive playing, often on the C-melody, which surely influenced the beautifully sonorous playing of Frankie Trumbauer. Adrian Rollini is rightly remembered as a leading player of the bass saxophone. It is interesting to note that several women can be numbered among performers at this time.

One of the effects of the popularity of the saxophone in the 1920s was its reluctant inclusion by New Orleans style bands. Fortunately for the survival of the genuine New Orleans style, this was but a stepping stone on the way to the dance bands and new forms of jazz very suited to the saxophone's rich blending sound. During the 1930s, makers vied to introduce advanced features in an effort to maximise a drastically curtailed market, and saxophonists benefited greatly from this competition, with soloists exhibiting sounds and styles hitherto unexplored. By this time Marcel

Mule, following his appointment to the Garde Républicaine, had formed an SATB quartet whose excellence was to encourage the writing of some of the great classical repertoire for the medium (see chapter 5). The period was particularly fruitful: Sigurd Rascher, Mule and Cecil Leeson all engendered fine pieces for the saxophone and this in turn encouraged others to play classical repertoire. The typical classical sound differed considerably from that produced on mouthpieces designed for jazz, and the sound and its production will be discussed below.

The saxophone continued to evolve during the 1940s. Saxophone production was considerably curtailed until the second half of the decade, but the army bands and the big bands of America flourished as public and troop entertainment media. Dance bands often sported the full AATTB saxophone section in close harmony; Marcel Mule reopened Conservatoire classes in 1942; and Charlie Parker presaged a whole new jazz era, at first misunderstood but destined to be followed and refined throughout the rest of the century. Before 1950, the Selmer factory in Paris had already surpassed pre-war production. The much-beloved Mark VI, destined to reign for twenty-one years, was soon to appear as the culmination of a development since 1935. For jazz and classical players alike, this model was to prove a firm favourite.

Dance bands flourished in many countries after World War II, boosted both by radio and the advent of television. Many saxophonists were able to find full-time employment, and the amateur and semi-professional likewise could find plenty of work. Learning was largely by imitation, and teaching was *ad hoc*, particularly with regard to jazz, yet there was no shortage of playing talent. In the post-bop era jazz idols influenced many of the amateur dance-band saxophonists both in sound and style. A potential disaster arrived towards the end of the 1950s in the shape of rock and roll, ousting hundreds of the dance bands which provided saxophonists with somewhere to grow. Twenty years later the rhythmic world frequented by the saxophone could acknowledge considerable enrichment by the rock era, without applying brakes to a steady increase in interest.

Since 1950, the classical world has embraced many fine exponents like Deffayet, Londeix, Rousseau and Hemke, all teachers and performers of high standing who have encouraged major works to be written. Gradually over this period the repertoire, standards of performance and quality of teaching have expanded to the extent that in 1969 the first World Saxophone Congress was held in Chicago, to be followed by others in later years, and the British Saxophone Congress is now a regular feature of our calendar.

Three-quarters of the way through the twentieth century, American manufacturers amalgamated and rationalised to become more world-competitive. The large European centres of manufacture were actively producing cheaper saxophones for an increasing student market, and the Japanese were already gaining considerable expertise. In America high school bands and an increase in effective teaching encouraged the playing of the saxophone, and universities pushed standards higher in both jazz and classical idioms. In Europe, too, the saxophone enjoyed increasing popularity from school through to conservatory. The most satisfying outcome has been the growth of good quality teaching, combining a classical discipline with enriched knowledge of jazz, rock and pop.

Greater interest in the classical and quartet repertories has encouraged manufacturers to apply their technical expertise to the neglected soprano saxophone and this has transformed a difficult-to-master instrument into a much more approachable member of the family. Even the bass, Sax's original invention, has been the subject of some updating, and new sopranino designs have appeared.

Acoustical elements

It has frequently been said that the saxophone is a relatively easy instrument to master. This is at once both true and deceptive. Musicians glibly talk of large bores, hard and soft reeds, and ease of response, without any specific reference points. It is always difficult to delineate substance which is composed of mechanics and art, and the saxophone and its player undoubtedly constitute exactly that. The following discussion attempts to enable the player to appreciate more readily where the manufacturer's responsibility ends and that of the player takes over, to see the relativity of hard and soft, ease of response and resistance, simple and complex, so that mismatches can be avoided or the consequent difficulties at least better understood.

Relative to other woodwind instruments the saxophone has a large bore, and this is of great significance to many aspects of its sound capabilities and player response. The use of a conical tube renders the soundwave richly harmonic, yet the fingering system rivals that of the flute in simplicity. In common with other large-bore instruments the fundamentals are easily formed, yet the reduction in bore towards the mouthpiece facilitates both an evenness of timbre throughout the instrument, and the extension of the two-and-a-half-octave 'normal' range. Sax, as a master maker, always knew that the range surpassed three octaves and would probably be unsurprised to witness its growing use today.

The extended range was little used during the first fifty years or so. Acceptance of the saxophone as a useful member of the marching bands stemmed from its ability to produce a large volume of sound. Using a mouthpiece of large and round internal volume and a single reed, players soon realised that everything from a whisper to full-blooded support of the brass section was possible. Today, players expect to achieve even greater volume, more focused projection and crisper texture, without sacrificing the ability to control extremely soft nuances. This ability to soar into distinctly soloistic mode from one largely of a supporting role reveals the true greatness of Sax's invention, and begins to give credence to the multitude of quite different and distinctive sounds produced over the years of this century from an instrument so often maligned as an easy option.

A tube of large diameter in relation to length favours production of the fundamentals. Moreover, to facilitate a scale of fundamentals the holes will also be relatively large. The consequence of this to the player, assuming a suitably efficient excitation medium, is the ability to effect a great range of volume, flexibility of intonation, and considerable influence over the tonal quality. *Notice how much these three factors demand player responsibility, awareness and expertise.* The astute clarinet player, for instance, will recognise that the relatively small French-bore clarinets favoured today offer, by comparison to earlier examples, more accurate and stable intonation. Such a luxury is much less easy to achieve on the saxophone. Indeed, the desire to create great intonational nuance in playing styles of the 1930s, together with suitable mouthpiece and reed combinations, reflects in designs of the time. The unthinking now frequently blame (top-class) manufacturers for producing out-of-tune saxophones, or may unwisely recommend such an instrument to a raw recruit.

Whilst this book is not a technical treatise in acoustics, some basic tenets specific to the behaviour of a conical pipe stopped at one end, together with cognisance of the complexities introduced by requiring that tube to produce more than a single pitch, should help the player to command control and avoid all-too-common mismatches in equipment.

The air stream from the blower constitutes an energy source, hence the direct relationship between the *speed* of air passing the reed and the ultimate *volume* of the sound produced. The reaction of the reed, held on the mouthpiece table, constitutes an excitation system which sets up vibration of the air column contained by the mouthpiece chamber and the tube. *Furthermore, the oral cavity constitutes a couple on the outer side of the reed, influencing basic pitch and tonal light and shade.* The intensity of the sound depends on the amplitude of the vibration and the pitch depends on the number of vibrations per second, or frequency. In common with other sounding bodies, air columns may produce tones of different

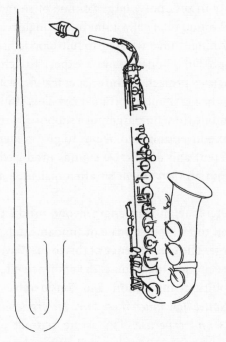

Fig. 2.3 Viewing a design sketch to incorporate four cones and their relationship with the complete saxophone

frequencies simultaneously and of different strengths, so that the ear hears a complex note. For a given fundamental pitch the relative strengths of these harmonic frequencies, adhering to the physical laws of the pipe in question, determine the timbre or tone-colour which the ear distinguishes as belonging to, say, a clarinet or an oboe.

Consider the conical air column of a saxophone. Without the mouthpiece the cone is truncated, and the mouthpiece of necessity has to provide the equivalent volume of the missing completion of the cone (see Fig. 2.3). Under resonating conditions the stopped, or mouthpiece, end has an antinode formed, where the motion of the air is a maximum at constant pressure. The open, or bell, end communicates directly with the atmosphere and the air is still, with rapidly alternating pressure – a point called a node. As the soundwave reaches the atmosphere to reflect back again it extends beyond the end to a degree dependent on the tube's diameter, so the length of pipe calculated to produce a given pitch will require some adjustment by shortening.

Musical instrument makers, particularly those of good quality recorders, are well versed in the process of constricting or widening the bore locally in order to lower or raise the pitch of a note which requires slight attention. The principle involved, applied to the conical air column, is that enlargement of the diameter at a node will produce a rise in pitch; conversely, a reduction in bore at a node will lower the pitch of the note.

The degree of conicity for a given length will determine the veracity of the complete series (both odd and even) of harmonics within a sound of the pitch required. Richness and ease of emission demand that the harmonic strengths are well defined, and that the degree of conicity enables an exact octave higher in pitch on overblowing. A cone that is too closed renders the upper harmonics progressively sharp, whilst a cone that is too open will overblow flat.

All this procedure would be relatively straightforward if the instrument was only required to play a single pitch, but an embryo sketch has to be made of a cone which will best support a chromatic scale, say, from low D to high C♯. The necessity of raising toneholes from the body, flat-topped to enable a mechanism to effect good sealing, adds volume to the basic cone. Each one will flatten or sharpen the sounding note according to whether it coincides with an antinode or node, and therefore constitutes an area of the designers' art equal in importance to the tube itself. A simplification of the above constraints, always observing first principles, might be to imagine, say, two adjacent cones – one correct for low D to middle C♯ and the other correct for middle D to high C♯.

On pursuing this idea (see Fig. 2.3), Adolphe Sax's preference for a parabolic bore becomes clearer and his grasp of an instrument's acoustical behaviour, a quarter of a century before Helmholtz presented his basic wave theory, is quite amazing. The greatest degree of alteration to a right cone in converting it to parabolic shape coincides substantially along the length of the saxophone's crook, and this has great significance for the discerning player.

Perhaps the best philosophy for the player to follow, irrespective of his degree of understanding of the acoustics of his chosen musical companion, is one of regarding the crook and mouthpiece as the 'business' end, to be treated with great respect. Oboe players soon learn that because the oboe's bore is so small the upper part in particular needs to remain spotless. Saxophonists appear generally to be less fastidious in this respect, and in extreme cases severely malign the embouchure in attempts to maintain reasonable intonation – all quite unnecessary with a little good housekeeping!

The crook then, or the upper end of a crookless soprano, will exhibit greater conicity than the main body of the saxophone in order to obtain optimum accuracy for the second register of each note, and this also affects the relative strengths of the partials in the sound spectrum. The fact that different makes have different inherent tonal characteristics and emissive response can be largely attributed to the design of this part of the tube. It is a simple though somewhat scientifically flawed exercise to transfer the crook of one make to an earlier model and to note the different characteristics produced; totally opposed designs will reveal the extent of mismatch to the discerning player. It should come as no surprise, therefore, given musicians' penchant for choosing from a vast variety of available mouthpieces, to find that some are working very hard to produce what they desire while others find a much more suitable choice. The best acoustic match of mouthpiece to saxophone may simply fail either to be comfortable for a player or to have the ability to generate the characteristics which that player desires, and in some cases a player could find improved intonation by wearing a palette to decrease the oral cavity.

The original mouthpiece, part of the saxophone patent and constituting the missing termination of the conical tube, consisted of a round chamber somewhat larger than in later designs. In general it can be said that any intrusion upon this plain round bore will favour the upper partials and thereby 'brighten' the sound rather in the manner of increasing treble dominance on a hi-fi system. Taken to extremes this will result in bright but projectionally thin sound emission. Saxophonists of the 1930s soon discovered that raising the baffle (using plasticine) to restrict the entry into the chamber caused an increasing sense of ambience, or 'presence,' to the blower, with perhaps less exciting results to the more distant listener. The effects on intonation, predictably and distinctly non-linear throughout the scale, produce an added distortion, often negating the painstaking work of the saxophone manufacturer. It is, of course, quite feasible in theory to start the saxophone design at the mouthpiece, so that the tube is scaled to suit the most exciting jazz mouthpiece, though in practice the differences in embouchure control necessary between various characteristic mouthpieces are the province of the player, and the design of a tube as near acoustically perfect as possible is the domain of the experienced manufacturer.

Elements of a mouthpiece are shown in Figure 2.4; the contribution of these elements to the sound is very important to players. The table and the mating face of the reed need to be absolutely flat so that the minimum of restraint is required to hold the reed in place, and various ligatures have been designed to do so with the minimum constriction of vibration. Beyond the table and extending to the tip, the dimensions of the rails forming the lay should be exactly even to enable undistorted propagation. This propagation starts by means of the reed vibrating across the opening made by the lay, trajecting to and reflecting from the baffle into the chamber. If the baffle is raised, as in so many jazz mouthpieces, there will be several deflections before reaching the chamber, tending to emphasise the higher partials or favour the treble end of the spectrum – musicians often refer to this propensity as 'edge'. More often than not they will use an

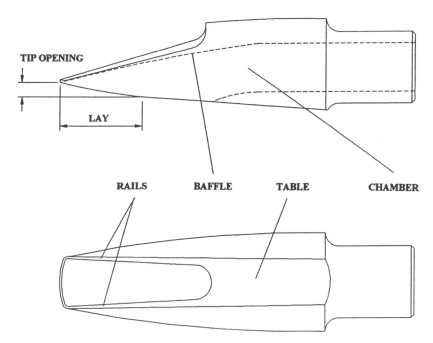

Fig. 2.4 Mouthpiece elements

American- or straighter-cut reed which also favours edge, whereas the classical players favour French- or multi-cut 'long heartwood' reeds with lower baffled, closer lay mouthpieces in order to suppress the edge and favour the purity of fundamentals (see Fig. 2.5).

Early jazz and popular music players found the sounds they wanted by using softer reeds, more open lays, and more restricted chambers than their classical counterparts, helping to distinguish between the sweet clarity of Marcel Mule, the masterful nuances of Rudy Wiedoeft, and the soft engaging auras of Ben Webster. Gradually jazz soloists worked on harder reeds, to produce the delicate brittleness of sound typified by Paul Desmond on alto, and to favour the wonderfully projective richness of Stan Getz's tenor playing. By 1950, Selmer's D-chambered Soloist mouthpieces, ideally matched in design to their Super Action saxophones, enabled a flexible and full projection from *pp* to *ff* with an adequately bright tone, thereby suiting a range of players from dance bands to orchestras. The American equivalent which enjoyed great popularity was designed by Arnold Brilhart. This type of mouthpiece, in conjunction with French-cut reeds, is well suited to today's classical players, the best of whom are thoroughly conversant with other types of music and may only need to change the cut of reed to feel comfortable outside the orchestra or recital situation. Both Otto Link and Selmer metal mouthpieces, together

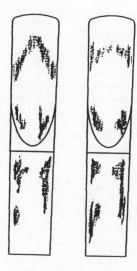

Fig. 2.5 A French-cut reed reveals a longer heartwood (left)
which suppresses the edge associated with the American cut
equivalent on the right

with the British Berg Larsen and Lawton makes, were much in demand in
the 1950s and 1960s, and continue to have many firm adherents.

Since that time jazz soloists have demanded mouthpieces with a somewhat searing quality – reminiscent of Michael Brecker's playing against
amplified electronic instrumental accompaniment – without losing the
full tonal qualities normally associated with high baffles and restricted
chambers. Many specialists offer variations on this theme, using
combinations of fine handwork and computer-controlled precision in
manufacture. The degree of influence attributable to the material used in
the manufacture of the mouthpiece is the subject of many rather over-
stated claims, yet classical players rarely choose metal, whose relative
rigidity is likely to favour the higher partials. Ebonite has long been a universal mouthpiece material, to be joined by metal and plastic about
midway through the twentieth century, but never ousted. Player comfort
should be the deciding factor here; of far more import is the choice of lay,
tip opening, and internal design. In general classical players prefer the
control of closer tip openings with more supportive reeds, whereas jazz
players take on board the problems associated with small-bore chambers
and choose much greater tip openings in order to control intonation and
tonal nuance by embouchure. It is important for a player to realise just
what choices are being made, particularly when teaching or advising
beginners.

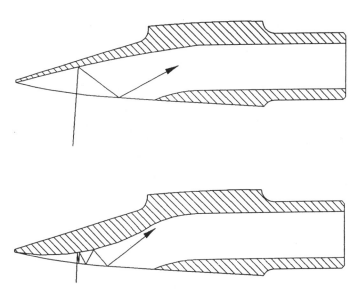

Fig. 2.6 Baffles and chamber designs considerably influence the characteristics of the sound by different propagation

Developments and choices

As far as possible the fingering mechanism necessary to operate an instrument should be straightforward, since the interpretation of music is demanding enough without requiring the player to negotiate awkward fingering. The saxophone system, except for the fact that like many other instruments it is somewhat illogically built around the key of C, benefits from its relative youth, and the improvements and additions throughout the twentieth century have not destroyed its simplicity.

Right into the 1920s some cheaper models sported double-octave key operation, though most had the familiar automatic change-over mechanism from around 1900. This was usually achieved by a system of two levers, one operating and one intermediary, plus the two actual octave keys, and relied on the different strengths of four springs not counting that of the G key which changed from lower to upper vent halfway up the second register. It was in the early 1930s that the major manufactories of Conn, Buescher and Selmer all devised a simpler knuckled link requiring less pressure, the shape of the Selmer link giving rise to the famous Cigar Cutter sobriquet. Urged on by the Wall Street crash and the loss of saxophone sales, these companies led the way to many mechanical improvements which did not spoil the earlier simplicity of fingering.

The provision of a 'front F' key was universal by the early 1900s (by contrast a top F♯ key became almost universal only three-quarters of a

Fig. 2.7 Modern front F spatulas facilitate a technique similar to clarinet throat A operation, and the left little finger now benefits from G♯ to low note articulation incorporating a C♯ and B♭ link via a tipping B♭ spatula. Introduced by Selmer in 1935, this ensures that the spatula remains close to the level of the finger on depressing low C♯

century later), though many companies produced cheaper instruments under stencil names, omitting some of the niceties. In the early 1930s the G♯ key became the subject of much design work. This normally closed key, opened by its own spring, needed a strongly sprung lever with short leverage to keep the G♯ shut, placing strain on the left-hand little finger. A requirement to articulate this lever to low C♯, B and B♭, particularly useful for the fifth patterns common in baritone parts, motivated basic design changes which culminated in Selmer's removal of the bell keys to the opposite side of the bell, thereby easing the leverages and taking the keywork away from the player's clothing at a stroke. The Balanced Action of 1935 created a modern layout which, peculiarly, the Americans did not follow until years later. The alternative E♭, fingered 1–2–3–4–6, disappeared at this time after a relatively short lifespan – it had had a propensity to go out of adjustment and cause leakage.

Both the left- and right-hand main keys have largely remained in their respective stacks – with few exceptions, the right-hand main keys have employed a single steel axle rod since the first saxophones. From about 1935 the G♯ key was frequently hinged on its own axle to avoid the old short leverages, and both Selmer and Conn saxophones favoured the B♭ *bis* key and G key, each supported separately from the main upper stack; this arrangement remains common. Longer keys are usually supported on point screws of various designs, and in fact because the basic methods of keywork hinging pre-date the invention of the saxophone, it is not surprising to find little change other than in materials and precision throughout its life. Because the pillars holding the screws and needle springs are soldered on to the metal body, their rigidity precludes many of the problems arising on wooden instruments. Many manufacturers soft solder each pillar in place, but Selmer have always made extensive use of straps combining many pillars without detriment to the acoustic of the tube; in fact, Selmer's use of the hardest brass of all no doubt influences the sound, and certainly contributes to a crisp key action. Because saxophone tubes are pierced with relatively large holes, good sealing is only effected by the use of considerable skill, and strongly made keywork helps to keep the action regulation at its optimum for longer periods.

Around the time of Sax's death, Buescher was constructing C. G. Conn's first soprano saxophone, and within a decade or so Conn, King, Buescher and Martin all offered both straight and curved sopranos, the last displaying less tendency to a rather raw nasal quality. French manufacturers also made curved models in the early 1920s, though the American Conns and Bueschers are the most common survivors. At the time of writing, a number of cheaper curved sopranos are available, but the Japanese Yanagisawa is possibly the only quality one. In the late 1920s, Conn heralded the ill-fated mezzo-soprano in F, which together with the mythical sopranino and baritone in F might have completed a whole F/C family, for the soprano in C and C-melody 'tenor' are not rare.

All sopranos require dedication for any degree of mastery, and their sparse use after 1930 until a revival around the mid-1960s did not encourage the sort of design research which has spawned the excellent Selmer Paris, Yanagisawa and Yamaha models of today. By comparison, the alto and tenor saxophones have been the subject of continuous acoustical development so that one may choose either from a number of characteristic earlier sounds or from current models; some explanation of these choices may be useful. Instruments of the 1920s are still in abundance and the primary consideration should be wear in the mechanism, since a complete retube and new axles may prove prohibitive. Otherwise, the main ingredient to look for is a delicacy and purity of sound, matched ideally by a mouthpiece of the time. Particular attention should be paid to the crook, remembering the importance of the upper cone; Conns whose patent tuning slides have been removed irresponsibly may exhibit impossible intonation problems.

As already noted, the mid-1930s was a period of transition. C. G. Conn produced their 'underslung' model (upper octave key slung underneath the crook) with rolled toneholes, in conjunction with L-shaped metal rings built into the pads which pulled the leather covering tight and flat. These helped to keep the seals healthy for a lengthy period as long as the holes remained undamaged. Factors which reduce the longevity of these sonorous and free-blowing favourites include irresponsible polishing of the body during subsequent relacquering, particularly from an initially frosted silverplated finish; denting close to toneholes; or removal of the rings on repadding. Buescher Aristocrats from this period arguably display the most free-blowing properties of all, with rich, full tones and the ability to produce a markedly full subtone from the lower notes. Some players will find the ability to bend notes, a well-used feature of the era, all too often makes for less easy intonational control. The Buescher bore has seen little change to this day, and was used in 1948 as the basis of the remarkable Grafton venture into plastic moulding. Almost by contrast the Selmer Balanced Action of 1935 featured a less easy full subtone than its forebears, in favour of a brighter (but not thinner) upper end and a well-balanced roundness of harmonic spectrum throughout the whole range. Classical use of the saxophone during mid-century was subordinate to the big band sections and developing jazz soloists, no doubt influencing designs in the quest for richness and brightness, with the ability to sing hard against large brass teams and to respond flexibly to the smallest of oral nuances.

The classical player has undoubtedly benefited from all this acoustical and mechanical activity, and indeed has also been able to contribute to design during the latter half of the century. Perhaps the most notable examples of this are the collaboration between Selmer and Marcel Mule towards the birth of the Mark VI, and the growth of Yamaha models under the player input of Eugene Rousseau. His advice to a determined and scientifically orientated team has produced a top-class saxophone with a distinctive purity of tone, yet bright in character. Any claim to being the easiest responding of saxophone tubes, particularly on lower notes, would be hard to refute, rendering them excellent instruments for young beginners. Because of this ease of response they are often unwittingly chosen by classical clarinet players who feel the need to be 'saxophone familiar', without recognising that all saxophones require considerable skill and familiarity on the part of the player in order to fashion a high personal standard of tone and delivery. That a Yamaha saxophone is capable of satisfying the highest musical demands is evident in the playing of the likes of Rousseau, members of the Northern Saxophone Quartet, and many others.

Since World War II, the American musical instrument industry has undergone considerable change, as a result of Conn's financial troubles and other makers' avoidance of the same fate through amalgamations. This has resulted in 'corporation' models rather than the specialist saxophone typified by the Conn Underslung, though seekers of tubes with a darker and more mellow character may wish to explore this area. In the midst of much activity in the cheaper lines from French, Italian, Czech and German centres (their saxophones often carried importer-designated names – for example, East German manufacturer Weltklang would supply instruments carrying a name specified by quite small

Fig. 2.8 Toneholes being raised from a saxophone tube at the Yanagisawa factory in Japan

importers), the Selmer company in Paris developed the legendary Mark VI. The Mark VI's richness, brightness and sheer weight of sound, combined with a precision of action, ensured its place in both professional and semi-professional circles alike; the baritone offered the now universal concert low C and a crisp delivery throughout the range. The Conn baritone continued without this facility until very late, but it remains a firm favourite with jazz soloists because of its rounded lyrical qualities. After some twenty-one years of Mark VI production the less-loved Mark VII Selmer lasted only five years, before the S80 – a much more refined and flexible instrument reminiscent of the post-war Super Action – became the latest epitome of saxophones for many of the world's top exponents in both classical music and jazz. The Selmer company has developed its concurrent Series III models in order to offer an alternative tonal option.

As we enter the twenty-first century, world markets have been inundated with cheap Far Eastern saxophones, some of which defy description, though there are now signs of improved technological input with factories such as KHS and Greenhill producing better models. At the same time there are small but diligent companies, notably Keilworth of Germany, who, having now considerable experience of making

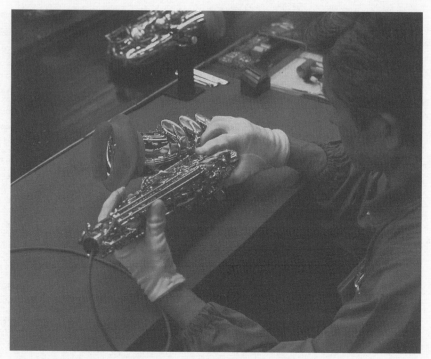

Fig. 2.9 Testing for the integrity of pad seating on a Yamaha saxophone

saxophones under contract, are offering quality products under their own name for the discerning player, as part of the Boosey & Hawkes organisation. The demand for saxophones is greater than ever, and the inevitable result of this interest will be better saxophones, better players and more improvement in the availability and quality of teaching.

3 Influential soloists

THOMAS DRYER-BEERS

This chapter surveys artists who have exerted, and continue to exert, significant influence upon the direction and acceptance of the 'classical' saxophone and its repertoire.[1]

Before the emergence in the late 1920s of Marcel Mule and Sigurd Rascher came the inspiration and tireless efforts of Adolphe Sax himself[2] and a number of contemporaries.

Early soloists

Belgian-born Henri Wuille (1822–71) was a contemporary of Sax and one of the most ardent proponents of the new instrument. He toured widely, performing on both clarinet and saxophone to great acclaim, and his tours with impresario Louis Antoine Jullien led to his being credited as the earliest solo performer on the saxophone to play both in England and the United States.[3]

M. Souallé (dates unknown), also Belgian, attracted the praise of Hector Berlioz after a concert in Paris in 1851, following his return from several saxophone performances in London in 1850. Souallé's artistry was proclaimed, as were the saxophone's then already obvious (at least to Berlioz) 'incomparable and expressive qualities; the trueness and beauty of sound which can be produced when one really masters the technique are such that it can, in slow pieces, challenge the finest singers'.[4]

Louis-Adolphe Mayeur (1837–94) earned a first prize for clarinet at the Paris Conservatoire and became an accomplished saxophonist after studies with both Klosé and Sax. He performed regularly with the Paris Opera and taught widely, contributing a tutor, the *Grande Méthode*, for saxophone published in 1867.

Edouard Lefèbre (*c.* 1834–1911) was without doubt the most outstanding soloist in America from the 1870s through to the 1890s. His performances as a soloist, for nearly twenty years with the Patrick Gilmore Band and later as 'The Saxophone King' with the John Philip Sousa Band, established him as a most remarkable player.

Several saxophonists rose to prominence in the USA and were introduced to a worldwide audience through their association with the Sousa Band. The tradition of featuring the band's fine instrumental soloists in their concerts did much to popularise the saxophone. Following Lefèbre as a featured soloist was Belgian-born Jean Moeremans, who also had the distinction of being soloist with the United States Marine Band from the 1890s to early 1900s. Benjamin Vereecken joined the Sousa Band around 1910; his tutor *Foundation to Saxophone Playing*, published by Carl Fischer in 1917, became a standard teaching method. H. Benne Henton (1867–1938) came to be considered by many to be the greatest saxophonist of his day. He performed with the Conway Band, another of America's famous touring ensembles in the early part of the twentieth century, and he followed Vereecken as soloist with the Sousa Band. He was particularly renowned for his tone quality and brilliant execution. Jascha Gurewich (1896–1938), promoted as the 'Heifetz of the Saxophone', performed briefly with the Sousa Band and made his career with a number of symphony orchestras, as well as presenting the first recital of serious saxophone music in New York City's Aeolian Hall in 1926.

A unique position in the development of saxophone repertoire is held by amateur performer and champion of the instrument Elise Hall (1853–1924). Both her commissioning of works from major composers, including Claude Debussy, and her remarkable turn-of-the-century performances for the Boston Orchestra Club gained significant notice amongst musical high society during the early 1900s.

Rudy Wiedoeft (1893–1940) thrilled many thousands of listeners from the late 1910s through to the end of the 1930s. His legendary facility on the C-melody instrument and his flair for showmanship caught the imagination of the American public during an era of widespread growth in the popularity of the saxophone (see Chaper 2). Wiedoeft made over a hundred cylinder recordings and his many compositions and arrangements became the standard repertoire of the many players whom he inspired.

In France, the prominent position of the Garde Républicaine meant that its saxophonists, and particularly the appointed soloists, were widely heard and highly regarded. François Combelle (1880–1953) held the post of soloist for many years and has the additional distinction of encouraging the young Marcel Mule, who eventually became soloist himself, to undertake the audition for the Garde.

Mid-century developments

Five American saxophonists should be acknowledged for the wide-ranging and long-lasting effect their artistry has exerted upon later performers and their repertoire.

As an influential freelance performer and teacher, saxophonist and clarinettist Vincent Abato (*b.* 1920) is acknowledged by many players as having been an inspiration, opening their ears to the expressive potential of the saxophone. His performances with some of America's greatest orchestras, and his early recording of Glazunov's *Concerto* and Ibert's *Concertino da Camera*, form a legacy of beautiful playing still relevant and remarkable today.

The contribution of Joseph Allard (1910–91) to the development of the saxophone, aside from his many years as an acclaimed performer on radio and within the New York City scene, resides principally with his many pupils. Saxophonists and clarinettists from all musical backgrounds and walks of life came to regard him as a mentor and guru of the instrument. He taught at the Julliard School, New York University, Mannes College and in his private studio.

Alfred (Al) Gallodoro's (*b.* 1912) live performances with ensembles ranging from theatre orchestras to top swing bands (including the Paul Whiteman Orchestra), and the large volume of recorded material on clarinet, bass clarinet and alto saxophone for ABC studio's popular radio broadcasts – including the Metropolitan Opera Auditions of the Air – thrilled listeners across the nation. His phenomenal articulation and technical execution inspired and challenged all those who heard him to strive for high standards of achievement.

Cecil Leeson (1902–89) was a saxophone pioneer in many ways. His interest in the classical saxophone, which he championed in spite of the American public's insistence upon the saxophone's 'correct' place in lighter, more commercial musical genres, is inspirational for all those who now take for granted both a repertoire and an audience for the instrument. His New York Town Hall debut in 1937 was the first appearance of a saxophonist in that renowned venue. His work with composers Paul Creston, Lawson Lunde, Burnet Tuthill and others left a rich legacy of commissions and dedications. Leeson taught for many years in private studios and major universities, including Northwestern University (1955–61) and Ball State University (1961–77). His dedication to scholarship and historical research has resulted in the establishment of the Leeson Archival Saxophone Collection, now at the Shrine to Music Museum in South Dakota.

Laurence (Larry) Teal (1905–84) played a number of instruments to a high standard and excelled in the fields of radio, commercial and studio music, and was noted particularly for the quality of his sound and his fine musicianship. His appointment as the first Professor of Saxophone at the University of Michigan (1953–74), a 'Big Ten' university, and his establishment of the first doctoral programme in saxophone in the US are

Fig. 3.1 Cecil Leeson

milestones in the acceptance of the instrument as a course of study. Teal's textbook *The Art of Saxophone Playing*[5] remains one of the best sources for general information on saxophone pedagogy.

In Britain, Walter Lear (1894–1981) was a performer on the clarinet and saxophone families with the orchestras of the Royal Opera House, the BBC and the Royal Philharmonic Orchestra, as well as having an active chamber music and solo career. His artistry was widely heard and highly regarded. In a teaching career spanning fifty years as Professor of Saxophone at Trinity College of Music, London, he influenced generations of pupils.

Michael Krein (1908–66) and Walter Lear have been credited with being the first serious saxophonists of this century in Britain. An accomplished clarinettist who worked for the BBC for over twenty years, Krein formed his very influential and groundbreaking saxophone quartet around 1941, and proceeded to entertain and educate audiences until his death, when Jack Brymer (*b.* 1915), one of Britain's most respected musicians, took over the leadership of the group. Krein was Professor of Saxophone at the Guildhall School of Music and Drama for many years.

Stephen Trier (*b.* 1930) has been a performer in London orchestras since the 1950s. A pupil of Frederick Thurston and Walter Lear, Trier was encouraged to learn the saxophone by Michael Krein, and has since performed and recorded most of the major orchestral saxophone repertoire. He taught for many years at the Royal College of Music and at the Guildhall School of Music and Drama in London.

From the very earliest days of the saxophone a lively tradition of performance and instruction has existed in Belgium. The historical, political and musical rivalries between Belgium and France resulted, quite understandably, in the creation of a proudly independent school of saxophone performance. The saxophone has enjoyed virtually uninterrupted availability of instruction at the Royal Conservatory in Brussels. François Daneels (*b*. 1921) gained a First Prize with Great Distinction in 1939 there, and afterwards had an international performing career. He formed the Quatuor Belge de Saxophones in 1953 and was appointed Professor of Saxophone at the Conservatory in 1954. The artistry of Daneels has long been a focal point for those wishing to identify a uniquely Belgian style of playing. Many composers have dedicated works to Daneels and he has been a tireless proponent of the artistic position of the saxophone. He established a reputation for musical sensitivity and finesse. Elie Apper (*b*. 1933) – a pupil of Daneels – gained First Prize at the Royal Conservatory and was appointed Professor of Saxophone (Flemish section) in 1970. He has performed as a member of the Quatuor Belge de Saxophones and leads his own quartet and saxophone ensemble.

Clive Amadio (*d*. 1983) gave many first Australian performances of standard works for saxophone and in 1941 became Professor of Clarinet and Saxophone at the Sydney Conservatory of Music. Peter Fraser (*b*. 1927) has been a pioneer of the classical saxophone in Australia. He was enthralled by recordings of Marcel Mule and, though self-taught, quickly achieved very high standards. In 1948 he was the first saxophonist to reach the finals of the Australian State Concerto Competition and went on to give many recitals for the ABC. In 1957 he formed the Adelaide Saxophone Quartet and in 1960 became a saxophone soloist with the Adelaide Symphony Orchestra.

Central figures

The influence and position of Sigurd Rascher and Marcel Mule are central to any discussion of the development of the classical saxophone in the twentieth century. They have been responsible both for attracting significant contributions from composers and for the dissemination of these works via live performance, broadcast and the teaching studio. Each artist's personal musical style has been repeatedly chronicled as influential by their fellow musicians and can now be viewed as a legacy passed to following generations.

Sigurd Rascher

Sigurd Rascher was born in Germany in 1907. He trained initially on the clarinet and received a diploma from the Stuttgart Musikhochschule in 1930 in preparation for a career as a professional clarinettist. However, his interests changed and he devoted himself to the saxophone. Beginning in 1932, his performing career, to which he devoted much of his energy and attention, took him to many corners of the world and provided the principal showcase for his extraordinary command of the instrument.

After leaving Germany as a result of Nazi prejudice against the saxophone, Rascher was appointed teacher of saxophone at the Royal Danish Conservatory in Copenhagen in 1934 and later also served in a similar capacity at the Malmo Conservatory in Sweden. After relocating to America in 1939, Rascher continued to build his career by performing with some of the world's finest orchestras, including the Boston Symphony Orchestra (his American debut in 1939), the New York Philharmonic, the Philadelphia Orchestra and the Cleveland Orchestra. The list of composers who have written or dedicated works to him is most impressive; from their pens have come many of the finest masterpieces of the saxophone recital repertoire. Works by Dahl, Glazunov, Husa, Milhaud, Cowell and many others acknowledge the inspiration of Sigurd Rascher. The influence his playing held over many composers is often evidenced by the inclusion of passages in the altissimo register, including perhaps most notoriously in the *Concertino da Camera* (1939) by Jacques Ibert. Rascher's lifelong efforts passionately promoting the utilisation and mastery of the altissimo register have resulted in the acceptance of a range of over four octaves[6] by both composers and performers.

Rascher also influenced saxophonists worldwide as a result of numerous teaching residencies, notably in the USA at the Manhattan School of Music, the University of Michigan and the Eastman School of Music. Recordings of the Rascher Saxophone Ensemble, comprising instruments from sopranino to contrabass, have served to inspire the formation of many similar groups, creating both enthusiasm and literature for the saxophone orchestra.

Rascher's particular concept of a proper saxophone sound was always based on his desire to stay true to Adolphe Sax's original intentions. This pursuit led both him and his followers to perform on instruments and mouthpieces modelled closely upon Sax's own. Older Buescher saxophones were particularly favoured for their tonal character, ease of response and accuracy in the production of the overtone series. Rascher's idealism of approach, a consequence of which was his rejection of many developments in musical literature and performance styles, has meant that in recent decades his name and the playing tradition he symbolised have been marginalised by some, and no longer considered 'mainstream'. Such a dismissal, without placing his contribution in a historical context, is an unfair reflection upon the enormous legacy of dedication, musical scholarship and artistic integrity associated with Sigurd Rascher from which both the saxophone and its repertoire have benefited greatly.

Performers and teachers with a musical background and approach traceable directly to the artistry of Sigurd Rascher include:

> **David Bilger** (USA), Professor, Lebanon Valley College, Pennsylvania, member of the Saxophone Sinfonia and the Bilger Duo.
> **Ronald Caravan** (USA), lecturer at Syracuse University, editor of the *Saxophone Symposium* (Journal of NASA), composer, author and member of the Saxophone Sinfonia.
> **Kenneth Deans** (USA), Professor, University of Southern Mississippi.
> **Lawrence Gwozdz** (USA), Professor, University of Southern Mississippi, member of the Saxophone Sinfonia.
> **John Edward Kelly** (USA), international soloist, member of the Rascher Saxophone Quartet.
> **Lee Patrick** (USA), Professor, University of Louisville, member of the Saxophone Sinfonia.
> **Carina Rascher-Peters** (USA/Germany), leader of the Rascher Saxophone Quartet.

Marcel Mule

Marcel Mule was born in 1901. He showed early precocity on the saxophone having been introduced to the instrument at the age of seven by his father, an accountant and keen amateur musician. He later studied violin and piano and demonstrated ability on each. He studied to become a teacher but in 1921, shortly after completing his training, he left for Paris, joining the Fifth Infantry Regiment, and subsequently its band.

The active musical environment of Paris inspired him and his prowess was quickly noted. He encountered and studied with numerous fine classical musicians and became involved in the Parisian jazz scene of the 1920s. Mule took inspiration from the many artists he heard, and while his own reputation grew he continued to observe others and to cultivate a very personal playing concept. In 1923 Mule won the competition for entrance into La Musique de la Garde Républicaine, beginning a thirteen-year tenure with the ensemble, and shortly thereafter he succeeded François Combelle as solo saxophonist.

Marcel Mule and colleagues from the Garde formed the first

Fig. 3.2 Marcel Mule

saxophone quartet in 1928 and established the now familiar soprano, alto, tenor and baritone instrumentation. This ensemble, eventually named the Marcel Mule Saxophone Quartet, always with Mule on soprano, performed to enormous acclaim for nearly forty years with remarkably few changes in personnel.

In addition to being a featured soloist with the Garde, Mule began to be sought after as a soloist with other ensembles, and by 1936, at the time of leaving the regiment, he had already established a career as a solo performer, inspiring those who heard him and receiving many dedications and giving numerous première performances. His unparalleled artistry was further acknowledged when, in 1942, he was appointed Professor of Saxophone at the Paris Conservatoire, only the second saxophone teacher in the history of the Conservatoire, after Adolphe Sax who left in 1870 without a successor being appointed. Throughout his tenure until his retirement in 1968 Mule worked to adapt and build a repertoire for teaching the classical saxophone. He was aided in this undertaking by the requirement that a new competition piece be written for the Conservatoire students, and by the many works written for and dedicated to him:

> His success as a teacher was to match his achievements on the concert stage. During his twenty-six year tenure at the Conservatory, no fewer than eighty-seven of his pupils attained the first prize. But even the many first prizes do not convey the true measure of Mule's influence on his pupils. His profound kindness, dedication, and wisdom as a teacher inspired his pupils personally as well as musically.[7]

The late twentieth century

The significance of the Paris Conservatoire and other regional conservatories in the creation of a performance repertoire through the commissioning of examination pieces cannot be overlooked. The influence of the studio class, with its emphasis on excellence through competition between selected outstanding students, and regular contact with master teachers, is responsible for creating an environment where progress towards placing the saxophone on the same artistic, intellectual and compositional foundations as other traditional orchestral instruments has been possible.

In this context one can speak of the emergence of a stylistically coherent French School of saxophone playing by the 1950s, which exerted great influence upon a generation of players who sought out the tuition and inspiration of Marcel Mule. Linked directly with Mule and the Conservatoire class tradition are many widely renowned soloists and artist/teachers, each of whom has made their own contribution to the further development and advancement of the saxophone.

France

André Beun, member of the Garde Républicaine, soloist and lecturer.

Serge Bichon, Professor at CNCR Lyons from 1956.

Daniel Deffayet, outstanding protégé of Marcel Mule and his successor as Saxophone Professor at the CNSM (1968–88).

Claude Delangle, award winning soloist and Saxophone Professor at the CNSM from 1988.

Jacques Deloges, CNRM Versailles from 1975.

Georges Gordet, member of the Mule Quartet, Professor at the Ecole National de Caen from 1971.

Marcel Josse (1905–96), member of the Mule Quartet, Professor at CNRM Versailles 1948–76.

Guy Lacour, member of the Mule Quartet and Ensemble de Saxophone Français, composer and lecturer.

Jean Ledieu, member of the Deffayet Saxophone Quartet, Professor at CNRM, Nancy.

Jean-Marie Londeix, international soloist, Professor at CNRM Bordeaux, founder of the Ensemble International de Saxophones, Selmer clinician and consultant to the Selmer company (Paris), adjudicator, writer and arranger. As a performer he has toured the world giving thousands of recitals championing the saxophone and its repertoire, and especially promoting new works by contemporary composers. His Bordeaux classes have been an artistic haven for many international students, and his reference books on music for saxophone are recognised as the authoritative source for repertoire listings.

Jacques Melzer, Professor at CNSM Nice, founder of the Ensemble de Saxophones Français.

Fig. 3.3 Claude Delangle

Michel Nouaux, member of the Garde Républicaine, renowned soloist, member of the Ensemble de Saxophones Français, lecturer.
Paul Pareille, founder of the Quatuor d'Anches Français, lecturer.
Henri-René Pollin, member of the Deffayet Saxophone Quartet and the Garde Républicaine, lecturer.
Georges Porte, member of the Quatuor de Saxophones d'Ile-de-France.
Jacques Henri Terry, member of the Deffayet Saxophone Quartet and the Garde Républicaine Band, lecturer.

USA
Frederick Hemke, international soloist, adjudicator, author, editor, highly respected educator, clinician and consultant to the Selmer company (Paris), consultant to Rico Corporation (USA), past President of NASA and host of the 1979 Evanston World Saxophone Congress, Professor of Saxophone and Chairman of Wind and Percussion, Northwestern University, Evanston, Illinois.
Eugene Rousseau, international soloist, author, highly respected educator, co-founder of the World Saxophone Congress, Yamaha design consultant and clinician, past President of NASA, Distinguished Professor, University of Indiana, Bloomington, Indiana.

Switzerland
Iwan Roth, international soloist, Professor at Basel Conservatory, member of the Quatuor de Saxophones Suisses.

Netherlands
Jules de Vries, soloist, lecturer.

Algeria
Marcel Perrin, soloist, founder of the Quatuor de Saxophones d'Alger, writer, lecturer.

Fig. 3.4 Eugene Rousseau

Canada
Pierre Borque, Professor at the Conservatoire de Musique Quebec.
Remi Menard, faculty of Ecole de Musique, University of Laval.

Japan
Arata Sakaguchi, self-taught from the recordings of and correspondence with
Marcel Mule, he became the seminal figure in promoting the classical
saxophone in Japan.

Within traditions built principally on the pioneering efforts of Larry Teal
and other American artist/teachers but embracing a stylistically broad and
less identifiably national perspective are performers and teachers such as:

Paul Brodie (Canada), international recitalist who has sought to extend
awareness of the saxophone to a worldwide audience, and co-founder of
theWorld Saxophone Congress.
James Dawson (USA), international soloist and lecturer.
Steven Mauk (USA), soloist, lecturer, Professor at Ithaca College, New York
State, regular contributor to *Saxophone Journal*, founder of the Empire Quartet.
Donald Sinta (USA), internationally acclaimed soloist, adjudicator, Selmer
clinician, highly respected educator and successor to Larry Teal as Professor of
Saxophone at the University of Michigan, Ann Arbor.

From a widespread net of influences and exerting a positive promotional message for the saxophone have been musical statesmen such as:

Peter Clinch (Australia) (1930–95), Professor at Canberra Conservatory and lecturer, Melbourne State Conservatory, founder of the Peter Clinch Saxophone Quartet.

Harry Gee (USA), author, soloist, adjudicator, Professor at Indiana State University.

Percy Grainger (Australia) (1882–1961), saxophonist, arranger, composer.

Wolfgang Graetschel (Germany), Professor at Nuremberg, host of the 1982 World Saxophone Congress in Nuremberg, member of the Arbeitsgruppe Saxophon.

Paul Harvey (UK), former Professor of Clarinet and Saxophone at the Royal Military College, Kneller Hall, London. Founder of the London Saxophone Quartet, and host with the LSQ of the 1976 World Saxophone Congress in London. An active studio and commercial performer, composer, author, arranger and leading music educator. He has been a regular contributor to journals worldwide on matters of interest to both clarinettists and saxophonists.

Joseph Viola (USA), Professor at Berklee School of Music, Boston, Massachusetts, author and regular contributor to *Saxophone Journal*.

Ever since the efforts and enthusiasm of Paul Brodie and Eugene Rousseau brought about the first meeting of the World Saxophone Congress in Chicago in 1969, this forum has done much to foster communication and awareness amongst artists and enthusiasts of the saxophone the world over. Regional meetings and activities of members help to keep a good 'grass roots' spirit and momentum going in the interval between the worldwide gatherings. The journals of the respective organisations, the North American Saxophone Alliance, the Association des Saxophonistes de France, the Clarinet and Saxophone Society of Great Britain and others have contributed scholarly articles, reviews, product information and developments of interest regarding the instrument. Membership of one or more of these organisations is of great value to any saxophonist.

Amongst the many notable players and performer–teachers in the classical saxophone tradition who are active today, truly far too many to be listed in this chapter, a number deserve mention for their ongoing contributions to the presentation of the saxophone to a worldwide audience. All of these artists have benefited from the efforts of their predecessors, whose contributions helped bring about the growth of a repertoire, the establishment of musical credibility for the saxophone and the setting of standards of instrumental achievement which are now widely accepted and often taken for granted. These performers now endeavour to pass on a tradition of excellence and a respect for their beloved instrument and its music to their pupils and audiences.

Recordings are available of almost all the artists mentioned previously and below. *Listening is highly recommended.*

USA
Raymond Beckenstein, Robert Black, James Boitos, Frank Bongiorno, Nicholas Brightman, Joseph Briscuso, Paul Bro, Paul Cohen, James Cunningham, Philip Delibero, David Demsey, Richard Dirlam, Steve Duke, Elizabeth Ervin, Kenneth Fischer, Brad Foley, Christopher Ford, James Forger, Roger Greenberg, Tedd Griepentrog, David Hastings, Ted Hegvik, James Hill, James Houlik, Laura Hunter, Reginald Jackson, Michael Jacobsen, Steven Jordheim, Jean Lansing, Lynn Klock, Rita Knussel, Trent Kynaston, Thomas Liley, Gary Louie, Joe Lulloff, Douglas Masek, Brian Minor, Michael Nascimben, Harvey Pittel, Leo Potts, Ken Radnovsky, Neil Ramsey, Al Regni, Debra Richtmeyer, James Riggs, James Rotter, John Sampen, Thomas Smialek, James Stoltie, Dale Underwood, George Wolfe, Joseph Wytko, Elaine Zajac

Australia
Mark Walton

Belgium
Norbert Nozy, Luc Schollaert

Britain
Rob Buckland, John Harle, Simon Haram, Kyle Horch, Richard Ingham, Gerard McChrystal, Martin Robertson

Canada
Claude Brisson, Marvin Eckroth, Masino Rene, William Street

Denmark
Pere Egholm

Finland
Pekka Savijoki

France
Jean-Pierre Baraglioli, Alain Bouhey, Jean-Pierre Caens, Jacques Charles, Marie Bernadette Charrier, Jean-Yves Fourmeau, Jean-Paul Fouchecourt, Daniel Kientzy, Pierre Leman, Daniel Liger, Jean-Denis Michat, Jean-Pierre Vermeeren

Germany
Linda Bangs, Detlef Bensmann, Johannes Ernst, Gunther Priesner

Holland
Ed Bogaard, Henri Bok, Arno Bornkamp, Leo van Oostrom

Italy
Federico Mondelci, Massimo Mazzoni

Japan
Musato Kumoi, Keiji Munesada, Ken-Ichiro Muto, Fumiyoshi Miyasawa, Ryo Noda, Yuichi Omuro, Yuji Sasaki, Keiji Shimoji, Nobuya Sugawa, Keiji Ueda

Norway
Erik Tangvold

Poland
David Alan Pituch

Russia
Lev Michailov, Margarita Shaposhnitova, Anatoly Vapirov

Spain
Pedro Iturralde, Manuel Mijan, Adolfo Rodriguez Ventas

Switzerland
Marcus Weiss

Yugoslavia
Oto Vrhovnik

4 The repertoire heritage

THOMAS LILEY

Introduction

The indispensable bibliographical index *150 Years of Music for Saxophone* catalogues 'more than 12,000 works of "classical music" for saxophone, 1844–1994. Not included are the 3,000 symphonic or operatic works in which one or several saxophones appear in the orchestration.'[1] The index lists music from dozens of countries by composers of all levels of recognition and of widely diverse aesthetic approaches. These men and women have written concertos for saxophone with band and with orchestra, sonatas for saxophone and piano, unaccompanied pieces, saxophone ensembles of various sizes, and works for saxophone in unusual combination with instruments such as voice, percussion, organ, tape and synthesizer.

The great majority of these works were written for the alto saxophone; only in the first and the most recent decades of the instrument's existence have composers given serious consideration to the other members of the family. This chapter will attempt to trace the growth of the saxophone literature, to identify influential compositions, and to create a sense of the heritage of the performing repertoire.

Much of the core of the saxophone repertoire dates from the 1930s and provides a striking parallel with that of the clarinet. Mozart's clarinet Concerto, K.622, written in 1790, is the first masterpiece for the clarinet, an instrument created around 1700.[2] The saxophone first appeared around 1840; Ibert's *Concertino da Camera* was written some ninety years later in 1935, and is a comparable landmark in the history of the saxophone literature. Each composition has important predecessors, but the saxophone repertoire had an important advantage: Adolphe Sax.

The saxophone repertoire to 1900

Adolphe Sax realised that repertoire must exist in order for his newly created instruments to survive. To this end he owned and operated a publishing house in Paris from the late 1850s until the bankruptcy proceedings of the late 1870s. Sax published almost 200 compositions for his

Fig. 4.1 Cover of *Fantaisie* for soprano saxophone by J. B. Singelée, published by Adolphe Sax in 1863

instruments, including at least thirty-five for various saxophones and piano.

Seven composers supplied music for saxophone and piano, including famous cornetist Joseph Arban, renowned flautist Jules Demersseman, clarinet virtuoso Hyacinthe Klosé and – most prolifically – Jean Baptiste Singelée. A large number of their compositions were *solos de concours* used by the Paris Conservatoire for their annual examinations. The majority of the works are harmonically and structurally conservative; most often an increasingly virtuosic set of variations or a *fantaisie* follows a brief piano introduction. Many of the compositions are solidly constructed and were intended to ensure that the saxophone – soprano, alto, tenor and baritone – would have both a small but important body of literature and the performers to present it.

This legacy of Sax remains little known. Several works by the composers in Sax's catalogue have been recommended as worthy of performance today: *Solo sur la Tyrolienne* by Leon Chic; Demersseman's *Premier solo, andante et bolero*; Jean-Nicholas Savari's *Fantaisie sur des motifs du Freyschutz*, and four works by Singelée – the *Fantaisie*, Op. 89, the *6e solo de concert*, Op. 92, the *7e solo de concert*, Op. 93, and the *Fantaisie*, Op. 102. Demersseman's *Premier solo* and Singelée's *6e solo de concert* are for tenor saxophone; Singelée's *7e solo de concert* is for baritone and his two *Fantaisies* are for soprano. As Bruce Ronkin states, 'Many performers feel that nineteenth-century music is accepted by a wider audience than more contemporary works. Perhaps by adding the Sax publications to the saxophonist's recital repertoire, a broader audience for saxophone concerts might be found, thus enhancing the instrument's acceptance in classical music circles.'[3]

To World War I

No composer of international stature wrote solo works for the saxophone in the last half of the nineteenth century. But, of course, almost no internationally regarded composer other than Brahms contributed to any other portion of the woodwind literature during that period.

Claude Debussy was one of the earliest important composers to write for the saxophone and is probably the most famous musician ever to have written for the instrument. His association with the Bostonian Elise Boyer Hall is mentioned in chapter 3. The *Rhapsodie Mauresque for Orchestra and Principal Saxophone* may fail to demonstrate the full capabilities of the saxophone, but does demonstrate the unique colours and qualities of Debussy's music. Comprised of two principal sections, the work has easily recognisable themes that are treated in a free, fantasia-like manner; the vivid Spanish rhythms reflect the original title.

In addition to Debussy's score, Hall commissioned works by composers such as André Caplet, Philippe Gaubert, Charles Martin Loeffler, Georges Longy and Florent Schmitt (see Appendix 1). For years much of the music associated with Hall was unavailable for performance and the manuscripts could 'be viewed by request only on the premises' of the music library of the New England Conservatory.[4] Several of these works have only recently become available, often with piano reductions of the accompanying ensembles.

World War I to 1930

Undoubtedly the best-known saxophonist and most prolific composer for the instrument in the years immediately following World War I was Rudy Wiedoeft. Much of his fame was built on the dozens of novelty solos he wrote for the C-melody and alto saxophones. Strongly associated with the ragtime style popular in the 1920s, such technically demanding and cleverly titled works as *Saxarella, Saxema, Saxophobia* and *Sax-O-Phun* caught the attention of the public. Various effects such as false fingerings, slap-tonguing, and the 'laugh' created an image of the saxophone that still persists. Other popular works by Wiedoeft include a number of florid waltzes such as *Valse Erica* and *Valse Vanité*.

In Europe the saxophone was utilised differently. Three works by German composers and one by an English composer in the 1920s merit mention. The earliest of these, *Façade* by Sir William Walton, dates from 1922; it remains his most famous work. Twenty-one poems by Dame Edith Sitwell are accompanied by a small chamber ensemble consisting mostly of winds. The jazz rhythms capture the spirit of the time and often recall the gaiety of the English dance hall.

Paul Hindemith's Trio, Op. 47, of 1928, is a challenging work for two of the instruments involved. The viola part is a reminder that Hindemith was a world-class violist whose compositions are an important part of the viola literature. The piano score is typically dense and contrapuntal, but the third score, for the now obsolete heckelphone or tenor saxophone in C or B♭, is much less challenging. The piece, however, is a major work by one of the century's great composers and is satisfying both to hear and to perform.

Anton Webern's Quartet for violin, clarinet, tenor saxophone and piano, Op. 22, was conceived as a concerto for violin, clarinet, horn, piano and string orchestra, to be written in the spirit of Bach's Brandenburg Concertos. The Quartet was composed in 1930, and Berg described it as 'a miracle. What amazes me above all is its originality.' Today theorists regard the Quartet as a classically organised masterpiece of formal construction.[5] Sigfrid Karg-Elert, one of the major organ composers of the twentieth century, also wrote *25 Caprices*, Op. 153a, and an unaccompanied *Atonal Sonata*, Op. 153b, for saxophone in 1929. His interest in the saxophone dates from his service in a regimental army band during World War I. 'Fourteen years ago [1915], the author [Karg-Elert] ... devoted a great part of his attention and time to the saxophone, a favourite instru-

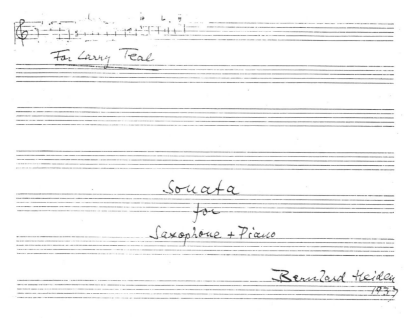

Fig. 4.2 The title page of the Sonata for Saxophone and Piano (1937) by Bernhard Heiden, with dedication to Larry Teal

ment of his. . . .'[6] Karg-Elert's studies remain pedagogically valuable and his sonata provides an insight into the musical ferment of Germany between the World Wars I and II.

1931–40

The fourth decade of the twentieth century remains a golden age of serious composition for the saxophone, with lasting contributions by numerous composers. Many of these works were written for Marcel Mule or Sigurd Rascher, but the most important and most frequently performed sonatas for saxophone and piano were composed for two American musicians – Larry Teal and Cecil Leeson.

Bernhard Heiden wrote what has been described as 'the first substantive sonata for the instrument'[7] for Teal in 1937. The Sonata, Op. 19, by Paul Creston, written for Leeson in 1939, is regarded as 'one of the definitive works for saxophone and piano'.[8] Two works with orchestra were among several written for Rascher – in 1934 the Concerto in E♭, Op. 109, from the Romantic master Alexander Glazunov and the *Concertino da Camera* by Jacques Ibert of 1935, which is 'often cited as an example of the perfect composition for a solo instrument'.[9] These four compositions, which form the core of the saxophone repertoire, have received numerous performances, scholarly discussions,[10] and theoretical analyses,[11] as well as commentary by their composers and dedicatees.[12] All saxophonists are indebted to the creators of these works and the artists who inspired them.

The 1930s also saw the creation of important works by such significant composers as Paul Hindemith, Frank Martin and Darius Milhaud. Hindemith's *Konzertstück* for two alto saxophones was written in 1933 but not performed until 1960 and not published until 1970. The first of five *Ballades* for various instruments composed by the Swiss-born Martin is for alto saxophone and orchestra. Written in 1938, the *Ballade* is a powerful work which accelerates and climbs through the registers of the instrument. Like the Hindemith it was composed for Rascher and, again like the *Konzertstück*, for years was not readily available until a piano reduction was published in 1981. The best-known and most popular of the three composers' works is Milhaud's *Scaramouche*, Op. 165b. Originally written for Mule for saxophone and orchestra in 1937, the well-known version for two pianos was created by Milhaud the same year.[13]

Two small-scale works for saxophone and piano dedicated to Mule have become repertoire favourites. Eugène Bozza's *Aria* of 1936, based on Bach's *Pastorale* for organ BWV 590, is a lyric masterpiece. Originally for saxophone, the *Aria* has appeared for other woodwind instruments, including flute, oboe and bassoon. The *Sonatine Sportive*, Op. 63, written by Alexander Tcherepnin in 1939, is in three brief movements. According to the composer the work attempts to portray in music the surprise elements found in sport. Mule tells us that the *Sonatine* was originally for bassoon and piano and was adapted to the saxophone by the composer.[14]

The *Harvard Dictionary of Music* describes an arrangement as 'the adaptation of a composition for a medium different from that for which it was originally written, so made that the musical substance remains essentially unchanged'.[15] Arrangements, or transcriptions, have been an important part of music since the early fourteenth century, and have played a significant role in the saxophone's history since its beginning. It was an arrangement by Berlioz of his *Chant sacré* that introduced to the public a sextet of Adolphe Sax's instruments. This first performance, which included a bass saxophone played by its inventor, took place in Paris's Salle Herz on 3 February 1844.[16] Hemke notes Thomas Ryan's performances of transcriptions of music by Schubert, Verdi, Donizetti and Rhode in Boston in the 1860s.[17]

Because of the paucity of original recital works, concert artists such as Leeson, Mule and Rascher adapted music of earlier periods to the saxophone. It is said that it was Rascher's performances of Bach that first interested composers such as Edmund von Borck to write concertos for him. In addition, Mule found in the music of the Baroque, Classical and early Romantic periods excellent pedagogical materials for the teaching of various historical styles.

Some of the earliest and most successful transcriptions by Leeson were of music by Bach, Kreisler and Schubert. Among Mule's more than a hundred *Pièces célèbres* are short works by Gluck, Lully and Mendelssohn as well as complete sonatas by Bach and Handel; many of these are still available to students and performers. Several arrangements by Rascher remain in print, ranging from short teaching pieces to concert-length works.

Saxophonists have long enriched their programmes with music of different periods. This trend will undoubtedly continue as music of the late Romantic and early twentieth century eras enters the public domain. A recent phenomenon is the use of music originally for other media which is transposed at sight by the performer rather than rewritten in the appropriate key; this is especially true of flute and oboe works performed on soprano saxophone.

1941–50

The decade of the 1940s is, in many ways, similar to the 1930s; among the rapidly growing repertoire are two important concertos – one written for Leeson and one for Rascher – and several works composed for Mule. Although undoubtedly slowed by the Second World War, interest in the classical saxophone continued in France and the United States. The last and longest of the compositions which resulted from Paul Creston's collaboration with Cecil Leeson is the Concerto, Op. 26, of 1941. The work is characteristic of the best of Creston's music – long melodies, rich harmonies, flamboyant rhythms and a virtuoso solo score – and amply demonstrates his declaration that 'the saxophone is the perfect solo instrument'.[18]

Ingolf Dahl's Concerto of 1949 for Rascher is a landmark in the repertoire of solo instruments with wind accompaniment, and is one of the earliest works to fully utilise the potential of the complete symphonic band. A dearth of performances caused by the formidable difficulties of both the solo and the accompanying parts prompted Dahl to revise the Concerto in 1953. Dahl is said to have made a second unacknowledged revision in 1959 which reduced the length of the Concerto by approximately a quarter, and this is the version which has been published.[19] A protégé of Stravinsky, Dahl also conducted the Collegium Musicum at the University of Southern California where he was a faculty member. The latter influence can be found in the first two movements – Recitative and Adagio (Passacaglia) – and his close association with Stravinsky can be heard in the texture, diatonicism and virtuosity of all three movements.

Another work for the same instrumentation as Dahl's Concerto, but of a decidedly more popular flavour, is the *Introduction and Samba* composed for Rascher in 1950 by Maurice Whitney. The work exploits the saxophone's agility and its upper register while the band's role is considerably less demanding. It has recently been reprinted with the original saxophone part and a piano reduction.

Four works inspired by Mule have entered the repertoire from this decade. Pierre Lantier's brief and bittersweet *Sicilienne* of 1943 is a melodic gem that captures Mule's singing approach to the saxophone. The *Improvisation* and *Caprice* of Eugène Bozza are the sixth and seventh of his *Etudes caprices*, Op. 60, written in 1944. The *Caprice* is a homage to Mule's remarkable technical facility, as is another difficult but idiomatic work for solo saxophone, the *Caprice en forme de valse*, written in 1950 by Paul Bonneau. Bonneau had studied the saxophone with Mule 'for a brief period, primarily so that he would be proficient on a band instrument when he entered military service. A talented man, he became a respectable saxophonist in about six months.'[20]

Heitor Villa-Lobos' *Fantasia*, Op. 630, of 1948 is undoubtedly the most important work for the soprano instrument. Scored for soprano saxophone, three horns and strings, the *Fantasia* contains many of the Brazilian composer's most famous characteristics – vigorous native rhythms, long languid melodies and Bachian counterpoint. Although the work is dedicated to Mule, he never performed it.[21] Rousseau tells us that when he produced the first and definitive recording in 1971 there was no evidence that the orchestral parts had ever been played.[22]

1951–60

The growth in the saxophone repertoire, begun in the 1930s and slowed by the Second World War, regained its momentum after the conflict and accelerated through the next two decades. Several of the works composed during the period have demonstrated their worth and have remained in the repertoire. More French contributions appeared, with Jeanine Rueff's *Chanson et passepied* of 1951 among the first of the decade. This brief and charming work uses the same material in each of its two sections, closing with a brilliant syncopated flourish. More substantial compositions for Mule include the *Tableaux de Provence* by another of his colleagues at the Paris Conservatoire, Paule Maurice, wife of Pierre Lantier. The suite, in five colourful movements, depicts the area in the south-east of France where the Lantier and Mule families spent several summers and to where Mule retired. Written during the years 1954–9, the reduction of the orchestral score is unusually idiomatic to the piano. During Mule's years at the Conservatoire twenty-five compositions were written for the Conservatoire's annual contest. Perhaps the best known of these compositions dates from 1956: the *Prélude, cadence et finale* of Alfred Desenclos; its cadenza is a 'must' for all serious saxophonists. This virtuoso work requires the refined approach and complete command of the instrument which exemplify Mule's students.

An outstanding product of Mule's classes is Jean-Marie Londeix, for whom Pierre-Max Dubois wrote a Concerto in 1959. A remarkably prolific composer, Dubois has written more than fifty works for the saxophone in various settings, ranging from solo saxophone to ensembles of eleven players. The Concerto is unusual because of its slow introduction and lengthy opening cadenza and is notable for its kaleidoscopic shifts of tonality.

The middle movement of Warren Benson's Concertino of 1955, the *Aeolian Song*, was written for Rascher and requires a flexible and assured control of the altissimo register. Also composed for Rascher was Karel Husa's *Elégie et rondeau* of 1960; it is in one movement, with the élégie leading directly into the rondeau. In the élégie, which is drawn from an earlier work written in 1957 for solo piano, Husa sought to display 'the legato, beautiful expressive sound of the saxophone'. The contrasting rondeau starts softly and becomes progressively stronger to capitalise on the 'incredible power' of the instrument.[23]

1961–70

The repertoire continued to increase in quantity and quality as new artists continued to appear and as saxophone teaching positions at major schools of music were created. In 1967, Eugene Rousseau, who had studied with Mule in Paris, received *Quattro Lirich brevi*, Op. 61, from his colleague at Indiana University, the Chilean-born Juan Orrego-Salas. Leslie Bassett composed his *Music for Saxophone and Piano* in 1968 for Donald Sinta; Sinta, a student of Teal at the University of Michigan, would later succeed Teal at that school.

Composers also continued to write for already established performers such as Mule and Rascher. Ida Gotkovsky's brilliant Concerto was written for Mule in 1966 and is an outstanding example of the saxophone contest pieces created at the Paris Conservatoire. Henry Cowell wrote his *Air and Scherzo* in 1961 as another demonstration of Rascher's mastery of the altissimo register. In an interesting reversal of expectations, the 'gay' minor scherzo contains a 'sad' trio in the parallel major key.

Rascher also gave the first performance of what many regard as the

Fig. 4.3 Sketches from the Concerto for Alto Saxophone and Concert Band (1967) by
Karel Husa

most important composition for saxophone in the second half of the
twentieth century.

The impetus for the Concerto for Alto Saxophone and Concert Band
of 1967 by Karel Husa originated with Donald Sinta. Husa and Sinta were
both residents of Ithaca, New York. Sinta, however, took a new teaching
position elsewhere and Rascher, who was already well known to Husa, was
selected as the soloist for the first performance. By 1976 the Concerto was
already considered 'a classic in the literature of the saxophone'.[24] The

three-movement work consists of a heroic, recitative-like Prologue; an intensely rhythmic Ostinato; and an Epilogue which begins from and ends with *niente* (nothing).[25]

The end of the decade saw the first of the World Saxophone Congresses, assembling performers, teachers and students from around the world. Beginning with the first Congress in 1969, premières of new work have been an important feature at each gathering. The first new composition to be heard was by Bernhard Heiden, whose Sonata has long been a mainstay of the repertoire; his *Solo* is dedicated to his colleague Eugene Rousseau and to the first Congress. The second Congress, held in 1970, heard two important new sonatas: Robert Muczynski's Op. 29, written for Trent Kynaston, is very American in its melodies, harmonies and rhythms; whilst the Russian composer Edison Denisov used complex metres and quarter-tones in his sonata for Jean-Marie Londeix; both sonatas unmistakably share the influence of jazz.

The most recent decades

At the beginning of the twenty-first century, the saxophone repertoire continues to receive significant contributions. The instrument will, of course, never have original music by Bach, Mozart or Schubert, but the heritage of compositions written since the instrument's creation around 1840 is the equal of any other wind instrument in the past 150 years. It may yet be too early to determine which works of the most recent decades will establish themselves as permanent members of the repertoire. Several compositions, however, seem to have the musical worth and performer interest to join the works already mentioned.

Ross Lee Finney's Concerto, written in 1974 to commemorate the retirement of Larry Teal from the University of Michigan, is both substantive and compelling. John Anthony Lennon's atmospheric *Distances Within Me*, first performed at the 1979 World Saxophone Congress, employs a contemporary harmonic language to speak persuasively to contemporary audiences. Robert Muczynski's Concerto, Op. 41 (1981), is a noteworthy heir to his highly successful Sonata, and concertinos written by Paul Harvey (1974) and Walter Hartley (1978) reflect the renewed interest in the tenor saxophone generated by James Houlik. Several of the numerous and complex works by the French composer Christian Lauba have attracted much attention, which may well be sustained.

In recognition of the substantial fees commanded by renowned composers, several saxophonists have occasionally combined resources to

For Eugene Rousseau

JINDŘICH FELD

SONATA

for Alto Saxophone and Piano

(1989 - 90)

Durata cca 21 min.

Fig. 4.4 The title page of the Sonata for Saxophone and Piano (1990) by Jindřich Feld, with dedication to Eugene Rousseau

attract finances for major commissions. Among the results are sonatas from William Albright, William Bolcom and David Diamond in 1984; in 1987, Morton Subotnick's *In Two Worlds* for alto saxophone, computer and orchestra;[26] and in 1988 the *Partita*, Op. 100, for alto saxophone, violin, violoncello and piano by Juan Orrego-Salas.[27] Each work was funded by the National Endowment for the Arts.

The compositions of the Czech Jindřich Feld hold considerable

Fig. 4.5 Manuscript of Feld's Sonata, as used at the first performance

promise of establishing themselves as notable members of the repertoire. Feld's music contains both forceful melodic lines and sophisticated rhythmic structures. His Concerto of 1980 – yet another work first performed at a World Saxophone Congress – and his Sonata of 1990 present the most contemporary compositional techniques in an accessible manner that should maintain his music in the twenty-first century.

Both of the Feld pieces were written for Eugene Rousseau, who has suggested an aesthetic by which the saxophone's future repertoire may be determined:

> If the saxophone has a future as a classical instrument, it will be because of its melodic use and not because of *avant-garde* pieces, great though they may be. The basic human spirit responds emotionally to melody. With the other music we might say the music is 'interesting', or that we were 'on the edge of our seats', but we're not sure if we want to hear that piece again or not. Or maybe we do hear it again and then we're *sure* we don't want to hear it any more, or maybe we want to hear it many times. Regardless of the final decision, the music still doesn't evoke the same response.[28]

Adolphe Sax understood in the 1850s that the saxophone, in order to be sustained, must have a repertoire worthy of the instrument and its audiences. A century-and-a-half later there exists a body of literature which has established the saxophone as a significant concert instrument, while the number of pre-eminent composers of high merit and international renown who have written for the instrument has grown conspicuously. They 'are making the saxophone an instrument capable of answering the highest musical demands of the time [and] have finally made the instrument indispensable to "classical" music and justify the involvement of our best musicians in the rendering of this concert music'.[29]

5 The saxophone quartet

RICHARD INGHAM

The saxophone quartet as a medium is generally thought to have dated from 1928, although earlier works were written for the combination by Jean-Baptiste Singelée (1812–75), including *Allegro de Concert* (AATB), *Quatuor en 4 Parties* (SATB) and *Grand Quatuor Concertant en 3 Parties* (SATB). Another early introduction of the ensemble was by Edouard Lefèbre (1834–1911). He was born in Holland of French parents and was a soloist with the New York based Gilmore band from 1873. The band featured a saxophone quartet in 1878, consisting of Lefèbre, Walrabe, Steckelberg and Schultz. In 1905, Lefèbre established his own quartet, which toured the USA, Alaska, Europe and the Philippines; their repertoire consisted of transcriptions.

The major push to establish the saxophone quartet was by the French virtuoso Marcel Mule, whose ensemble gave its first performance in La Rochelle on 2 December 1928. Le Quatuor de la Musique de la Garde Républicaine consisted of Mule (soprano), René Chaligné (alto), Hippolyte Poimboeuf (tenor) and Georges Chauvet (baritone). When Mule left La Garde in 1936, the group became known as Le Quatuor de Saxophones de Paris, and in 1951, the group took the name Marcel Mule Quartet, under which it was known until its disbandment in 1967. The original grouping remained the same until 1932, and subsequent members were Paul Romby, Fernand L'homme, Georges Charron, Marcel Josse, André Bauchy, Georges Gourdet and Guy Lacour.

With a celebrated figure such as Mule behind the artistic development of the ensemble, the grouping did actually create its own chamber music category. Because of Mule's own soloistic virtuosity and resultant contact with composers, many of these composers were forthcoming with works which formed the basis of the classic French repertoire. The nature of the ensemble was already apparent – well balanced in tessitura like a string quartet, and homogeneous in texture. Mule himself was still experimenting with the introduction of vibrato into classical saxophone performance at this time, and the quartet played for the first four years of its existence without vibrato.

Initially relying on transcriptions for programmes, the Mule Quartet rapidly incorporated new works into their repertoire. The very first was

Fig. 5.1 Saxophone Quartet of La Garde Républicaine, 1927: soprano, Marcel Mule; alto, René Chaligné; tenor, Hippolyte Poimboeuf; baritone, Georges Chauvet

by Pierre Vellones (1889–1939), entitled *Au Jardin des bêtes sauvages*, completed in 1930. Perhaps the most significant and popular are:

1930 Robert Clerisse	*Cache-Cache*
1932 Alexander Glazunov	Quartet, Op. 109
1936 Gabriel Pierné	*Introduction et Variations sur un thème populaire*
1937 Jean Absil	*Prémier Quatuor*, Op. 31
1938 Eugène Bozza	*Andante et Scherzo*
Jean Rivier	*Grave et Presto*
1941 Florent Schmitt	*Quatuor*, Op. 102
1946 Eugène Bozza	*Nuages*
1954 Jean Absil	*Trois Pièces*, Op. 35
1955 Jeanine Rueff	*Concert en Quatuor*
1961 Claude Pascal	*Quatuor*
1964 Alfred Desenclos	*Quatuor*

The Glazunov quartet is an extensive work in three movements, dedicated 'Aux artistes des saxophones de la Garde Républicaine', completed four years before the Concerto, and in similar late Romantic style to the latter. Bozza's *Andante et Scherzo* opens with a restrained slow movement before bouncing through the Scherzo, for which rapid staccato playing is essential. *Nuages* on the other hand is like a seamless garment of chromatic bursts thrown around all the instruments – a character piece of great effect. Jean Rivier's *Grave et Presto* is one of the highlights of the repertoire, written in the traditional French style of thoughtful introduction exploiting the colours of sustained saxophone chords, followed by a virtuosic finale – yet it succeeds as a highly original piece of writing. The

Presto section itself is beautifully balanced between flowing effortless bravura episodes and lyrical moments of reflection.

Pierné's *Introduction et Variations* is a very early quartet and also quite original in its concept. The fragmented opening allows for sustained ensemble playing as well as occasional bursts of solo activity; the variations themselves follow standard variation options, and are well crafted for the instruments, particularly when one considers that Pierné had almost no precedent to follow – the Mule Quartet won Le Grand Prix du Disque for their 1937 recording of this work. Claude Pascal and Alfred Desenclos have contributed two of the most substantial works in the French repertoire. Pascal's opening movement is one of great urgency, and, as throughout the whole work, the composer displays a sensitive awareness of strengths and timbres, not only of each instrument, but also within each instrument's range. The second movement is marked 'Choral' and contains very unusual, intense gestural writing. The waltz movement which follows is a deceptive light antidote in sound, which is none the less a challenge in control for performers. The finale shares the impetus of the opening movement and closes in grand style. Alfred Desenclos writes long complex chromatic lines but the rhetorical nature of his writing is undeniably traditional, and ultimately rooted in tonality. The opening movement of his *Quatuor* initially pits the soprano against the other three in a surprising conflict so early in a piece, yet this feature is developed throughout the movement: a separation of smaller groups within the quartet, providing timbral contrasts, both in terms of individual instrumental colour as well as textural variety. The slow movement begins as an innocent melody in song form, and develops into one of the most effective examples of musical climax writing in the whole repertoire. The third movement opens with a powerful recitative section for all four instruments in unison rhythm, before giving way to a traditional, albeit episodic, finale.

Mule himself contributed numerous arrangements to the embryonic repertoire, the most notable of these being the Andante from Tchaikovsky's first String Quartet and *Trois Pièces* by Albéniz. His example in establishing a quartet was to be followed by many throughout the world. Mule's pupil Daniel Deffayet, who was later to succeed Mule as Professor of Saxophone at the Paris Conservatoire, established his own group (Quatuor de Saxophones Daniel Deffayet) in 1953, along with Jacques Maffei, Jacques Terry and Jean Ledieu. After Maffei's departure in 1956, Henri-René Pollin joined what was to become a very stable ensemble. Composers who wrote for this ensemble included Damase, Dubois and Jindřich Feld. Also in France the Quatuor de Saxophones Fourmeau, led by Jean-Yves Fourmeau, was formed in 1979.

In 1969 the great soloist Sigurd Rascher founded the Rascher

Saxophone Quartet with his daughter Carina Rascher, Bruce Weinberger and Linda Bangs. On Rascher's retirement in 1981, his place was taken by John Edward Kelly. The Quartet has dedicated itself to the promotion of many contemporary works from its German base, and extended techniques are a speciality of the ensemble; numerous works have been written for them.

The USA has produced many outstanding quartets, including the Chicago Quartet (established 1968), the Harvey Pittel Quartet, the New York Saxophone Quartet (1959) and the Prism Quartet. The first professional quartet in Canada was led by Mule disciple Arthur Romano from 1949 until 1964. Gerald Danovitch, who had been a pupil of Romano and a member of his quartet then led his own ensemble from 1968.

Michael Krein (1908–66) established the pioneering Krein Quartet in Britain in 1941 with Chester Smith, Hugh Tripp and Ken Warner. Subsequent members were Norman Barker, Phil Goody, Gordon Lewin and Jack Brymer. Krein himself contributed many compositions and arrangements to the repertoire including *Valse Caprice*. In 1969 the London Saxophone Quartet was formed under the leadership of Paul Harvey and was an influential ensemble which remained together until 1985. Paul Harvey was a major figure in the popularisation of the saxophone in Britain, renowned in particular for his ensemble writing. His quartet played at the World Saxophone Congresses in Toronto in 1972 and Bordeaux in 1974, and hosted the 1976 Congress in London. The English Saxophone Quartet (established 1975) were recitalists at the World Saxophone Congress in Nuremberg in 1982, and the Scottish Saxophone Quartet led by Philip Greene was established in 1976. In 1976 the Myrha Quartet was formed by John Harle at the World Saxophone Congress in London, and despite its short life span contributed enormously to the acceptance of the quartet as a chamber ensemble, being the first quartet in Britain to commit itself to contemporary works. The Northern Saxophone Quartet was formed in 1980, and presents programmes of French classical repertoire, jazz, medieval and contemporary music. They were recitalists at the World Saxophone Congresses in Washington (1985), Tokyo (1988), Pesaro (1992) and Valencia (1997). Led by Alistair Parnell, Mistral Quartet has enjoyed a successful career since its establishment in 1984.

Choreography played a part in saxophone arrangements when the Fairer Sax began their barn-storming series of successful recitals from 1982. Quality playing, quality arrangements and effective media exposure also helped the cause of other quartets, and it is noticeable that since they became popular as concert and cabaret artists, there are now many more quartets in Britain sharing what one had originally thought was a small recital market area. Their recital at the World Saxophone Congress in Tokyo in 1988 was followed by a less formal event demonstrating their dancing skills alongside Frederick Hemke and Jean-Marie Londeix. Slightly less choreographed but using stage space and memorising charts have been features of Saxtet, formed in 1985. Their original and versatile programming has taken them on many tours of recitals and street busking throughout the world, including a very successful presentation at the 1992 Congress in Pesaro. The Apollo Quartet, established in 1985, has specialised, like the Myrha before it, in commissioning contemporary works. Throughout Britain, the 1990s saw a tremendous rise in the number of amateur quartets, making great use of the extensive repertoire already available, including both original works and transcriptions. Many of these ensembles give concerts or play at functions, or just meet to enjoy playing chamber music.

In Japan, Quatre Roseaux (1974), the Tokyo Saxophone Ensemble (1980), the Harmo Saxophone Quartet (1982), the Trouvère Quartet (1987) and the Fine Arts Saxophone Quartet (1987) are examples of outstanding professional performers in a rich saxophone environment. Evidence of the popularity of the instrument and the pleasure to be gained from playing chamber music are to be seen in the worldwide proliferation of ensembles, some of which are listed below, with dates of formation:

Norway
Harald Bergersen's Saxophone Quartet (1982); Saxofon Concentus (1990)

Sweden
Stockholm Saxophone Quartet (1980); Rollin' Phones (1986)

Holland
Selmer Saxofoon Kwartet (1973); Aurelia Saxophone Quartet (1982); Saxofoonkwartet L'Imprévu (1993)

Belgium
Quatuor Belge de Saxophones (1953)

Ukraine
Kiev Saxophone Quartet (1985)

Germany
Akademie-Quartett Nürnberg (1982); Hannover Saxophon Quartett (1990); Berliner Saxophon Quartett (1983); Ensemble Atmosphère (1996)

Austria
Wiener Saxophon Quartett (1987); Danubia Saxophon Quartett (1995)

Spain

Quartet Sax de Barcelona (1982); Cuarteto Orpheus (1982)

Italy

Quartetto Italiano di Sassofoni (1975); Ensemble Italiano di Sassofoni (1983); Quartetto di Sassofoni Accademia (1984); Quartetto di Sassofoni di Perugia (1988)

Croatia

Zagreb Saxophone Quartet (1989)

Australia

Melbourne Saxophone Quartet (formerly the Peter Clinch Saxophone Quartet, 1977)[1]

The importance of establishing a repertoire can be seen by the example and quality of the Mule Quartet library. It is really due to the strength of what has become known as the classical French repertoire that the saxophone quartet as an ensemble was able to develop during the twentieth century. Chamber music groupings come and go, some seem like nice ideas at the time but are really dependent on strong personalities and occasional works; but to establish a medium it is important to create a stable high quality ensemble which will attract the best composers to write, thus preserving the instrumentation beyond the original grouping. Once a medium is established, succeeding generations of artists, composers and promoters have reference points. String quartets had a guaranteed future from Haydn and Mozart; Big Bands from Ellington, Basie and Goodman.

The French repertoire naturally also contains many works which were not written for the Mule group, including those by Françaix, Dubois and Absil. Jean Françaix' *Petit Quatuor* (1939) remains one of the most popular pieces. The opening Gaguenardise is best described as cartoon music rooted in 'Les Six', with explosions of dynamics and accents belying the steady pulse. The famous slow movement (Cantilène) is innovative in that it is written for only three instruments (no soprano), while the final Sérénade Comique is a metrical puzzle. The four movement Dubois *Quatuor* (1956) is in a similar style to the Françaix: witty and rhythmic. Its slow movement is based on a Spanish lament; the third movement is a classic light texture emphasising the upper registers; the finale is a bustle, more straight ahead than the Françaix yet with similar results. Absil's *Suite sur des thèmes populaires roumains* Op. 90 (1956) is a fine work. Needless to say there are French works which do not live up to the quality of those mentioned in this chapter – it would be surprising if that were not the case. None the less even some of the lesser works offer a good training ground for quartets as they become established, giving a variety of musical thought for the ensemble to test its balance and sensitivity.

Historically, the saxophone quartet as a medium is a relatively new concept, so it is rare for works to become 'established' – more prevalent is the hothouse atmosphere of a high proportion of new works being incorporated into programmes on a trial basis. One major work which has become a classic of the repertoire and also a classic of 'crossover' writing is *Three Improvisations* by Phil Woods (1980). He writes with classical discipline yet never loses the unmistakable drive of jazz rhythmic impetus, combined with authentic harmonic tension. An outstanding soloist himself (see chapter 8), Woods successfully combines developmental *and* riff-based writing in the first movement, and features an exciting passage led by the tenor (thus lifting the tenor part from its normal ensemble responsibility in order to allow a real jazz tenor sound to flourish). There is also an optional improvised soprano solo as a coda, accompanied by funk-based riffs in shifting metres. The central slow movement is a beautiful ballad with the melody shared between soprano, alto and baritone. The latter melodic section allows the baritone to soar into its infrequently used upper register, accompanied by much lower figures in semitonal clusters – an inspired piece of writing, reminiscent of the pioneering work by Harry Carney on the baritone instrument. The finale is a high energy series of chromatic and fourths-based ensemble sections, again in shifting metres, and broken by another wailing tenor solo.

Three Improvisations is one of few works which could legitimately be performed by a classical or a jazz quartet. This history of the quartet in the twentieth century has largely confined itself to ensembles and ensemble writing in the classical tradition, but since the 1970s, there has been a strong development of jazz quartets. These are covered in Chapter 8 and include the World Saxophone Quartet, the 29th Street Quartet and Itchy Fingers. One important feature of this blossoming of different disciplines is that young quartets are able to see and hear a much greater range of sound possibilities than were available to their predecessors. Likewise, composers are now encouraged to move freely within the classical and jazz/rock spheres, in the knowledge that their works will be performed.

The saxophone quartet was the most important representative of ensemble writing and performance in the twentieth century, but the impact of larger ensembles should not be ignored, and many of these have grown from the enthusiasm of players for what has become the standard quartet instrumentation. The popularity of the instrument itself in the early twentieth century can be traced to saxophone ensembles touring the vaudeville circuit. One of the most celebrated groups was that led by Tom Brown – The Brown Brothers Quintet began around 1911, and expanded into a sextet in 1915. The band toured until 1925 and was disbanded in 1933. The instrumentation varied, and certainly used everything from soprano down to bass, but most publicity photographs showed two altos, tenor, two baritones and bass. Beyond the small groups, saxophone choirs have been led by, amongst others, Sigurd Rascher (the Rascher Saxophone Ensemble) and Jean-Marie Londeix (L'Ensemble International de Saxophones de Bordeaux, established 1977).[2] The repertoire for these ensembles consists of original works (now numerous) and transcriptions, whilst the sound is quite unexpected, often remarkably similar to a string ensemble. Economically these groups are difficult to put together, and even more difficult to hold together; consequently they appear most often at major congresses and established masterclass and clinic courses. Extremes are possible – The World Saxophone Congress in London in 1976 presented an ensemble of over a hundred players, and at the Washington World Congress in 1985 an ensemble of 300 played on the Capitol Steps. This author was inside the ensemble at the time and was unable to hear the full impact – however one listener did comment that the band sounded very good, and became more attractive the further away one walked.

London Saxophonic have produced one of the most exciting original programmes, including pieces by Will Gregory, and have devoted programmes to the music of Michael Nyman. Urban Sax, an ensemble who take vaudeville, street theatre, concert performance and digitally controlled abseiling to extraordinary lengths, have certainly laid a marker for originality. Many colleges and conservatoires have saxophone choirs – these are responsible for producing a wide range of both new works and transcriptions – some of which develop into more permanent groups (for instance London Saxophonic from the Guildhall School of Music, London).

Quartet performance

Playing in a saxophone quartet, whether as a professional or amateur is a highly recommended experience. Making music in a group small enough to be intimate yet large enough to be able to share different ideas and approaches is most satisfying. With the development of repertoire following the establishment of the medium, quartets of any playing standard can expect to find more than enough performance material.

The ideal instrumentation is naturally that of soprano, alto, tenor and baritone, but for ensembles who have no soprano available, there is plenty of material for two altos, tenor and baritone. If the *baritone* is not available, the problem is more serious. It is almost worth saying don't start until you have a baritone, because although some bass lines are possible on the tenor, they do not sound very attractive and are very demanding (and frustrating) for the tenor player. Seating is an important considera-tion; the two most popular plans are two facing two, or four spread in a semicircle, as with a string quartet. The former is useful for rehearsal pur-poses, but is quite alienating in a live performance. The most common distributions of voices (stage right to left in semicircle) are SATB, STBA, BTAS. The first option allows the voices to move across the physical space in descending order; the second option enables the two upper voices to be opposite each other, highlighting any alternating melodic writing; the third retains the descending line in the opposite direction, but ensures that the baritone production moves into the ensemble rather than directly out to the audience, avoiding any lower domination.

Good intonation is naturally something a quartet should aim for, and a prerequisite of this is that each player should be aware of his/her own intonation throughout the instrumental range. It isn't really any use tuning to a concert A if the players are unsure of their own relative tuning beyond that. Presuming the ensemble is sensitive to saxophone tuning, a useful exercise is for the baritone to play low (written) F♯, followed by each of the other instruments playing their own low F♯s. This exposes fifths, allowing 'beats' to be heard and counteracted. Then try the two lower instruments on low F♯s and the two upper on middle F♯s. This gives a good spread of typical quartet range, and *should* have the same intona-tion as the previous exercise. If not, then it is possible there are individual problems. For further checking, repeat the previous exercise on F and then E. Success here will begin the blending process. Bear in mind also if using tuning machines that the ear prefers to hear the low notes of a bari-tone slightly flat, and the upper notes of the soprano slightly sharp, as in the pianoforte 'stretch'. The ensemble should be aware of the use of vibrato within the quartet – certainly used for French repertoire, but probably not for Renaissance transcriptions. Classical vibrato will not work in jazz pieces and vice versa. Unless indicated, subtone should be avoided on alto, tenor and baritone, but may be used sparingly on the lowest notes of the soprano, whose harmonic spectrum can tolerate it, whereas in the others the blend is disturbed. The soprano player should lead confidently without dominating, the alto should support the soprano at suitable volume and intensity levels, at the same time being prepared to take over the lead when the music demands. The tenor is the most decep-tive regarding volume – both that given out and perceived by the player – and should be carefully monitored in the early days of the quartet. Baritone players should be aware of their enormous responsibility –

missing notes are much more obvious than on the other instruments, and sense of timing should be very keen, as the baritone drives the group and provides harmonic 'answers' (the larger instrument also takes fractionally longer to speak, and this needs to be compensated for by the player).

Many ensembles flourish today, from the most avant-garde concert quartets to those providing cocktail music at social functions. So thanks are due to Marcel Mule for his legacy of the saxophone quartet.

6 The mechanics of playing the saxophone

Saxophone technique

KYLE HORCH

Saxophone technique consists of the physical actions required to play the instrument – a simple definition, but this is nevertheless a very wide and often daunting subject, both because of the large number of actions and parts of the body used in playing, and because of the bewildering variety of styles and idioms in which the chameleon-like saxophone family of instruments is used. However, I believe that it is possible to identify a few important common fundamental principles, and that observations can be made with regard to saxophone technique which are widely applicable throughout the members of the saxophone family and across all styles of playing.

A framework of approach: breaking music down and using models

Instrumental technique does not exist in a vacuum. Rather, it is one aspect of musical performance; others include phrasing, interpretation within an historical and stylistic context, and of course sheer flair for communicating with listeners. It is a cliché that music is like a language, yet the analogy is a useful one. Like music, spoken language has both spoken and written forms; it can express ideas ranging from banal to profound, can be used either improvisationally or in set forms such as poems, stories, plays, novels or speeches, and there is a performance aspect to speech which we see most obviously in actors. In speech the simplest unit is the word, enunciated by a variety of vocal and oral actions. Words are connected by conventions of grammar into meaningful arrangements (phrases, sentences, paragraphs) which communicate ideas, large or small, of a practical or artistic nature. Musical performance, in my view, is the art of communicating through a sort of language based on sounds of varying pitches, lengths and colours. As the word forms the basic unit of speech in all languages, the single note is the basic unit of music in all its styles. Notes can be created by a variety of means, either vocally or instrumentally. Notes relate to one another within theoretical contexts to create larger ideas – narratives, abstract shapes, patterns, moods. Technique is the 'how' of music – it is the physical process by which individual notes are created and, under the guidance of an interpretative imagination with a flair for performance/communication, related to one another in meaningful ways.

Any individual note begins in a performer's mind. Instrumental playing is essentially concerned with using an instrument as a vehicle for realising an ideal – producing sounds which the performer 'hears' in his/her aural imagination, whether placed there by a composer, or by their own composition or improvisation. We can imagine a huge range of sounds, of different pitch, length and quality, yet every note we dream up will have three common attributes – a beginning, a middle and an end. I refer to these parts as attack, sustain and release, respectively; they can be modelled using a simple syllabic system. For example a note may be imagined in a number of different ways:

HAAAAAAAAAH
DAAAAAAAAAH
TAAAAAAAAAH
HAAAAAAAAAT
DAAAAAAAAAT
TAAAAAAAAAT
HOOOOOOOOH
DOOOOOOOOH
TOOOOOOOOT
DEEEEEEEEH
and so on...

The goal of good saxophone technique is to offer ways of achieving all of these mental constructs in reality on the saxophone, as efficiently as possible. In common with the other wind instruments, this process has three major aspects: sustaining a sound on a single pitch (i.e. tone production), defining and inflecting the attack and release of the note where necessary (i.e. articulation), and moving that sound between different pitches fluidly (i.e. finger technique). Using this modelling system as a framework of reference and approach, a description of playing fundamentals becomes fairly logical.

Creating a sustained tone

Turn now to perhaps the simplest possible note model – a long tone modelled on the syllable HAH. We can examine this note with reference to the nuts-and-bolts areas of saxophone playing such as breathing, embouchure and so on. How is sound created on the saxophone? Simply by an airflow into the instrument, through the reed/mouthpiece opening, of sufficient velocity to cause the reed to vibrate back and forth against the facing of the mouthpiece. In this note model, the attack is simply the moment when the necessary velocity is reached, and the release is the moment when the air velocity stops being enough. Between these moments is the 'sustain', which is the main and longest part of any note, and the part I will examine first.

Breathing

To create a sustained tone, the airflow that goes into the instrument obviously comes from the lungs, so breathing is of massive importance in playing. The inhalation before our note should be relaxed and quite full, taken through the sides of the mouth rather than the nose, thereby quickly obtaining a large reservoir of air to draw upon. Physically, the air is drawn into our lungs by the action of our diaphragm, the muscular wall at the base of the lungs, moving downward; exhalation is caused when the diaphragm reverses this motion, moving upward, compressing the lungs and forcing air out of the body. The position of the diaphragm is such that it feels as if it is more part of the stomach than the chest. So, when breathing in during playing, I try to feel that my stomach expands outwards, perhaps then followed by my chest if I need a large breath, so that I have a sensation of my lungs seeming to fill from the bottom upwards. This is the sort of breathing one can observe when watching a sleeping person, lying on their back, breathing deeply. When only lightly active, people often breathe to much less than full lung capacity, with the sensation of air travelling to and from the top of the chest only – this is to be avoided in wind playing as the reservoir created is not large enough for long notes, nor is the support of the exhalation adequate from the diaphragm. When exhaling, blowing the air from my lungs into the saxophone, I try to have the sensation of steady gentle pressure from my stomach region (bottom of lungs) rather than from my ribs/chest (top of lungs). I aim to reach the required air velocity as quickly as possible and then maintain and keep the velocity constant. It is useful to have a sensation of blowing the air not just 'to' the saxophone but 'through' it. This process of inhalation and exhalation ensures a sufficient, even airflow to the instrument which sustains a steady, unwavering, 'supported' note, as well as adequate circulation of oxygen to the rest of the body during playing, which after all is a physical exertion.

Throat and tongue position

As the air travels up out of the lungs, it must pass through the throat and oral cavity before it reaches the saxophone. The main goal in this area of the body is simply not to obstruct the airflow by creating a narrow area, a bottle-neck in the flow. Internal bottle-necks tend to have the effect of forcing the diaphragm to compensate by pushing harder than necessary, and of changing the quality of the tone produced, usually to its detriment. Musicians often speak of the necessity of having an open throat. For most of the course of the trachea this is no problem; our lives depend on an open trachea and it is actually quite impossible to close it. The danger area is at the top of the throat, where the trachea opens into the back of the oral cavity. Here, it is possible to have a sensation of 'closing' the throat. To avoid this, some players try to imagine the throat as being as open as when yawning. Personally, I try to have my throat feel as open and relaxed during blowing as it was during the inhalation of the previous breath.

In my experience, however, the real culprit in most internal bottle-necks is actually the tongue, which can easily arch either backwards out over the throat opening, or upward towards the roof of the mouth. The syllable method is a useful tool in creating practice models. The tongue position used in saying vowel sounds such as AH or OO allows an unobstructed airflow, as opposed to, for example, EE or IH, which cause the tongue to rise, narrowing the flow and changing the character of the vocal tone from an open, relaxed quality to a more restricted, intense quality. The tongue positions used in pronouncing these syllables can all be used when blowing into the saxophone, with very similar effects on the tone. There may be reasons to use a more intense sound at times, but most players use the more relaxed, open sound created when the tongue is in the AH position as a fundamental basis. Whatever the method used, the tongue should generally be low and long in the mouth, out of the way of the airflow. The tip of the tongue can be held fairly close to the reed – this keeps the tongue long and has the added benefit that when it is required for articulation it will not have far to travel.

Embouchure

Having passed from the lungs through the throat and oral cavity, the airflow then reaches the saxophone, where the airflow is turned into sound by the action of the reed/mouthpiece under the control of the lips, teeth, jaw and facial muscles, the positions of which are together referred to as the embouchure. Embouchure is of crucial importance in controlling the sound and in determining its quality, depth and colour. It is also a rather vexed issue, which is, perhaps more than other aspects of technique, down to personal comfort and is also partly dependent on the equipment being used and the idiom within which you are working. However, a simple description and some observations may be useful.

Most saxophonists place their top teeth directly on the top of the mouthpiece roughly one quarter to one third of the way up the slope from the tip. The lower lip is placed against the reed, and beneath the lower lip the lower teeth and jaw press up gently, usually causing the distance of the reed/mouthpiece opening to narrow slightly. The lips seal around the reed/mouthpiece so all of the air is directed into the instrument rather than being lost escaping from the sides of the mouth. The facial muscles around the mouth and cheeks should be held firm enough to assist in centring the sound, and the cheeks should not puff out, unless a particularly wide and potentially wild sound is desired. The combination of jaw and muscular pressure should create a sensation that the embouchure is a circular support to the work of the reed, mouthpiece and airflow, a gently firm valve regulating the airflow by focusing the air column and allowing the tip opening to be a certain size.

Perhaps the main issue of embouchure is: how firmly should the mouth grip the saxophone? The pressure of embouchure around the mouthpiece/reed must fall at least within a certain range, because if gripped too tightly the tip opening will close entirely, not allowing any reed vibration, and if held too loosely air will travel through the saxophone but not create a sound. Once within the range needed to create a tone, embouchure pressure is dependent on several factors: reed strength (harder reeds require more pressure), mouthpiece design, personal comfort, personal taste in tone quality and requirements of tuning individual notes (firm embouchure will be relatively sharper, loose embouchure relatively flatter). In my experience as a player and teacher, however, I have more often come across the problem of the embouchure being too tight, creating a bottle-neck just as the air enters the instrument and, as a result, a tone which is restricted in colour, dynamic potential and is consistently sharp. It is worth remembering that the tip opening is usually quite small and creates enough resistance to regulate the airflow without excessive pressure from the embouchure. A useful image common among teachers is to encourage an airflow which feels 'warm' and not too tightly focused, as opposed to an intensely concentrated 'cool' airflow. This usually means allowing the embouchure to be fairly passive and letting the velocity of a steady, unobstructed airflow do most of the work of tone production. It is possible to hold the embouchure in a controlled position yet open enough so that a small proportion of air passes into the saxophone without being turned into tone, giving the tone a faintly airy quality. This sense of ratio of airy quality/sound is used by many players to a greater or lesser extent to give a sense of depth to the tone, so that our example note

becomes perhaps better represented by

Vibrato

Vibrato is an expressive device, which can add resonance to a note or a phrase. It gives the tone an undulating, rippling quality and creates the illusion that the notes on which it is used are spinning or shimmering, literally 'vibrating'. Physically it is made by a slight, regular undulation of intensity or pitch, or both. The speed of the undulation depends on the context of the note/phrase and the taste of the player. To create vibrato a number of methods are technically possible, for example by varying the intensity of support from the diaphragm or by trilling with a key or keys which will alter the timbre but not the pitch of a note. By far the most commonly used method, however, is based on the embouchure – varying slightly the pressure of the jaw/lower teeth/lower lip on the reed, moving the jaw in tiny motions up and down, therefore making the pitch of the note relatively sharper and flatter.

Possible models are:

Straight tone

Tone moving sharp and returning to normal

Tone moves above and below normal pitch

Tone moves below pitch and back to normal

I personally use the third vibrato model, because imagining the vibrato this way helps to prevent excessive pressure on the reed, which in addition to sharpening the note might possibly constrict the tone. It is worth remembering that, whatever model is used, the effect created might better be visualised as:

because, after all, the tone of the saxophone has a certain depth and the vibrato should be conceived as 'inside' the tone rather than as in this representation:

which usually produces too strong an effect, particularly at quick speeds. The pitch variation required for vibrato is actually quite narrow, so small that it often feels more like a variation in quality than in pitch.

Dynamics

Those, then, are the major physical aspects of tone production on single notes. On our example note

HAAAAAAAAAH

air travels from the lungs at a constant rate, through the throat, oral cavity and embouchure, into the saxophone, producing a tone, either straight or with vibrato. The note may be produced at different dynamics, depending on the volume of air used: more air = louder, less air = softer. It is important to point out that, for softer volumes, air velocity must be maintained at least up to a point and that the smaller amount of air used for a *pianissimo* note should still be inhaled from and supported from the diaphragm, otherwise tonal quality will suffer.

Attack and release: articulation and the tongue

In actual music, simple notes such as our model

hah

where the attack is created by the breath alone, are quite rare. It is much more usual to define the attack with the aid of the tongue, for example as in the models

dah

or

tah

For the listener this gives the note a clear beginning and while for the player articulating the note in this way is an added technique to think about, it is useful in gaining an immediate response – both because it eliminates the split second of airflow before the velocity required for reed vibration is reached in a breath attack, and because it offers, psychologically, a discrete point of attack. The technique is quite simple: a spot very close to, but not absolutely on, the tip of the tongue (the same spot used when pronouncing the syllable DAH against the roof of the mouth) touches the tip of the reed just at the moment the airflow begins, and comes away again, allowing the reed to vibrate freely during the sustain period of the note.

Some players touch the flat part of the reed rather than the tip, but I generally prefer to use the tip because it offers great clarity and, of course, the tip of the tongue has only a small distance to travel from its usual resting place long and low in the mouth which places it close to the reed. This is an aid when speed is necessary for quickly repeated attacks. It must always be remembered that the tonguing merely defines the point of attack and that the airflow continues to do most of the work of beginning the note.

Release is a slightly more complicated subject, because various options are used regularly. Much of the time, notes end with an 'open' release, i.e. the note ends when the air stops flowing as in the syllable TAH. This is appropriate for many long notes, and also for repeated tonguing, if the tempo is slow enough.

It is sometimes necessary, however, to end notes by stopping the reed's vibration by placing the tongue on the tip of the reed, as in the syllable TAT. I call this a 'closed' release. This is most often used in a classical context for quick staccato playing, when the speed of the tongued notes does not allow for each note to be created by a fresh attack from the diaphragm; support in this case is constant from the diaphragm and the staccato gaps are made by the tongue stopping each note, resting on the reed to create a gap, then coming away to allow the next note to speak.

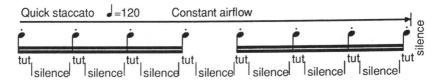

Notes stopped with the tongue, of any length or speed, are also commonly used in jazz and popular music.

Another common situation is connected or legato tonguing, where, like the quick staccato, the airflow is constant. In this case, however, the tongue does not rest on the reed to create a gap; it merely defines the attacks of successive notes, which may be imagined as not having a release as such.

Lastly, in the case of slurred notes, attack is obviously created by the tongue only on the first note, and successive notes require no tonguing. The airflow must be sufficient and embouchure steady to allow a smooth connection between notes.

Moving the tone from one pitch to another – finger technique

I use the concepts outlined above for producing tone on all of the notes of the saxophone, whether high or low in range, no matter which fingering is chosen. As music is usually composed of groups of different pitches, a large aspect of saxophone technique is involved with developing dexterity in moving the hands from one fingering arrangement to another. This dexterity usually develops naturally with practice and experience, however some observations may be useful. The job of the hands in saxophone playing is to move from one fingering to another fluently at whatever speed required, allowing the music to flow with an evenness of rhythm and tone. To do this, it helps if the fingers, hands and arms are relaxed, with fingers curved as if preparing to pick up a tennis ball. The curved position helps keep the fingers supple. It can be useful to think while playing that one is 'squeezing' the keys rather than 'slapping' them. In gaining speed of movement it is essential that the movements of the fingers be as small as possible – this means keeping the fingers on or near the keys rather than allowing them to lift some distance away when in the 'pad raised' position. Usually the fingers should be thought of as moving simultaneously if a finger change of several fingers is required. The major exception to this idea is the left thumb (octave key) which may sometimes move slightly out of sync with the other fingers. For example, if slurring an interval such as

the left thumb may move a split second before the other fingers in order to ensure that the lower note speaks immediately. Like the other fingers, the movement of the left thumb should be minimal, using only the end of the thumb on the octave key and leaving the majority on the left-hand thumb rest.

Holding the saxophone

Generally, it is worth remembering that the weight of the saxophone is supported by the neck sling, unlike the clarinet, flute and oboe which are held up in playing position by the hands. Once the sling has been adjusted to a height that brings the mouthpiece easily to the mouth, the left thumb pushing against its thumb rest and the contact between the upper teeth and mouthpiece anchor the instrument in a stable position. This, apart from ease and speed of motion, is why it is essential that the left thumb remains on the thumb rest rather than lifting and shifting to depress the octave key and why the top teeth should remain on the mouthpiece at all times instead of lifting while breathing – if these anchors are shaky the tone may not be steady. The right thumb rest, in contrast, is merely a convenient place to rest the right thumb, which needs to take no really active part in playing or supporting the instrument (the straight soprano saxophone is an exception). Since the hands are not the main means by which the weight of the instrument is supported, this factor assists in keeping them relaxed and supple.

Summing up: inter-relations

In short, the techniques of producing notes, singly or in groups, involve actions and interactions. To produce this note

or the examples:

There are only five possibilities for co-ordination/independence between the three areas of playing, shown above.

1	Blowing, tonguing and fingering all in co-ordination
2	Blowing and fingering in co-ordination (constant), tonguing independent
3	Blowing and tonguing in co-ordination, fingering independent
4	Blowing independent (constant), tonguing and fingering co-ordinated
5	Blowing, tonguing and fingering all independent

requires three types of activity: producing the tone, articulating the tone and fingering. The tone quality of the note or notes to be produced is influenced by: airflow and relative 'warmth' or 'coolness'; position of the back/middle of the tongue; shape of the lower lip; pressure of the jaw and lower lip; the factor of resistance created by the reed/mouthpiece. Saxophone playing is a complicated business, with many parts of the body doing different tasks, often not visible to the eye (unlike, for example, the piano, stringed instruments, percussion instruments). The tasks of playing notes together may require that the blowing, tonguing and finger-ing are done either independently or in co-ordination. All of these tasks are most easily accomplished when the instrument is supported by the sling, anchored by the top teeth and left thumb, creating an even airflow, unobstructed from diaphragm to instrument; articulation is effected by the tip of the tongue; reed/mouthpiece are appropriate for the idiom and player, and embouchure shape and pressure are appropriate for the mouthpiece; the fingers are relaxed and supple. At all times, the technically adept saxophonist will seek to avoid wasted effort and to let as much of the work as possible be done by the airflow.

The inter-relatedness of the actions involved in saxophone playing means that sometimes a problem in one area of playing will cause a reaction in another. Two brief examples: (1) the attempt to support the instrument's weight with the hands may lead to arm and shoulder tension, reducing the ease of fingering and, more importantly, creating general upper-body tension which can close the throat and discourage diaphragm breathing. (2) Failure to aid the anchoring of the saxophone with the left thumb can cause the embouchure to compensate by gripping the mouthpiece too tightly, constricting the tone (especially on open C♯ and the high 'palm key' notes), as well as causing general sharpness. Fortunately, once an understanding of this type of problem is arrived at, a solution is usually straightforward.

I believe that the ideas I have outlined in terms of breathing, throat position and finger technique are generally applicable to all idioms of playing and sizes of saxophone. Articulation and embouchure are areas which require sensitivity and adjustment. With articulation, the technique of using the front of the tongue can be generally applied, but the weight and patterns of articulation differ widely between classical and jazz/popular styles. In classical playing articulation is mainly concerned with clearly, lightly defining the beginnings of notes and phrases and then allowing attention to be focused on the sustained part of the notes or phrases. With jazz, however, attention is often focused directly on articulation and the inflections given to individual notes; often a heavier attack is used and the tongued release is common. For further discussion on the subject of embouchure see pages 88–9.

A brief note on practice

The mastery of saxophone technique requires regular practice over an extended period of time. Practice should include a mix of work (at least at one time or another) ranging from long tones to scales and arpeggios (played from memory over the full range of the instrument), short exercises in limited ranges for fingering and tonguing, studies such as Ferling, Mule or the *Charlie Parker Omnibook*, repertoire which places the technical work into an expressive context and involves work with piano or other instruments, and improvisation.

Such a regime includes both work which requires music-reading and that which does not. This encourages good listening, attention to detail and a relating of the individual techniques and notes represented on a written page to an internal aural imagination. Practically speaking, the use of a metronome at least part of the time is invaluable. Playing from memory or by ear is a great confidence builder. Again, the use of a syllabic modelling system and regular singing of different types of phrases and articulative patterns assist greatly. Rather than having to view technique as a large number of independent yet inter-related actions which we may have trouble consciously controlling, this method offers a form of mental shorthand; a person who is able to sing a phrase is likely to be able to play it, or at least to diagnose where they are going wrong, since the actions used in singing the syllables are so closely related to those used in playing the saxophone. With the building up of good habits through regular practice, good technique gradually becomes second nature, carrying out the actions required to produce the sounds called for without too much involvement of the conscious mind.

Conclusion

In the end, technique becomes a personal matter. Each player will find some aspects which come easily and some which do not. Through maximising strengths and minimising weaknesses, one hopes that all saxophonists can aim not just towards competence, but to excellence and the development of a unique voice on the instrument. There is, of course, leeway for bending the rules – each person is physically different and adjustments may be necessary. Musical context and personal taste play a huge role in directing the actions of technique and the use of musical judgement is of paramount importance. For example, while 'relax' is a mantra word of guides such as this one, even tension is sometimes a part of musical expression. For this reason, a teacher is an invaluable resource, helping in the long process of learning the *parameters* and *ranges* of what is 'appropriate' and 'inappropriate' (words which should replace 'right' and 'wrong' to an increasing extent) in music and technique. Good technique is based on a few fundamental principles, and it is important to get the basics correct. But our general approach to technique should not be overly dogmatic – our musical imaginations should not be stunted by limited views of what is possible on the saxophone. Rather, it should be firmly rooted in a wider understanding of musical context and related always to producing the sounds we hear in our minds – the servant of personal musical expression, not its master.

Jazz and rock techniques

DAVID ROACH

Basic instrumental technique and control are as much prerequisites of jazz and rock as they are of classical music. Most classical players can and must be able to play scales and arpeggios throughout the range of their instruments, but jazz and rock musicians must expand their knowledge to every type of broken chord in sevenths, ninths, elevenths and thirteenths, every mode, every diminished, half-diminished, augmented scale and so on, for so much of these styles is based on a player's ability to improvise. Inasmuch as the art of classical music aspires to perfection of execution, jazz and rock aspire to something less easily defined but which is none the less great performance; and although jazz is at times as diametrically opposed to rock as it is to classical music, in terms of the saxophone they share many techniques.

Embouchure

The embouchure is the player's most sensitive point of contact with the instrument, and as such must perform the job of cushioning the reed's vibrations and controlling fine pitch and tone variations (along with the throat cavity). The main difference between a jazz or rock player's embouchure and that of a classical player is the positioning of the lower lip; in classical sax playing it is more common for the lower lip to be slightly curled over the lower teeth providing the firmness necessary to control pitch and sound in that style, however in general, jazz and rock players turn the lower lip outwards. This used to be heavily frowned upon by educators, but now it is almost universally agreed that, even in the classical style, the tenor sax in particular needs the extra freedom afforded by the turned-out lower lip. The sound is broadened, allowing many more partials to appear in the tone; the reed vibrates more freely in the mouth, and more of the lower lip comes into contact with the rest of the reed, providing a different quality of damping. This creates a suitably more relaxed feel to the tone and its production, although some players build the strength to play very hard reed/wide mouthpiece set-ups in this way.

On some mouthpieces, the upward pressure on the reed of a turned-in lower lip is likely to produce squeaks. This is due to the small area of lip pressure being applied nearer the tip of the mouthpiece where the baffle is closest to the reed, accentuating vibrations where the high frequencies are strongest. An experienced player with a strong embouchure can control this, and some players who use the altissimo register a great deal find it easier to do so with a turned-in lower lip. Listen particularly to David Sanborn and Tom Scott, both of whom use a turned-in lower lip at times.

The mouthpiece and reed

Mouthpieces and reeds are probably a saxophone player's most critical and often-changed pieces of equipment. Most players possess at least two mouthpieces (each suited to different styles of music) and some many more, for the mouthpiece and reed combination can make an immense impact upon the quality of sound and ease of playing.

This is the point at which the basic timbre of the instrument is generated and aside from the obvious effects of a player's embouchure and breath support, is one of the most critical influences upon the timbre. Mouthpieces are made in various materials, tip openings, lengths of lay, baffle heights, rail and tip thickness, bore and chamber sizes.

Tip openings generally range for soprano sax from around 1.10 mm (for a close classical lay) to 1.80 mm (for a wide jazz or rock lay), for alto sax from 1.50 mm to 2.80 mm, for tenor sax 1.60 mm to 3.50 mm, and for baritone sax from 1.80 mm to 3.50 mm. The length of lay will generally increase in proportion to the tip opening. These more open measurements are the widest practical mouthpieces (according to the majority of players) when taking into consideration the breath and embouchure compression necessary to play the instrument in tune. The wider the tip opening, generally the more freely the reed will vibrate; however, the player must work harder to produce a sound.

A correspondingly softer reed is used on a wide mouthpiece, but in extreme cases the lip pressure necessary to bring the reed close enough to the mouthpiece tip for it to vibrate is also enough to dislodge the intonation in the upper registers. The player must flatten the upper notes by pulling the lower jaw down or by enlarging the throat cavity (a little of this is necessary on all set-ups), which can cause problems in the stability of pitch and tone. However, many players feel that the extra work involved in controlling a wide set-up is worth it for the increased weight of sound. Generally, harder use of the tongue is required in order to overcome the higher resistance which wider mouthpieces present, and the increased air pressure this generates can be sufficient to override some difficulties, but this is tiring over long periods.

The next most influential aspect of a mouthpiece is the baffle; this upper inside wall is critical in its height or distance from the reed. It is almost totally responsible for the amount of upper partials audibly present in the timbre and together with the side walls, chamber and bore size, governs the tone colour and internal compression of the mouthpiece.

Care must be exercised in choosing a mouthpiece to suit the particular music being played. If too gentle a set-up is used (a close lay with a 'low' baffle) then the player will waste energy forcing a hard bright sound from a mouthpiece that simply does not possess those qualities. Conversely it is immensely difficult to tame and refine a rock and roll set-up (a wide lay with a 'high' baffle) to play more gentle music.

The English mouthpiece makers Berg Larson have made a tenor saxophone mouthpiece with a tip opening of 4.60 mm – an incredible beast, although not altogether unplayable – but as far as I know nobody in Britain has dared to use it professionally, for in general it is accepted that a compromise between size of sound and stability of intonation is necessary for the player to be at ease and not over stress the embouchure.

The increased compression generated by many jazz and rock mouthpieces (particularly ones with a high baffle) is inclined to produce 'squeaks' (super high uncontrolled notes) at unpredictable moments, particularly when such a mouthpiece is used with classic, thin-tipped French reeds. Thus the 'American' style of reed is favoured by many jazz and rock players; it has a thicker tip and a flatter heart which impart a greater stability and aggression of tone at the expense of some refinement.

Although the basic technique of tonguing remains the same in all saxophone playing, the choice of mouthpiece and reed can vastly change the clarity of articulation, and, coupled with a generally more open embouchure, jazz and rock players generally sacrifice some cleanness at the start of a note for the sake of the basic tone colour, particularly at the lower end of the instrument.

Subtone

Subtone is generated by pulling the jaw down and back towards the tip of the reed, allowing the reed to come away from the mouthpiece, whilst the player fully supports the air column. This gives a very warm tone with much less definition than normal, and only works really effectively in the lowest octave. One of the finest exponents of this was jazz master Ben Webster. In quiet passages a player often will use subtone at the bottom of the instrument, generally hardly using the tongue at all and avoiding staccato (which involves re-energising the instrument for each note). Instead, a form of damping is used in which the player allows the tongue to return partially to the reed, not completely stopping the sound but deadening it to a level considerably lower than the start of the note, thus imitating staccato. This technique, when used with a normal embouchure, is available as an expressive articulation in other registers creating a tone-change effect upon the sound. Listen to David Sanborn's recordings for examples of the latter usage.

Ghosting

Ghosting is the technique in which some notes in a line of regular quavers are given more weight according to the main rhythmic/harmonic structure of the phrase, and others are almost not played, or are ghosted, often using subtone. This technique is akin to speech, in which less important words are glossed over to bring into high relief the overall point of what is being said, and it adds contour to a line that if played with equal weight could sound pedantic or contrived. Some care must be exercised because this effect is produced in the lower register, in effect, by insufficient support of the air column or an overly loose embouchure, which if adopted in normal playing leads to bad intonation and poor tone quality.

Slap-tongue

This effect occurs as much in the classical saxophone repertoire as anywhere, and true slap-tongue is less commonly used nowadays than in the past. The technique is to lay the tongue flat on the reed prior to starting a note, and, after bringing the air pressure to the mouthpiece, smartly release the tongue in a downwards movement – the reed strikes the mouthpiece hard, and the player stops the air pressure, thus creating a short pitched slapping sound. A real slap-tongue is only easily produced with a fairly soft reed on the lower instruments and many players find it difficult, if not impossible, to produce with hard reeds or on wider mouthpieces, due to the sheer physical distance of the reed from the mouthpiece tip. A much used variation to slap-tongue comes about quite naturally if the player gives insufficient breath support to a note, particularly in the lower register. Slap-tongue is used in Jean Françaix' *Petit Quatuor pour Saxophones*, and also in the extraordinary baritone playing by Andrew Findon in Michael Nyman's music.

The bend

Also called the smear, the bend is probably the most familiar technique in jazz and rock, and is achieved by starting a note flat and returning it to the correct pitch. At the start of the note the player's jaw and lower lip are pulled downwards whilst still retaining the air-tight seal around the mouthpiece; most players also open their throat cavity somewhat (from the relaxed 'ah' position of normal playing to the wider 'aw' similar to a yawn). Thus a flatter pitch is produced, the player only needing to control the degree of flatness and the speed of return to normal embouchure and pitch. Very wide bends are made by fingering a lower pitch as well as flattening in the previously described manner; the return to correct pitch is then made partly by a chromatic run and partly by embouchure: this is more correctly called a gliss (glissando). Bending notes is so endemic to jazz and rock, and easy to perform, that many players become recognisable for the ways in which they use this technique; beginners in particular tend to over-use the bend, due to lack of embouchure control, whilst skilled players use it sparingly, but most of all it becomes unselfconscious and a naturally expressive part of a player's technique. Listen to Johnny Hodges's sublime and extreme use of the bend on Duke Ellington's recordings, or Jan Garbarek's use of the bend – haunting, delicate, sparse.

Growl and flutter-tongue

Growl is created by the player singing into the instrument at the same time as playing. The note sung is low (in order to avoid unisons with the instrument which tend to cancel out the effect) and is generally on a monotone. The pitch differences and the disturbance to the air column generate a rough tone particularly suitable to rock and roll. Some players reject growling as vulgar, but a discreet touch here and there can be effective in adding more projection to the sound.

Flutter-tongue is a more extreme form of the previous technique. The player rolls an 'R' with the tongue on the roof of the mouth whilst playing, introducing an even greater disturbance into the air column and 'grit' into the sound. Good examples are Jim Horn's playing on Duane Eddy albums of the 1960s, or Clarence Clemons on Bruce Springsteen's *Born to Run* from the 1970s. For a more romantic and integrated approach to growling, listen to Gato Barbieri's records of the 1970s. Occasionally players find it very difficult or impossible to perform either of these effects, in which case an alternative is to allow some air to escape on one side of the embouchure, close to the mouthpiece; if this is carefully regulated the lips will vibrate (as in the trumpet embouchure) producing a pseudo-growl.

False fingerings

This effect is calculated to produce variations in tone colour and intonation on a note by adding extra keys to the basic fingering, or taking alternative fingerings for the same note. Fingered adaptations (as opposed to changes in embouchure and throat) can be used in technical passages as an augmentation to the basic notes available in a scale. A very commonly used example would be the addition of the first three fingers of the right hand to the regular fingering for A (in either octave) of any saxophone. Some notes are easily altered, whilst others require either careful working out or use of the harmonic series available on any of the fundamental notes of the instrument, for example fingered G and G♯ in the upper octave can be generated by the second harmonic of low C and C♯ respectively. In fact many saxophone players use this practice as a way of improving tone and intonation by matching the harmonic series to fingered notes. Listen to American saxophone superstars Michael Brecker, Bob Berg and David Sanborn to hear this effect.

Styles

Part of a player's learning process is to recognise different styles, and much detailed rehearsal time can be spent agreeing on interpretation of note lengths, etc. Part of what makes a saxophone section great is the agreement on style which comes through many years of playing together and listening to each other. Fine examples of this are the Ellington and Basie bands, and the Frank Sinatra–Quincy Jones collaboration. The point of most of the techniques outlined here is to give music a more natural and conversational feel, and without doubt they came about through generations of players' instinctive need to shape music in a very personal way. Today jazz is more widely taught in music colleges, and many players are able to switch convincingly between one style and another, or even more importantly, to carry their own styles through many different types of music. For sheer diversity, the saxophonist should listen to Jan Garbarek's collaborations with Indian and Pakistani classical musicians and Michael Nyman's extraordinary fusion of high European classical music and rock and roll delivery.

The saxophone family: playing characteristics and doubling

NICK TURNER

The idea of creating a family of instruments is a very old one. One thinks immediately of the family of recorders and the 'chest' of viols. Indeed, the ophicleide, the largest in the family of keyed bugles, leads directly into the development of the bass saxophone and the present set of instruments. Sax was obviously keen that players should develop their skills on different saxophones (and saxhorns), and instigated the system of keeping all the instruments in the treble clef, regardless of their size, to facilitate reading and to retain uniformity of fingerings. This simple idea was so successful that by the 1920s there emerged the 'saxophone technician' capable of playing several saxophones as well as clarinets.

Defining saxophone sound is not easy as it varies so much from one player to another; more than on any other wind instrument the player has a very marked effect on the acoustics of the saxophone and consequently no two players sound alike. However, there are some characteristics which are common to all players to a greater or lesser extent.

The alto saxophone

The alto saxophone is possibly the most popular member of the family; what makes it so distinctive is its light, slightly reedy, yet somehow broad tone which lacks the penetrating intensity of projection associated with the oboe. It manages to achieve the sensuality and mystery of the cor anglais while retaining an innocent simplicity in its voice. Its essentially vocal style ranges from a very full and rich lowest register to an otherwise focused and delicately understated sound in the middle and upper reaches. The latter is a characteristic particularly developed in the so-called 'French School', and indeed by all players sensitive to its musical potential. The vocal element is reinforced by the use of vibrato; the classical player choosing to emulate the controlled, continuous vibrato of singers and string players, while the jazz performer utilises the terminal vibrato (vibrato increasing towards the end of the note) and subtle pitch bending of the great jazz singers.

To create this gently modulated and finely controlled sound many players choose a mouthpiece of only a moderate tip opening and with not too hard a reed (a general guide being a Selmer C*, Rousseau NC4 or

Vandoren A25 with a Vandoren 2–3 reed) – this also helps to control intonation as any sort of biting will send the higher notes very sharp, as well as the notorious 'D, 4th line'. A flexible embouchure and a good ear are both essential to help accommodate equal temperament within the confines of a natural acoustic system, refined though it is. The alto is normally held right of centre when standing and can either be held in front or to the right side when seated. The latter is personal preference, but when changing instruments quickly it is usually easier to keep it to the right rather than having to lift it over your right leg.

The tenor saxophone

The tenor saxophone possesses a rich, cello-like quality. After the gentleness of the alto the tenor has a much more masculine strength in its tone which is nevertheless capable of producing a very great range of tone colour. From the delicate and veiled sounds of its upper register played *pianissimo* it can descend to a good trombone *fortissimo* in the lower reaches. And vice versa: strident and forceful in the high and altissimo registers contrasting with the suggestive subtoning of its bottom notes. Most players relate very easily to the upper register as it shares its pitch and registration with the alto and much of the clarinet. It is the lower register which usually needs attention: to pre-hear the notes at that pitch and then to 'voice' them correctly with the oral cavity, resonance and placement of the air. It is a common mistake to try to think of the tenor as a large alto; it may only be a fourth lower but it has a considerably larger volume of air to activate and control as well as a different harmonic structure to the sound. It is therefore very important to discover what elements exist within the sound, and to reinforce these defining qualities rather than trying to create some preconceived notion of how it ought to sound and respond.

The answer lies, as it does with all woodwinds, in a close study of the lower register. Consequently, it is better to commence with a relatively soft mouthpiece/reed set-up to facilitate the playing of these notes. This may cause the higher end to be slightly thin in tone and flat in pitch but with better use of air support, voicing and embouchure this soon improves, and results in easy facility across the whole range of the instrument. One will also begin to discover how much more stable the tuning is on the tenor compared to its smaller cousins.

The embouchure is obviously more open and offers rather more gentle support than on the alto, the emphasis being much more on breath support and tube control. Posture plays an important part in this. Since the tenor is nearly always held down the right side of the body it is worth ensuring that it is the mouthpiece, crook and sling that are adjusted to fit the player and not the other way round. When adjusting the sling, one should always have the sensation of resting one's head on the mouthpiece, never having to reach up or forwards.

The soprano saxophone

The soprano saxophone has a more nasal quality about its sound, which is unique in the saxophone family. At times it can sound rather like an oboe, an instrument of similar length and sharing a conical, but considerably narrower, bore. However, the soprano is a very sensitive instrument and a careless player can easily sound raucous, out of tune and generally rather unpleasant. The shortness and width of the tube make it difficult to fill the sound with the lower and middle partials. Fullness can be achieved but often at the expense of its expressiveness, akin to playing the violin with overly thick strings. A very fine balance has to be achieved. The soprano became more popular in the 1970s, and as it has increased its share of the mainstream musical instrument market, so manufacturers have become more competitive in terms of playing quality and pricing. Although these modern instruments are of a much more stable tone and pitch they still possess the strange 'ethnically tempered' scale which attracted jazz players in the 1950s. Whole tones and semitones should not be *assumed* to exist on the soprano, slow practice and a good ear being the key elements for success. *The Saxophonist's Workbook* by Larry Teal contains excellent material to cover this point, as well as being useful for saxophone playing generally.

The embouchure obviously has to be a little smaller and tighter than that of the alto, and control has to be more finely tuned. However, it should never be pinched and must always remain circular to control the pitch at the top of the instrument, and to maintain some fullness in the sound. A hard, straight lower lip seems to suppress the middle harmonics and makes for a very brittle sound. Breath control is somewhat easier because of the greater resistance of the soprano, and this is perhaps why it is easier to move from clarinet to soprano than to the other saxophones.

The soprano comes in a range of shapes. The most familiar is the straight soprano, and this is the preferred shape for leaders of saxophone quartets and soloists generally. In recent years a slight curve at the top of the instrument has been introduced to facilitate the use of a sling which would otherwise interfere with the left thumb, and possibly affect the angle of incidence between mouthpiece and embouchure. The fully curved soprano can still be found, its exponents believing it to sound if not better than the straight version then at least different. Obviously the player's perception of the sound is changed by the upward-pointing bell, the sound no longer going into the floor, and one should take care to remember that bore size and taper can vary between different makes of instruments and also from one era to another, so that it would be a mistake to attribute the different tone colour simply to the altered shape of the instrument.

The baritone saxophone

This instrument is pitched in E♭, one octave below the alto. Its rich bass/baritone voice has something of the cello in it, but with a slower vibrato requirement and possessing a quiet strength and depth rather than the fragile transparency of its stringed counterpart. Comparisons with the cello continue with both instruments having the same range of notes, and both occupying the same chair in their respective quartets; in general terms the cello is a very good role model for its tone colour and vibrato. The octave pitch difference with respect to the alto results in an enormous increase in size of instrument and volume of enclosed air. Like the tenor, air control and particularly depth of air, voicing and resonance, are important factors, embouchure strength only becoming significant at the top end of the instrument. Tube control and the practice of harmonics are important since there is no way of 'forcing' the instrument to respond without it becoming ugly and unmusical.

The bigger reed and mouthpiece can be a very tempting target for large amounts of tongue contact. Be careful to keep to the last 2 mm of reed to avoid any unwanted 'slap-tongue' effects. Always remember that it is the support from the air and energy from the abdomen that produce the sound and not a 'kickstart' from the tongue (see Fig. 6.1).

Imitation of cello pizzicato is a useful starting point for developing the air support/tongue release co-ordination. Strangely, rapid articulation is not difficult owing to the instrument's ability to speak even while the tongue is still in light contact with the reed. This means that the tongue does not have to clear completely from the reed before returning for the next attack, resulting in a potentially more rapid pulsation of the tongue.

Vibrato always needs to be used sensitively and practised methodically and musically. The baritone saxophone requires more awareness of technique in order to achieve control of the greater range of movement and the generally slower speed of vibrato used, reflecting the approach adopted by singers and string players. To create the same depth of vibrato

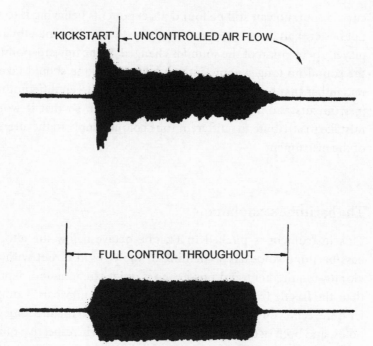

'KICKSTART' ⌐ UNCONTROLLED AIR FLOW

⌐ FULL CONTROL THROUGHOUT ⌐

Fig. 6.1

across the full range of saxophone, less jaw movement is needed at the top and rather more is needed at the very bottom. On the larger saxophones this difference in movement becomes much greater, ranging from a barely perceptible undulation for the highest notes to a very significant and visible jaw movement at the bottom. This can easily become uncontrolled and only constant critical and musical appraisal from the player will ensure an artistic result. If the embouchure is not supportive enough, then gaps will appear in the sound during the downward cycle of the jaw. Whilst baritone embouchure is very much more open and relaxed it should never become completely slack.

A hard reed can cause problems, especially with baritone parts containing a surfeit of low notes. But a word of caution: too soft a reed will have difficulty in handling the very strong pressure waves experienced at the very bottom of the instrument and the tone will begin to break below low D. Also, the highest notes have a tendency to 'break' resulting in an unmusical grunt, a situation made worse by soft reeds. Thirdly, such large reeds need a certain stiffness to maintain their shape when they become wet, very soft reeds tending to assume the curvature of the mouthpiece and thus produce a choking effect to the response.

The weight of the baritone necessitates good posture. It is played on the right-hand side of the body. Try not to lean forward or push the head forward but instead try to keep the pressure that is on the back of the neck over the heels if standing, or down the spine and into the seat of the chair if seated. An alternative is to use the old 'Selmer Jiffy' stand or the spike arrangement now fitted to several instruments. Various sling arrangements exist but one should be careful not to inhibit completely the movement of player and instrument, as slight changes in posture can bring into play a number of different muscle groups, which prevent the player from becoming frozen into one position and causing muscle spasms and cramps. Needless to say, the abdomen should never be cramped up as the ability to intake large amounts of air is paramount. Also, never leave the intake of breath until the last moment, lest the intake is insufficient.

Doubling

To play an instrument successfully requires the performer to develop an almost instinctive response to the acoustic characteristics of that instrument. This is developed over many years of playing. When doubling one has to know and understand these characteristics because to acquire these instincts on several instruments would take too long to develop and they would not necessarily be mutually enhancing.

The first practice to undertake when doubling on saxophones is to gain an understanding of the different embouchure tensions and air support requirements. The simplest way to do this is to play the mouthpiece alone (with a reed fitted, of course) and to produce a sound from the mouthpiece at *fortissimo* level. With correct use of air and embouchure the notes in Figure 6.2 should be produced at concert pitch.

Fig. 6.2

Do not try to alter the pitch by playing more quietly, but by altering the embouchure tension and the focus of the air in the oral cavity.

An effective method of developing a sympathetic response to a saxophone, and at the same time increasing the control of the air in the tube, is by the study of harmonics. This is not as advanced a technique as the term 'harmonics' would suggest. Put simply, a tube of fixed length (i.e. without changing the fingering) is able to produce several different pitches which are whole-number multiples of the first, lowest note played – the first harmonic or fundamental. The second and third harmonics are simply twice and three times the frequency (vibrations per second) of the first note, or, in musical terms, an octave and a twelfth respectively. For our purposes we shall use the third harmonic, or twelfth. Taking low B♭ as an example, begin by playing the twelfth above, F at the top of the stave. While sustaining this note add the fingering for low B♭, still with the octave key open and still keeping the F sustained. Achieve this not by biting or forcing the sound but by using the correct voicing in the oral cavity and diaphragmatic/abdominal support. This may seem to be a tall order, but the feedback from such a large tube will leave one in no doubt as to what one should be doing. Once this has been achieved in a confident and relaxed manner it will be found that, while continuing to blow, by releasing the octave key a wonderfully well-rounded and centred low B♭ will appear. If this does not happen then suspect biting or pinching the sound, and check that the tone is projected forwards and not held in the back of the throat.

It is obviously good sense to have mouthpieces with similar characteristics on all one's saxophones to keep embouchure adjustment to a minimum, and do not attempt any doubling work without some good instrument stands. Flautists move on to the saxophone without too many problems but should guard against flatness of pitch. Clarinettists venturing to saxophone tend to play sharp and with a pinched sound; the mouthpiece test should cure both players' problems. Saxophonists changing over to clarinet need to check mouthpiece/embouchure alignment – it is not a soprano so remember 'head up, clarinet down' and smile! Saxophonists taking up the flute? Buy the best affordable instrument, find a sympathetic teacher, and practise as much as you can.

7 The professional player

The saxophone in the orchestra

STEPHEN TRIER

The nineteenth century

In 1983, it was estimated that the composers of more than 2000 operas, ballets and symphonic works had by then included parts for one or more saxophones.[1] Only a very small number of these works were written between 1850 and 1900. I am sure that Adolphe Sax the designer, manufacturer, player and publisher was disappointed that his family of instruments had not found a much more secure place in the affections of classical composers by the turn of the century.

The eulogies heaped upon Sax and his inventions by Hector Berlioz, even before the patent was secured in 1846, should have helped to popularise them.[2] It is all the more strange that Berlioz only scored one piece including saxophone, an arrangement for six instruments, all designed or perfected by Sax, of one of his own vocal works, *Chant sacré* (arr. 1844). Few composers used saxophones in the orchestra in the nineteenth century. Their works are well known and frequently quoted; Ambroise Thomas in his operas *Hamlet* (1868) (alto and baritone) and *Françoise de Rimini* (1882), Bizet in *L'Arlésienne* (1872), Delibes in the ballet *Sylvia* (1876), and Massenet in *Hérodiade* (1877) and *Werther* (1892) all wrote effective and beautiful solos. These are mostly in the form of brief set pieces, although the saxophone plays throughout the whole opera *Werther*. *Hérodiade* requires an alto and a tenor. César Franck scored for a complete quartet (SATB) in his rarely performed opera *Hulda* (1882–5). Saint-Saëns included a part for soprano saxophone (in F) in his symphonic poem *La Jeunesse d'Hercule* (1877), but Sax complained in a letter to the Director of the Paris Conservatoire, Ambroise Thomas, that it was not possible to find a player since his saxophone class at the Conservatoire had been discontinued due to lack of funds from military authorities impoverished by the Franco-Prussian war.[3] Sax even offered to continue teaching for nothing, but this elicited no response from Thomas. Sax never held the position of professor; he only gave instruction to military musicians. The saxophone class was not re-opened until 1942, when Marcel Mule's enormously influential professorship began a new era for the instrument.

It is interesting to speculate upon this lack of early success. It is true that one thing all nineteenth-century orchestral saxophone parts have in common is their low tessitura. The lowest notes of conical wind instruments have always been notoriously difficult to control *pianissimo*. Even today, when instrumental design and manufacture have been so refined, this remains true. A glance at the alto saxophone solo by Delibes in his ballet *Sylvia*, with its frequently repeated low C's, will demonstrate clearly what I mean: a charmingly simple melody which strikes fear in the heart of the saxophonist who has to play it! There are many other such examples where repeated, delicate attacks are a hazard which would present no problem to the clarinettist. (I should add that the skills of today's players surmount these difficulties with relative ease.) Perhaps it was even more significant that players of a sufficient standard were not readily available. This led to an impasse: composers no longer wrote parts for saxophone because they were not certain to get their works played on the instrument of their choice; players, on the other hand, stopped learning the saxophone because there were no longer any parts to play.

The extraordinary life of Sax himself cannot have helped, because a man of such wide and unusual talents was bound to be a controversial figure. In spite of, or indeed because of, his talents, he made many enemies, and much of his life was spent defending himself from adversaries he had often helped to create when the time might have been better used in the promotion of his astonishing inventions. Competing instrument manufacturers were extremely jealous in guarding their products, which had often become outdated by Sax's more adventurous methods.

The twentieth century

It is certainly true that after its first faltering steps, the saxophone all but disappeared from the orchestra until the 1920s. This lengthy barren period has been graphically documented by Wally Horwood;[4] the snobbery and prejudice the saxophone had to overcome have persisted, in some cases, to the present day. This prejudice came about largely because of the easily accessible qualities of the saxophone. By this I do not mean that it is easy to play, but some modest results can be achieved quite quickly. People found that they could quite easily teach themselves to play tunes on it, hence its enormous success in early ragtime, jazz and popular music in the USA. This success became a 'craze', encouraged by the virtuosity of players such as Rudy Wiedoeft in the 1920s and 1930s.

I am aware that some of what is written above may not appear to have any bearing upon the orchestra and the saxophone. However, the snobbery such popular music engendered created a gulf, not to say a chasm, between popular and classical music which successfully barred the saxophone from the 'polite' company of the symphony orchestra.

At the very beginning of the twentieth century Richard Strauss wrote his *Symphonia domestica* (1903), and for reasons not entirely clear, he included a somewhat bizarre quartet of saxophones: soprano in C, alto in F, baritone in F and bass in C. Such instruments did indeed exist as part of Sax's proposed family of orchestral saxophones, but they have not survived, except that the tenor in C had a considerable vogue (as the 'C-melody' saxophone). Controversy surrounds Strauss's work. Amid the theorising and speculation, one thing is certainly true: Strauss marked the parts *ad lib.* and always dispensed with them in performances he conducted.[5] As a great admirer of Strauss's music, I find this a pity, but unsurprising. The extravagant double fugue in the finale scarcely needs further thickening of the orchestral texture!

Of the music that the saxophone was required to play in the symphony orchestra from about 1920, some derived from jazz or popular sources. Not much of this was caricature, as is often suggested, and the composer's affinity with the instrument is often apparent. Milhaud, in *La Création du monde* (1923), calls upon the jazzy and vocal qualities of the saxophone with great success. On the other hand, Ravel explores another quality, its evocative cantilena in *Il Vecchio castello* in his orchestration of Musorgsky's *Tableaux d'une exposition* (1922), and yet another in *Boléro* with solos for tenor and sopranino/soprano. (The latter solo is now always played on the soprano throughout.)

Composers gradually became much bolder, realising that, in spite of prejudice, the saxophone family possessed qualities they could no longer ignore.

The arrival on the scene of two undoubted virtuosi – Marcel Mule and Sigurd Rascher – can only have helped, the latter by his commissions from eminent composers. It is true that these commissions were for solo works, but everything helped to generate interest and from this time the cause of the saxophone in the orchestra began to gather some momentum.

The earlier case of the extraordinary American, Mrs Elise Hall, should be mentioned in this context. Told to take up the saxophone for her health, this indomitable lady's persistent efforts between 1900 and her death in 1920 to enlarge the solo repertoire had a lasting effect. The onset of deafness only increased her efforts to secure works from such as Debussy, Caplet, d'Indy, Schmitt and many others (see Appendix 1). Her playing was much derided, but in pursuit of her aim she advanced the cause of the classical saxophone at a crucial time.

By the mid-1920s it was not only one or two French composers who decided that the saxophone's tone colours were becoming indispensable to their orchestral palettes. In Britain, Joseph Holbrooke, whose work is unjustly neglected today, had been exploring the possibilities of the saxophones in his *Apollo and the Seaman* in 1908. William Walton had written music for the original version of *Façade* between 1922 and 1926; this was for a small group of five players. Later, in 1938, he scored several of the pieces to form the second *Façade* suite for orchestra, calling for cor anglais or alto saxophone. Walton told me that he had always preferred the saxophone in all his works where specified, but that it had often been difficult to find suitable players. *Belshazzar's Feast* (1931) was a case in point. By this time, although prejudice was still rife, other composers were joining the fray – Ralph Vaughan Williams for one. In 1930, *Job*, a masque for dancing, was first performed, part of which, the *Dance of Job's Comforters*, is a well-known set piece for the alto saxophone displaying the kind of affinity between composer and instrument mentioned earlier. As Wally Horwood has written,[6] conductors often try to make the saxophonist emphasise the sleaziness which they think the composer wanted in this solo (I believe he did not), so much so that at the Three Choirs Festival of 1948 in Worcester, 'the ecclesiastical authorities insisted the movement incorporating the saxophone be omitted rather than let the instrument's profane voice speak within the sacred edifice'.[7] I well remember the storm evoked by this bigotry. The saxophone still had its social problems! At any rate, Vaughan Williams was not deterred from scoring for saxophone again: a taxing and effective use of the tenor in two movements of the Sixth Symphony (1948), followed by parts for two altos and a tenor in the Ninth Symphony (1956–8). The latter was, and remains, unusual in the use of a group of saxophones deployed both as individual solo voices and as an ensemble.

Benjamin Britten was yet another British composer who found a place in a number of his works for the alto saxophone. Britten wrote idiomatic parts in *Our Hunting Fathers* (1936), *Mont Juic* (1937) (with Lennox Berkeley), *Sinfonia da Requiem* (1940), *Diversions* (1940), *Paul Bunyan* (1941), *Billy Budd* (1951) and *The Prince of the Pagodas* (1957). Everywhere the texture of the saxophone and the orchestra are combined with Britten's customary consummate skill and understanding of instrumental colour. Michael Tippett's opera *New Year* (1988) calls for a trio of saxophonists, originally including a bass in B♭.

French composers, although often more preoccupied with writing works such as *solos de concours* designed for academic competition, also began to use saxophones in the orchestra. As well as Darius Milhaud, Arthur Honegger (who was Swiss, though born in Le Havre) incorporated saxophones in many of his orchestral works. Noteworthy among these is *Jeanne d'Arc au Bûcher* (1934/5), a stage cantata where three alto saxophones replace the more usual three horns to great effect. Few composers have championed the cause of the saxophone more assiduously than Charles Koechlin, particularly in the orchestra. His *Seven Stars Symphony* (1933) – a tribute to seven stars of the silent cinema (such as Charlie Chaplin, Marlene Dietrich and Greta Garbo) – and *Les Bandar-Log* – one of several orchestral pieces inspired by Kipling's *Jungle Book* – both feature prominent saxophone writing.

Jacques Ibert's friendship with Marcel Mule probably led to several saxophone parts in symphonic works and film music. During the early 1950s he contributed a score for part of a ballet film by Gene Kelly made in London; it was to have been a full-length feature (for MGM), but all that survives is a short piece about a circus, *Invitation to the Dance*. Ibert's music, with busy alto saxophone part, survives.

Swiss-born Frank Martin featured saxophones in many of his works. Noteworthy among them are the Symphony (1936/7), *Rythmes* (1927), the Violoncello Concerto (1967), Piano Concerto No. 2 (1970), *Les Quatre Eléments* (1964), *Der Sturm* (1956) and *Monsieur de Pourceaugnac* (1963).

Lulu, the unfinished opera by Alban Berg (1937), includes a very important role for the alto saxophone. I use the word 'role' advisedly, since it is often on a par with the singers. *Lulu Symphonie* for soprano and orchestra (1934) contains music for the saxophone which is later sung by Lulu in the opera. The Violin Concerto (1935), with its delicate scoring, features another beautifully written part for alto saxophone (the saxophonist is also required to play clarinet in the Bach chorale 'Es ist genug' at the close of the second movement – an early example of doubling).

In entirely different style, Paul Hindemith, always ready to experiment, used alto saxophone in his operas *Hin und Zurück* (1927) and *Neues vom Tage* (1929). The tenor saxophone figures largely in the three-act opera *Cardillac* of 1926 (revised 1952).

During the Nazi era, foreign imports from 'negro music' such as the saxophone were banned from Germany. Kurt Weill left Germany in 1933, largely on account of his Jewish descent. Saxophones were essential elements of his orchestration in *Die Dreigroschenoper* (1928), *Happy End* (1929) and *The Rise and Fall of the City of Mahagonny* (1930).

Meanwhile, across the Atlantic, the very well-known works of George Gershwin have gloriously survived. '*An American in Paris*', wrote Eric Blom,[8] 'shocked the audience of the 1931 ISCM Festival in London by its excessive commonness'. But he does add that perhaps it was not the right audience for it! The *Rhapsody in Blue, Second Rhapsody* and the opera *Porgy and Bess* (1935) are scored with saxophones. In *Porgy*, all the saxophonists are required to double on clarinets.

Aaron Copland and Leonard Bernstein do not seem to have been as restrained as American composers. Both often emphasised the swing potential of saxophones in their works, for example Copland's Concerto for Piano, First Symphony (arranged from the *Organ Symphony*) and others. (During my professional career I was twice engaged to play alto saxophone in Copland's *Organ Symphony*. Although the full score listed saxophone in the instrumentation, no part was ever found in the music of the score!) Bernstein's *Symphonic Dances from West Side Story* (1960) are probably his most well-known pieces to include a saxophone, although there are many others: 'Kaddish' (Symphony No. 3) and *Prelude, Fugue and Riffs* are just two of them.

The Russians Rachmaninoff, Prokofiev, Kabalevsky, Khachaturian and Shostakovich all included saxophones in their music. The evocative alto saxophone solo in Rachmaninoff's *Symphonic Dances* (1940) is particularly well known: very short but very effective. Prokofiev nearly always favoured the tenor saxophone in his scores; for instance, in *Lieutenant Kijé* (1934), *Romeo and Juliet* (1938) and *Alexander Nevsky* (1938) the tenor is sometimes a soloist and sometimes scored with the bassoons. Shostakovich has written a fine solo soprano part in his *Age of Gold* (1930) ballet which is very difficult to control with its wide interval leaps.

Pierre Boulez scored for saxophones in a couple of his pieces. They are very much absorbed into the general texture of *Rituel* (1974/5) and the *Improvisation 1* from *Pli selon Pli* (1958/1962). On the other hand, the saxophone figures in nearly all Luciano Berio's large output of operatic and orchestral works. His opera *Outis* (1996) includes a full quartet. Hans Werner Henze employs saxophones in many of his stage works, either in the pit or in stage bands. These include his operas *Orpheus* (1977) and *The Bassarids* (1964–5/1992). Many of his orchestral works also benefit from the presence of saxophone, for example Symphonies Nos. 3 and 6 (1949 and 1969/1994). Peter Maxwell Davies wrote a unique solo for sopranino saxophone which appears in the suite from his film music for *The Boy Friend* (1971). Soprano saxophones feature largely in several of Harrison Birtwistle's major works, such as his opera *The Mask of Orpheus* (first performed in 1986), which asks for the three soprano saxophones to double on conches. Trumpeters actually played the conches in the performances, while the saxophonists doubled on bamboo flutes! An earlier work, his *Triumph of Time* (1972), requires an amplified soprano saxophone.

The cause of the saxophone has made great progress recently in Britain, through the writing of composers such as Jonathan Lloyd (Second and Fourth Symphonies), Oliver Knussen (*Choral*), John Woolrich (Oboe Concerto), James MacMillan (*Sinfonietta*) and Robin Holloway (*Divertimento*, First and Second Concertos for Orchestra). Another encouraging trend is for composers to form groups or bands of players to perform those of their works in which saxophones figure. Steve Martland, Michael Nyman and Graham Fitkin are exponents. Perhaps even more exciting is the work of Mark Anthony Turnage, who has shown his affection for the saxophones in numerous works of all kinds for chamber, symphony and opera orchestra; he exploits all facets of the instruments' colours in *Three Screaming Popes* (1989), *Momentum* (1991), *Drowned Out* (1993), *Dispelling the Fears* (1995) and *Blood on the Floor* (1996), not forgetting the operas *Greek* (1986/8) and *Killing Time* (1991).

In making a modest selection of works including saxophone, I have tried to choose those pieces which are likely to be available in some recorded form, so that the reader may explore the manifold styles employed by composers. Norman del Mar once described the saxophone as being an affiliated instrument as far as the orchestra is concerned.[9] This somewhat disparaging observation was certainly true when his book was written but, as I hope that I have been able to show, there has been much progress in recent years.

Technical change and evolution

During the past fifty years much has changed in the way that saxophonists have learned their skills. The majority of players in the past were either self-taught or learned their craft from clarinettists. Only comparatively recently have all colleges and schools of music had their own specialist teachers. Playing styles too have evolved over this time. In the 1940s and 1950s there were many dance bands manned by multi-instrument players, or doublers. In Britain, as opposed to Belgium, France and to a certain extent the USA, no exclusively specialist saxophonists existed. They could not and would not today earn a living as professionals or semi-professionals without recourse to doubling on flute and/or clarinet. The demand of the symphony orchestra for the occasional saxophone player is usually filled by one of a number of players with both the skill and the temperament required. In Britain, these were, and are often, 'in house', as it were – clarinettists or bass clarinettists who are already members of the orchestra, or freelance players brought in for the occasion. In the past, numerous saxophone players whose considerable abilities as players in dance bands did not really 'fit' in the more rarefied atmosphere of the symphony orchestra. I remember many conductors whose attitude to the saxophonist was intimidating to say the least. I can only assume that these maestros had had bad experiences of players unused to the disciplines of the orchestra, however skilled they may have been in their usual surroundings. It was also true until recently that dynamically and tonally there was often a jarring mismatch.

Saxophones are capable of an immense range of dynamics. A large industry has been set up to produce mouthpieces to help the player achieve these extra decibels. It is not possible to produce every type of sound from one mouthpiece and reed. There is no other wind instrument for which such a large choice is available. Every kind of material has been used: wood, crystal, ebonite, plastic, and a profusion of metals and alloys. Their object has always been to enable players to produce different qualities and quantities of sound. The saxophones are capable of an enormous variety of timbre, but players need the help of different kinds of reeds and mouthpieces to produce them. Metal and alloy mouthpieces do not necessarily mean louder sounds, but it is certain that many of them are expressly designed to that end. The latter would seldom be at home in an orchestra where, as remarked before, delicacy of attack and nuance is often required. One other vital factor in the player–mouthpiece equation is the control of intonation. It is difficult enough with an instrument so inherently flexible. The player can do a great deal, but it is certain that some mouthpieces do not match every instrument. In other words, a mouthpiece not originally designed for a particular make of instrument could create 'intonational' havoc when the two are combined, no matter how satisfactory to the player the dynamic and tonal qualities may be. It is, I think, a golden rule that the saxophonist should first try the mouthpiece designed by the instrument's manufacturer before purchasing one of the more weird and wonderful products, some of which are apparently designed to shatter glass at twenty metres! It is fortunate that current Selmer alto and tenor ebonite mouthpieces seem to be a good and suitable match for other makes of instrument. Suitable for an orchestral context they certainly are; mixing and matching is not always a disaster, but beware!

The advance of technical skills in recent years has in many ways been the equal of the demands made upon the players. It is still possible to hear inept playing in orchestras, but it is much less common than it once was. This is good news, because the better saxophonists play, the more likely it is that composers will write music for them.

The undocumented

GORDON LEWIN

Jazz saxophone, its music and its players are by now well documented, while the symphonic and recital repertories also appear in appropriate reference books; what, however, of the vast hinterland of light music which has been so little explored? Perhaps the very term 'light music' is misleading, for it overlaps into everything from vaudeville and popular dance music to theatre and semi-symphonic presentations, to say nothing of the numerous small ensembles and soloists who have beguiled us throughout the twentieth century on radio and records. To pin down light music with a definition would probably reveal it to be music which is neither pretentious nor profound; has entertainment value without being unduly cerebral; may be heard in the concert hall, recital room or restaurant, on radio, television or record; but which in its finest manifestation is a craft to be practised with taste and discernment by accomplished performers.

Where does the saxophone stand in this uncharted territory? The soloists range from Rudy Wiedoeft to Al Gallodoro; the composer-arrangers from Gershwin and Robert Russell Bennett to Bernstein and Hershy Kay; the large orchestras from André Kostelanetz to Glenn Miller and the Army Air Force Band; and those golden years from 1945 to 1970 when the BBC enabled us to hear more light music from the established orchestras and free-lance ensembles than either before or since. This has virtually disappeared with the formation of Radios 1 to 5, for the death of the Light Programme meant the almost total extinction of free-lance light orchestras and the jettisoning of much of the repertoire and its practitioners.

And what of those memorable moments of evocative saxophone playing in theatres and films which were highlights that enhanced the action? Who can forget the opening of *West Side Story* with the solo breaks for alto saxophone, later to be absorbed into the motifs for the *Jets and Sharks*; similarly with the cantering 'New York' theme in Bernstein's ballet *Fancy Free*, appearing again in the film *On the Town*; the gradual emergence of saxophone section scoring into the rhythmic phrasing of the ballet *Slaughter on 10th Avenue* from Richard Rodgers' *On your Toes*; the gritty tenor saxophone of Henry Mancini's *Pink Panther* theme, or the saxophone duet in thirds heard in the opening and closing credits for the television series of *Cagney and Lacey*? We surely have to make the assumption that the boundaries of light music can encompass such diverse idioms. So, is it the composer-arranger or the performer who weaves the magic moments? Of all orchestral instruments the saxophone is probably the most idiosyncratic. Style, and the listener's perception of it, changes over the years; pieces once regarded as jazz have worn coats of a different colour with passing decades. Jimmy Dorsey's *Oodles of Noodles* or Frankie Trumbauer's *Bouncing Ball* are more in the realm of light music now than they ever were at the time of their inception.

Players with their own personal styles put the stamp of recognisability on the orchestras and ensembles with whom they played. Peter Yorke, whose orchestra was heard regularly on the radio during the 1940s and 1950s, had a section of five saxophones, but their distinctive sound was entirely due to Freddy Gardner, the lead saxophone player. He was also a featured soloist on such standards as *Valse Vanité* and *Stardust*, soaring into carefully contrived harmonics with his own distinctive way of playing. That personal sound disappeared with his death, and although he was replaced by some excellent players, they did not use the same wide, fast vibrato that made Freddy Gardner so recognisable, and to Peter Yorke it was never quite the same again. The Geraldo orchestra of the 1940s and 1950s, which was famous for its *Dancing Through* radio series, owed much of its distinctive sound to lead altoist Dougie Robinson, whose meticulous playing gave polish to the section. Canadian alto player Bob Burns was a mainstay of the saxophone section with Robert Farnon's orchestra on radio, television and records. His positive lead set an accurate and carefully delineated sound, later to be transferred to the Jack Parnell orchestra in their residency as house band at ATV, Elstree. All these orchestras played music which strayed over the borders into neighbouring territories. Popular dance music, accompaniments to vocalists, dancers and variety acts, and semi-symphonic items for the orchestras constituted the mainstay of the repertoire. The music they played embodied typical saxophone scoring of the post-war years, with most saxophone sections having five players who, for economic reasons, were usually required to double on clarinet, bass clarinet or flute. Hence the musicianship demanded from the wind players during this period was of an extremely high standard. Fast sight-reading and familiarity with repertoire was essential, for most studio work was organised on tight budgets and stringent time-scales.

This diversity of idioms meant that there was considerable musical cross-fertilisation, with the expectation that players would have the expertise to embrace both straight and jazz styles in the appropriate manner. Probably one of the best solo saxophone examples is Eddie Sauter's composition *Focus*. Written for Stan Getz, it is scored for tenor saxophone, strings and percussion. It contains long sections of improvisation for Getz, with the jazz juxtaposed against highly organised string writing. This is without doubt a jazz work, but nevertheless the concept is basically that of light music. This was later to be emulated by Michel Legrand, who followed a similar pattern for the same soloist with *Communications 72.* Ronald Binge's Concerto for alto saxophone and orchestra is a work which, while serious in content, has more of the light music idiom to it than the solemnity of the concert hall – which brings us back to the listener's perception of the definition of light music. Like Alice in Wonderland, it begins to appear that it can mean anything one wishes. In the years between the wars the saxophone's popularity was due in no small measure to the efforts of American Rudy Wiedoeft, who not only was a brilliant technician on the instrument, but who also wrote a string of compositions, the most famous of which was *Valse vanité.* He published over thirty-five compositions and innumerable transcriptions. As well as exploiting some of the more bizarre effects of which the instrument is capable, as in the *Sax-O-Phun* and *Sax-O-Trix,* Wiedoeft was one of the finest exponents of virtuoso saxophone playing.

In the post-war years Al Gallodoro, who at one time was a member of the Paul Whiteman Orchestra, donated some of the most accomplished and superb playing heard on record. A master of fast articulation and possessor of a staggering technique, he is equally adept on clarinet, as is shown in his recording of *Concerto for Doubles.* For sheer brilliance of technique on alto saxophone his versions of *Carnival of Venice, Gigue,* Monti's *Czardas* and Haydn's *Gypsy Rondo* are incomparable.

The BBC's promotion of light music on what was known as the Light Programme, later to become Radio 2, was the golden period for free-lance broadcasting groups. From 1945 to 1970 staple ingredients of broadcasting fare included the large symphonic orchestras of Robert Farnon, George Melachrino, Peter Yorke, Geraldo, Philip Green, Stanley Black, Mantovani, Ron Goodwin, Frank Cordell and many others.

The small ensembles who became well known for their frequent appearances on radio and television included Max Jaffa and Tom Jenkins with the Palm Court Orchestra, Sidney Bowman and the Promenade Players, Norrie Paramor, Ray Martin, Wally Stott (whose orchestra was an integral part of the *Goon Show* and *Hancock's Half Hour*), Eric Jupp, Sydney Davey, Eric Robinson and the BBC Television Orchestra (with varying instrumentation according to programme requirements), Michael Collins, plus innumerable *Music While You Work* broadcasts of dance bands, light orchestras and Latin-American groups. The BBC Light Music Unit provided many ensembles, drawn from a pool of players who were split into smaller groups as the occasion demanded. Typical of these were the London Studio Players, the Majestic Orchestra, the Southern Serenade Orchestra, the Chameleons, and the 20th Century Serenaders. Permanent BBC orchestras included the Revue and Variety orchestras, later to be disbanded and replaced by the Radio Orchestra, and the BBC Theatre Orchestra, eventually renamed as the BBC Concert Orchestra. Regional orchestras included the Northern Dance Orchestra, the Midland Light Orchestra, the Scottish Variety Orchestra and the West of England Players.

There were small groups broadcasting from London which included a single saxophone, usually embedded in the ensemble as a solo or blendable voice – perhaps the best example was the Fred Hartley Sextet, comprising string quartet, baritone saxophone doubling clarinet, and piano. The baritone was used as a second cello or viola, or as a solo voice alternating with clarinet. Typical items would be *Molly on the Shore* or *These Foolish Things*, and although the music may have been light in content, the interpretation always conformed to the highest chamber music standards. The reed player with Fred Hartley was invariably Frank Reidy or Norman Barker, both of whom spoke of the exacting performance standards demanded.

Music of a different idiom came from the Latin-American groups, the most frequent broadcaster being Edmundo Ros; this was almost the only such band consistently to use a saxophone section. Music from Europe was played by the Gerald Crossman Players, utilising three accordions, tenor saxophone doubling clarinet, bass and guitar. Another popular programme was *Music Tapestry*, played by the London Studio Players, with a change of style and pace often being provided by the Michael Krein Saxophone Quartet. For many years this was the only saxophone quartet to make regular broadcasts, and their repertoire ranged through Spanish transcriptions, the lighter works of Tchaikovsky, salon pieces from France and Russia and contemporary composers. After Michael Krein's death the quartet was led by Jack Brymer, and it continued broadcasting until the early 1980s. The London Saxophone Quartet, led by Paul Harvey, began broadcasting in 1970, and contributed many new works to the repertoire. Several new quartets emerged from the early 1970s onwards, the most notable of which were the Northern Saxophone Quartet, the English Saxophone Quartet, and the Fairer Sax.

The fact that saxophone quartets have proliferated over the past fifteen years in Britain is in no small measure due to the acceptance by the Royal Colleges of the instrument as a first study, and provision of the Associated Board's wind syllabus and graded exams. This meant a drastic reappraisal in academic circles, for the saxophone had been a completely neglected instrument when compared with other wind instruments. Unfortunately this renaissance coincided with the BBC's decision to disband most of their house orchestras. In fairly quick succession we saw the demise of the NDO, the MLO, the Scottish Variety Orchestra, the West of England Players and finally the Radio Orchestra and the Light Music Unit, none of which has been replaced. Coupled with this was a change of policy which cut out all of the free-lance ensembles which had become so familiar. The house bands and record programmes began to monopolise the radio programmes, and with a national recession in full swing it also meant the cutting back of orchestras in theatres and studios. More doubling, trebling and quadrupling was being demanded from wind players, until the Musicians' Union took the matter in hand and placed an embargo on unfettered multi-instrumentalism. Theatres and studios had reached the point where it was becoming the norm to expect wind players to accede to these demands. For economic reasons it was easier to have a palette of tone colours and range of instruments in this fashion. It is perhaps significant that in no other section of the orchestra are such demands ever made – no string player has been expected to play violin, viola and cello, nor has it been the expectation for brass players to play trumpet, horn, trombone and tuba. Perhaps players in the wind sections themselves, having become adept on a variety of instruments, then found that the doubling of these instruments with saxophone became an economic necessity. Music directors, arrangers and composers, at the behest of those wielding the financial power, were not slow to capitalise on the talents of such musicians, who had in effect created the very chains by which they had become captive. Innumerable examples abound, and one has only to look down the instrumentation of many theatre shows, television and film productions to see this in action. The transition from being a willing participant in order to maintain a foothold in the commercial market, to becoming a victim of those very attributes is but a short step. Although we do not live in a cultural vacuum, it is amazing how often a restrictive budget and a fiscally minded producer can influence instrumentation and eventual booking of individuals.

Examples of this can be seen in the gradual diminution in the size of the studio orchestras for the *Carry On* films, the requirements for individuals in the wind section to play four to five instruments in the stage shows *Wish You Were Here* and *Chorus Line*, the minimal instrumentation used for the films of *Bonny and Clyde* and *Butch Cassidy and the Sundance Kid*, and the proliferating use of the smallest groups possible for background music for television, bolstered by synthesizers and other electronic means. The days of large orchestras for Dimitri Tiomkin are but distant memories.

The dividing line between dance band and light orchestra can often be somewhat blurred; are we listening to a dance band with added strings, an orchestra which includes a saxophone section, or just a light music ensemble? Some of the Ambrose recordings from the late 1930s illustrate this: *Caramba*, *The Piccolino* and *My Lost Love* surely come into the light music category, while Reginald Foresythe's compositions *Dodging a Divorcee* and *Lament for Congo* veer towards jazz. And how do we categorise Raymond Scott's *Reckless Night on Board an Ocean Liner* or *The Toy Trumpet*, Alec Wilder's *Neurotic Goldfish* or *Such a Tender Night*, and the excellent Hollywood Jazztette, directed by Jerry Field, playing *Skylark* and *Memphis in June*? All of them constitute admirable light music, but with a jazz influence. The Hollywood Saxophone Quartet epitomised this perfectly with their chamber music approach, jazz-flavoured arrangements (many by alto player Lennie Niehaus), and the addition of drums and bass to the quartet. Their version of *Cheek to Cheek* is a delightful example of 'cross-over', and the intelligent saxophonist's approach to playing in both camps of what used to be called 'straight and dance'.

Composer-arrangers Robert Russell Bennett, Ralph Burns, Henry Mancini and Leroy Anderson have all contributed generously to this area of music, while in England Robert Farnon, Angela Morley and Peter Knight have produced excellent compositions and memorable scores for the BBC Radio Orchestra. There has been a wealth of music arranged and composed by highly skilled musicians in the second half of the twentieth century, using the saxophone in a way which has moved it firmly from the stereotype of the early years into an instrument associated with a high degree of technical and musical literacy.

The whole meaning of the term 'light music' and the venues where it could be heard were changing by the time that the rock and roll era appeared in the late 1950s. Standard musical fare hitherto heard in restaurants, hotels, variety theatres and in the spas and seaside towns of Great Britain was disappearing. Hotels and restaurants were dispensing with live music, as muzak and recorded music increasingly displaced the musician. In spite of the efforts of the Musicians' Union as sole defender of the faith, the music halls and variety theatres were being turned into bingo halls and cinemas, while the old municipal orchestras were being phased out as uneconomic and wartime restrictions were held over into the post-war period. Harrogate, Bath and Cheltenham no longer supported permanent or seasonal music groups, and the seaside resorts of Blackpool, Margate and Worthing cut back on their previous musical commitments as more and more holiday makers were taking their vacations abroad. With this came the advent of the discotheque, which replaced the previous live entertainment centres – with a consequent loss of employment for musicians. Rock and roll brought about a change in fashion and public taste, particularly among the younger generation. Programmes no longer included works by Ketèlbey, Eric Coates, Ivor Novello, Friml, Haydn Wood or Romberg. The era of the keyboard, percussion and guitar-dominated smaller groups had taken over, together with a fondness for excessive amplification; for the saxophonist these groups rapidly became the only possible avenues for employment, usually in a solo or vocal-backing capacity. The big band era had vanished, so that social change indirectly led to a dearth of saxophone players for almost three decades, except for limited use in theatres and studios. It was not until colleges and examining boards revised their previously entrenched attitudes and admitted the saxophone as an instrument with the same potential as other orchestral instruments that the situation began to look somewhat healthier.

Through much of this decline, there were a few enlightened players who did not give up the struggle to gain acceptance of the instrument. From 1945 to 1975 the saxophone quartet scene was almost the exclusive domain of the Krein Quartet and the London Saxophone Quartet, but since 1975 a new generation of saxophone players has emerged. It is interesting to note that many of today's exponents of the saxophone are single-instrument players. Unless working in theatres or studios doubling no longer seems to be an essential part of one's trade. Before and immediately following the war, one would invariably find that the saxophonists in the featured light orchestras (Farnon, Melachrino, Yorke, Parnell, etc.) would be adept players of the clarinet, bass clarinet and flute (Frank Reidy, Keith Bird, Roy Willox, Al Baum, Ted Planas, Bob Burns, Norman Barker, etc.). This situation had changed dramatically by the 1990s, with a burgeoning in the number of technically outstanding young players and their quartets, many of them specialising in music of the light category: the Mistral, the Adelphi, Itchy Fingers, Saxtet, Saxology, Saxploitation, the Jazz-a-belles and many more. Although French players had mainly concentrated on classical and contemporary repertoire, with Marcel Mule and Jean-Marie Londeix as the outstanding virtuosi, Daniel Deffayet and his quartet had produced many light pieces to act as benchmarks (for instance *Valse chromatique*). Dance bands, including the Piccadilly Dance Orchestra and the Pasadena Roof Orchestra, are once again in demand, albeit within a smaller market.

The years after World War II saw the progressive influence of jazz in films and television, and a consequent increase in the use of the saxophone in studio work. American composers in this sphere were in many cases drawn from a jazz background, as the screen credits reveal the familiar names of Neal Hefti, Nelson Riddle, Quincy Jones and Bill Conti. The ground had been well laid by Elmer Bernstein, André Previn, Alex North and others. One has only to hear the scores for films featuring Gene Kelly, Fred Astaire, Cyd Charisse and Frank Sinatra to perceive the shift in style from the pre-war movies. Bob Fosse, Michael Kidd and the jazz-dance choreographers all had their influence on the type of music and the resultant scoring and instrumentation. Studio musicians in the USA (Toots Mondello, Bud Shank, Lennie Niehaus and Buddy Collette) all produced what we have come to recognise as a Hollywood sound, while latter-day television films and themes have been dominated by a different tonal concept, as exemplified by David Sanborn.

Over the decades, there have been changing perceptions of the sound, timbre and tonal qualities of the saxophone. In the symphony orchestra, or orchestral world, the role of the saxophone has been self-effacing and inconspicuous, blending with the wind section until, or unless, called upon to perform in a solo capacity. However, most of the recognisable stylists came from the jazz world, where players were instantly known by their individual tonal characteristics. One has only to cast one's mind back to recordings of Johnny Hodges (velvety vibrato, controlled slurring and pitching), Benny Carter (smooth, suave and sophisticated), Charlie Parker (more recognisable for his harmonic ingenuity and inventive bop phrasing than for his tonal quality), Lee Konitz (with his 'lean-warm' tone, to quote Gunther Schuller) and Paul Desmond (who described his own tone as 'trying to sound like a dry Martini'). Among the tenors were the full-throated sounds of Coleman Hawkins, the limpid straight sound of Lester Young (based on his own conception of Frankie Trumbauer's C-melody saxophone sound), the feathery sound of Ben Webster (sometimes described as 'more air than note') and the beautifully produced felicitous timbre (particularly in the upper register) of Stan Getz.

All these players were instantly recognisable by their own personal style, and their appearance in their own decade set the prevailing sound for the next generation of saxophonists. The various tonal perceptions as influenced by these players meant a new evaluation of the means of production, hence the variety of mouthpieces which were to become available. In the final analysis beauty lies in the eyes (or ears) of the beholder, and so a succession of 'sound-alikes' has inevitably appeared during the twentieth century. One has only to witness the Sonny Stitt/Charlie Parker comparison, the Sonny Rollins/Dexter Gordon/Lucky Thompson syndrome, the Ben Webster/Paul Gonsalves imaging, and the cool school as exemplified by Stan Getz and Bob Cooper. Perhaps the latest and most successful saxophonists to absorb the ideas of previous generations into a rhapsodic composite are the Americans Scott Hamilton and Ken Peplowski.

But to where does all this lead in the evaluation of light music and the role of the saxophone therein? Except for studio-based performances, or music-theatre, there now exists little light music of the type so predominant fifty years ago, and so the tendency of players in the 1980s and 1990s has been to forge an amalgam of the best from the jazz world tempered by the criteria for 'straight' saxophone as laid down by the colleges and examination boards.

Foremost in Britain for setting present trends have undoubtedly been John Harle as role-model soloist, Paul Harvey as leader of the LSQ (particularly with his varied compositions and arrangements for saxophone), Stephen Trier via his influence at the Royal College of Music, and now the recently appointed teacher-soloist Kyle Horch. All these players have set musical and technical standards for younger players, and bear some degree of responsibility for what we hear from today's generation. When we speak of light music players now, we are, in general, speaking of those who come from both classical and jazz backgrounds, and who ideally incorporate the best of both worlds in their playing.

Light music as a contemporary living force has changed over the years, and much that we now hear comes from soloists and small ensembles who are essentially entrepreneurial in character. So many of the old established avenues of employment have now been closed, and it is due to the efforts and individual enthusiasms of players in their search for new outlets that the saxophone flag is still flying. Many of our current groups feature light music in their programmes and travel worldwide: foyer concerts, music clubs, colleges and self-promotions have replaced the old circuits of yesteryear.

With recognition from the colleges it is no coincidence that there have been far more technically advanced and musically literate saxophone players who have appeared over the past two decades than ever before. Enlightened teaching enables the talents of today's generation to play music of all idioms – whether in chamber ensembles, recitals, bands, jazz groups or the theatre – in a more musically democratic fashion than ever existed in the first half of this century.

A most encouraging aspect of recent years has been the emergence of new repertoire. Although many of the familiar names among music publishers have been swallowed up by multinationals, nevertheless we have also seen the growth of many small music companies who are now providing new material for the saxophone. There has been a positive flood of new compositions and arrangements, and the players of today have many options for building programmes to satisfy all tastes.

The studio player

CHRIS 'SNAKE' DAVIS

A session player is a musician who is booked on a free-lance basis to work in film, television or recording studios. Almost all of us, however, combine our recording studio work with other activities such as gigs, tours, shows or teaching, and it is doubtful whether any two session sax players have matching careers. It's a life with little or no routine – most session work comes in at very short notice, maybe a week or so if you are lucky, but all too often the request is 'We need you now, how quickly can you get here?' This is especially true for sax players. A producer will know they are going to need a drummer, a keyboard player and a bassist, but it's often not until a piece is apparently finished, perhaps already being mixed, that someone says – 'Hey, a sax solo might be really good in that bit!'

Not knowing what's round the corner can make life exciting. One moment you are gazing at the phone wondering whether there really is a fault on the line, the next moment the phone finally does ring, and before you know it you are travelling to a top studio to play a solo for someone very famous, or flying to Tokyo to work on a live album for more money than you have ever dreamed of. The lack of routine can be disruptive, frustrating and worrying. In session work, for some reason, there always seems to be either a feast or famine. I am writing this on a flight to Belgium (all the way to Antwerp for a twelve-bar solo!), and this is the sixth flight in as many days. I have been working every day for at least twenty days, sometimes two or three jobs in one day, yet I had a couple of months in late 1996 when I hardly saw the inside of a studio.

Studio skills

Many of the skills required for session work are the same as those needed in other areas of performance – technical proficiency, a good sound, familiarity with many different styles, and of course punctuality; the ability to sight-read well is not absolutely essential, but without it the range of work available is very limited. It is more important in the studio than in other areas of performance to have well-maintained instruments. Clicks and clunks are so much more noticeable and may irritate a recording engineer to the extent that he or she may try to 'EQ' them out, thereby distorting your precious sound. It is possible to breeze happily through a jazz tour with a leaky tenor, not needing a soft bottom B♭, but in the studio you never know what to expect, and can get caught out (I was that red-faced tenor player!).

Doubling, like sight-reading, is almost a prerequisite. I play five different saxes as well as flute, alto-flute and wind synthesiser. That may seem a lot (it does by the time I've loaded them all into the car), but the truth is that by ignoring piccolo and the clarinet family I have made myself ineligible for many sessions, particularly in the field of television and film. Naturally a high standard is required on all the doubles (double, don't dabble).

Skills more specific to studio work are sometimes less easy to define. In my own specialist area (soul/pop soloing) a very important quality is the ability to get the 'feel' of a piece, so that what you play will sound natural and enhance, change or lift the mood. With this kind of work, and even more so in advertising jingles and corporate music, requirements include being able to translate the demands of the client, who is probably not very used to dealing with music and musicians, into some kind of performance. In other words, mind-reading needs to be on a level with sight-reading, and you need saint-like patience – 'Have you got a deeper one?' or 'Could you make it sound more biscuity on that bit?' As a session player your job is always to make the piece of music sound as good as possible. This may seem obvious, but it is not always simple. It means often suppressing your own ego, sometimes ignoring your own taste, and somehow getting into the producer's or artist's head, seeing and hearing from their angle.

The progression to studio work is usually a gradual one – most people start with the odd session here and there, but there are ways to speed the process up. It is certainly a good idea to send a c.v., photograph and show-reel to fixers (orchestral contractors), agents and management companies, and also to more established musicians, but the most important thing is to get out and play as much, and in as many different situations, as possible. Jam sessions, jazz clubs, rehearsal bands, function bands, singers' nights, church, school bands, auditions, youth orchestras, workshops etc. – get yourself out there and meet other musicians. Some of the players you meet may already be doing sessions, or they may go on to be session players, or they may have friends who work in the studio. Many session players have been to music college or taken courses of one kind or another; the actual qualification is of no relevance whatsoever to the studio player, but disciplined ensemble playing and contacts made with other musicians in college are invaluable.

Many studios, especially smaller ones, rarely see any acoustic instruments today; most of the work is done on computers, midi-keyboards and samplers, and often the recording engineer is also the writer, producer and studio manager. It is quite likely that the session player will be asked for advice on how best to record their instrument and what effects to use. There are no hard and fast rules for this; every situation is different, and it is good to experiment sometimes. Put up a couple of mics, perhaps a trusty Neumann U87 or AKG 414 and something less familiar, and see which one you and the engineer think sounds best with the track. *With* the track, because a microphone which sounds rich and warm might, for example, be fine for a ballad, but lack the presence to cut through on a fast dance track.

There is an almost infinite number of effects available in the studio, together with very sophisticated equalisation (tone control). Here again I am always happy to experiment, but in the vast majority of cases what I want to hear is a natural sound. This means recording the sax flat (no EQ), and playing it back with just reverb and perhaps some delay or echo (effects such as these won't be recorded with the sax in a multi-track situation, but added at the mix-down stage). Most of us are precious about our personal sounds, and we didn't spend the best years of our lives blowing long notes into broom cupboards to have those sounds distorted and effected out of recognition.

Many recording engineers will use a compressor when recording wind instruments. Compression squeezes the audio signal from both ends, making the quiet bits louder and the loud bits quieter, enabling higher levels to be recorded without fear of distortion when the player gets excited. This is a useful tool when used sparingly, and quality valve compressors can add warmth or richness, but beware of over-compression which can clip the attack of notes and rob the player of dynamic control. I occasionally have to ask an engineer tactfully to 'back off the compression a touch'.

An effect which can be created through performance is double-tracking; some sax lines benefit from being thickened up by overdubbing the original line. The effect is exaggerated if a different sax is used, and a double an octave down, perhaps set back and panned to one side, can work well.

The most common request for a session saxophonist is for a short solo take ('We just need an eight-bar solo') and this can introduce a new dimension to a piece of music. The shorter the solo the more critical each note becomes, and the more pressure there is for it to be absolutely perfect. Solo sessions can be so fragile, so fraught, that I am never sure how they are going to go. My favourite approach is to work fast; I'll have a quick listen to the track to get a feel for it and establish what key it's in, then watch the producer for a nod indicating that the solo is coming up, shut my eyes, let the music engulf me, take an imaginary step forward, get hit by the imaginary spotlight and go for it! If this works then everything's fine – smiles, nods of approval, and I'm almost out of the door before the tea has cooled. It often doesn't happen like this of course, and then things can start to get tricky. Guidance may well be offered by the artist or producer. Raf Ravenscroft had Hugh Murphy's string line to copy for the famous *Baker Street* solo, and King Curtis had Lieber and Stoller singing lines into one ear while he was recording those fantastic solos on The Coasters hits. If no guidance is offered, and you've had a few runs at it and no one is really knocked out, it's time to stop and think about it. To keep going over the same eight bars can quickly diminish inspiration, notes can start sounding forced and lifeless, and desperation creeps in, quickly sensed by the artist and producer. You've probably already tried coming in on a really high note, or the same note the singer finishes on; you've thought of the solo as having two halves with a change of gear into the second half, you've experimented with a really jazzy approach, and finishing on a crazy ascending pattern over two bars sounded awful. It's now time to take the advice given to me early on in my career by the crazy, zany and gifted producer–arranger–writer Richard Niles. Seeing me in a desperate situation on one of his sessions, he took pity on me and suggested that I detach myself by jumping out of my skin, standing a little way away from myself, taking a look at the situation from all angles and thinking 'What advice can I give this poor guy?'

The most obvious solution may have been overlooked. Perhaps you just need a ten-minute break, or maybe the tenor was a wrong choice – try the solo on flute. Learn or write out the chorus or verse melody, and try playing that in the solo section (if the chords or key are different, bend the melody to make it fit). Go back to the first couple of takes (which you hope are still on tape), and see if you and the producer can put something decent together with sections spliced from both of them. If nothing seems to work, don't despair completely. Heard with fresh ears the next day your solo may sound fine, and if not, then perhaps guitar would have been a better choice for the solo all along, and anyway, every one of us has the occasional bad session!

Touring, stadiums, television and film

I played to 50,000 people at Alton Towers with M-People in the summer of 1996. After my big solo someone turned to Andrew Mansi, the tour manager, and commented: 'Snake gets a lovely tone on that sax'. Mansi replied: 'Well, I don't know much about sax playing, but I know he always turns up on time and I never have to worry about him, so he's OK by me'. My next touring engagement is three weeks in Japan with pop/soul band Swing Out Sister. I know for sure that it is far more important to their management company that I send my passport photos back quickly for the visas, and turn up on time at rehearsals, than how accurately I play those hard brass parts, or how much applause my solos get.

Touring is an area where social etiquette, punctuality and team spirit are just as important as being able to play blistering solos every time the spotlight hits you. Hanging around airports, thousands of miles from home, jet lagged, unable to remember which country you are heading for, or crawling on to a sleeper bus after a show in Copenhagen for a sixteen-hour trip across Europe straight to the sound-check in Munich – these experiences can be draining and demoralising enough without having to contend with a band member who is constantly whinging, going AWOL or smoking on the bunk below yours. A degree of concern and consideration for other band and crew members is needed along with a respect for privacy.

One of the toughest things on a long tour is to keep the standard of performance high night after night, especially in venues such as stadiums. There is often a distinct lack of atmosphere from the stage end of these venues: the public are simply too far away for you to feel the buzz, and you often can't even see the eyes of the people in the front row, so it's unlikely that their excitement is going to reach you like it does in a club environment. Similarly, the audience at these venues can't see your eyes either, and they are not going to sense what a great gig it is from your changes of facial expression and the slight nuances of body language. Somehow you have to make everything bigger on this kind of show. Hurl the sound out into the audience, make every body movement so obvious that to you it feels ridiculously over-exaggerated, and your presence may just about be felt from 200 yards down the auditorium. I have a method I use sometimes when I realise that I am about to go on stage but the atmosphere is wrong and the adrenalin is not flowing. I picture myself as an actor playing the part of a sax player who is on stage, vibed up, going for it, giving his all, loving the audience and playing as though it was his last gig, in other words playing the part of me on a good night!

Recording theme tunes and incidental music for films and television may not differ from other session work when all the music is written, and the writer knows what is required. It gets much more interesting, however, when you are asked to work to picture, sometimes with a written part to use as a guide, often just improvising, attempting to reflect a mood, preempt a change of mood, or highlight a movement – 'Can you play a bit more darkly when the villain walks in?' Perhaps the theme could be played on baritone for the villain, flute for the heroine and alto for the love scene?

Live television work where the performer is in vision, perhaps as part of a house band, or part of a band doing a guest spot, is yet another discipline. Many chat shows and variety shows use a regular band to play their title music, walk-ons (short stings for guests to skip down the staircase to), and sometimes to accompany a singer, magician or escapologist. The Letterman Show from New York and shows hosted in the UK by Chris Evans and Jonathan Ross are good examples. There are depressingly few real live music shows on television today, but the tireless Jools Holland continues to deliver exciting programmes of quality music.

This kind of television work is not for those with weak hearts or nervous dispositions. It is a world where tedium turns into terror in less than one beat of a pounding heart, where 98 per cent boredom is cruelly juxtaposed with 2 per cent naked fear. The call may have been for 7.30 a.m., but the chances are that you sat in the dressing room or canteen doing nothing until about 11.00 a.m. Then to the studio, standing around until 11.50 a.m., and a quick sound-check before lunch. You couldn't stay on stage and run your number during lunch, because of union rules and electricians. The afternoon carried on in a similar vein except this time it was camera and lighting rehearsals. At 5.00 p.m. there is a dress rehearsal of the whole show. At last, after an argument between the director and the producer over the lighting, it's time to play (a chance to practise that change worked out in the dressing room). Three bars into the piece, however, you are flagged down by the floor manager: 'OK, that's fine, let's move on, time is running out . . .'. Now it's 7.00 p.m., showtime, and you have to be on stage ready and occasionally in vision, although you don't play until near the end. Feeling decidedly jaded, a little stiff and somewhat under-rehearsed, you still try to remain attentive and wear an interested and amused-at-the-right-time expression. Just as the mask is slipping, the eyes are glazing and you are slipping off to an imaginary tropical island, you become vaguely aware of some people clapping. Then suddenly, as if from nowhere, you hear 'two, three, four', you are on your feet, the horn is in your mouth, you have precisely two minutes to sock it live to three-and-a-half million viewers. Live – that means no re-takes, no repairs, no 'I think we could do a better one', and certainly no 'I'm really sorry, it caught me by surprise, I wasn't ready'.

Taking care of business

It's very quaint and English to think that a session musician can get by on talent alone, or to come out of music college with the attitude that the world owes you a living and that the job offers will roll in. The reality is that as a free-lance musician you are running a small business, and must promote that business, marketing the services it has to offer, namely your skills as a player, arranger, band-leader and whatever else you do. It is essential, especially in the early days of your career, to be able to supply, quickly, a concise c.v., a show-reel (normally a cassette tape with short examples of your playing), and a 10" × 8" photograph of yourself with horn. It's very important to be readily available, and it remains almost incomprehensible to me that some musicians still do not have answer-phones. A mobile phone or pager is essential for a studio sax player, perhaps together with a diary service (a company who will keep a copy of your diary, take calls and put work in your book for you whilst you are otherwise engaged). The more organised and businesslike you are, the easier it is to juggle as many jobs as possible, and keep everyone happy. Next month I hope to be rehearsing for a tour with Swing Out Sister, fitting in the occasional studio job around rehearsal times, and skipping the country at weekends to do shows with Lisa Stansfield. You can't be in two places at one time, but you can be in two or three places on the same day if you are well organised. And, of course, taking care of business can often include negotiating fees. 'How much will it cost me?' – this is the question I dread. I would rather run a mile barefoot over burning coals than have the discussion over fees which is inevitable in at least 50 per cent of my session work. Where a fixer, contractor or agent is involved, they will handle the negotiations. In radio and television the Musicians' Union rate is very often used, although if you are soloing you might seek a higher fee. With everything else, however, unless you are lucky enough to have a manager or a willing and business-minded partner, you are on your own. I have two pieces of advice on this thorny subject – first find out what your contemporaries charge, and then try to imagine it is someone else's ser-vices you are putting a price on, rather than your own. You may find that playing the saxophone is easy compared to negotiating fees.

8 Jazz and the saxophone

RICHARD INGHAM

A history of the saxophone in jazz is in many ways a history of jazz itself, inasmuch as many of the essential protagonists, those who took style and aesthetics forward, were saxophonists. This is also a story from the twentieth century, of an art form born in the early years and fast-forwarded through many of the changes that classical music history took much longer to experience. Perhaps that is in its nature as an oral art form, relying much more on spontaneous composition than on the written work for posterity. Jazz artists tend to be creators rather than interpreters, and consequently as much will be made in this chapter of performers' creativity as of their technical skills.

The story of jazz in the twentieth century is a story of music in the United States, of black and white popular culture. Latterly, Europe becomes important. Throughout, male domination of the creative process is self-evident. It is hoped that all of the significant saxophonists in jazz will be mentioned here – although some will be disappointed that their favourites have not been included. Rather than follow each career extensively, I have tried to indicate major soloists, along with the main features of their stylistic contributions.

Early soloists

The development of the saxophone in jazz from that of a negligible bit-player, through tonal feature, to essential requirement, includes influencing factors both from within jazz and from wider society. The early jazz ensemble evolved into front line and rhythm section instruments, where the front line consisted of cornet, trombone and clarinet, whilst the rhythm section used piano/banjo/guitar, tuba/string bass and drums. The rhythm section as a functional unit (bass – harmonic rhythm; drums – decorative percussion; piano – harmonic filling and clarification) remained fairly constant up to the 1970s, once the banjo had disappeared and the string bass eased out its brass cousin. The front line, however, was to undergo regular upheaval.

Initially the cornet carried the melody, with a counter-melody in the trombone, and the clarinet obbligato lines making great use of that instrument's flexibility and register contrast. The saxophone does appear alongside the other single-reed instrument in this context, but as an optional addition. When jazz musicians began to move out of New Orleans from 1917, mainly up to Chicago, they also colonised other centres such as Kansas City. Justifiably known as a saxophone breeding ground, Kansas City fostered the early careers of Coleman Hawkins, Lester Young and Charlie Parker.

The influence of vaudeville is vital to the early years of the jazz saxophone – for technical and availability reasons. Travelling saxophone ensembles, originally an offshoot from the Sousa Band, demonstrated virtuosity and instrumental possibilities to audiences across the USA and beyond. Sidney Bechet (1897–1959), a New Orleans clarinettist, had been greatly influenced by the soprano saxophone when only a boy. He tried to learn the instrument early in his career but found the intonation too much of a beast to tame. Having left New Orleans for Chicago, and then on to a tour of Europe, he returned to the instrument in London in 1920. Bechet's style on the soprano is unique, incorporating long flowing melodic lines with driving accents, and an unmistakable vibrato. His vibrato is as wide (and as wild) as one could achieve. At first hearing, this is an uncontrolled sound, yet in fact it is anything but. The vibrato of course assisted in conquering the soprano intonation problem, and Bechet had an instrument which would rival the melodic lead on the cornet or trumpet in intensity and volume. Bechet is sometimes thought of as a one-off figure, yet his influence is significant, if only for the fact that John Coltrane and Johnny Hodges listened intently.[1]

Johnny Hodges (1906–70) was a cultured player, influenced by Bechet when doubling on soprano, and surely aware of the power and potential of the saxophone as a lead instrument. He was to take part in what was one of the most outstanding ensembles of the century, the Duke Ellington Orchestra. Ellington wrote for his band as instrumentalists, rather than writing scores which an ensemble might play; Hodges was the new voice of the alto saxophone – rich and full of tonal depth in all registers, and lyrical in the extreme. His famous bends and glissandi (on *I Got it Bad and That Ain't Good, Black Butterfly* and many others) colour a melody in a way that few have successfully imitated and none surpassed. He was a member of the Ellington Band from 1928 until 1970, with only a four-year break in the 1950s. Forty-two years in the same company is a major achievement – within a jazz life style, it is astonishing. Hodges did much to define the role of lead alto within a saxophone section. His early solos were well-balanced contrasts of pace and movement, using smooth melodic lines interspersed with rapid arpeggio patterns, with the addition of dynamic layering. The pace slowed in later years as the solos became more ruminative, and to the end he showed classic examples of crisp articulation he can only have learnt from virtuosic vaudeville acts in his youth. Later in the century the work of Jan Garbarek and Eric Marienthal demonstrates more than a cursory nod in Hodges's direction, in their quest for making tone and pitch variation control essential parameters of sound.

Revered as the 'father of the tenor saxophone', Coleman Hawkins (1904–69) began his career in 1921 in Kansas City. By that time Rudy Wiedoeft had been recording for four years, and Hawkins began to transfer some of that virtuosity from the C-melody instrument to the tenor. Effortless movement around the instrument became one of his hallmarks, using a full range with a full sound. Wiedoeft had shown what was possible with vibrato, sustained full-voice notes, rapid tonguing and slap-tonguing, arpeggio and scale virtuosity, and musicianship in phrasing. The instrument itself was in an unparalleled period of popularity, even a craze.

Hawkins joined the Fletcher Henderson band in 1924 and remained for ten years, a move which propelled him into the public eye and ear. After leaving Henderson, he worked in Europe until 1939, initially as a guest with the Jack Hylton band in Britain. He returned to New York, touring and recording with small groups. Hawkins's big sound made him the voice to imitate; in his musical style he was equally at home with fast numbers as with sensuous ballads. He soon cut out the slap-tongue which became unfashionable in jazz; he used a wide and fast vibrato, narrower but not unlike Bechet's on the soprano. His ability to tell a story – expose a narrative in his improvisations – makes him one of the most influential jazz performers on any instrument. He would develop solos from single phrases and was very adept at incorporating sequential patterns as developmental figures, moving effortlessly through harmonic changes; he set the benchmark for ballad interpretation and creative improvisation in *Body and Soul* (1939). In keeping with the jazz style of the 1920s, he moved towards beats 1 and 3 in the bar, giving a period feel to his playing. His harmonic awareness was very alert, a skill which enabled him to retain his prominence during the musically turbulent 1940s. His recording with Dizzy Gillespie in 1944 is considered the first bop recording, and a few years later he was working with sidemen such as the young Miles Davis.

Lester Young (1907–59) began his career, like Hawkins, under the influence of the C-melody saxophone, this time as played by Frankie Trumbauer. Instead of, like Hawkins, *adapting* the C-melody sound on to the larger tenor instrument, Young took the sound of the C-melody and set about *re-creating* that on the tenor. Thus the light approach and higher tessitura. Initially a difficult exercise, because the tenor sound everyone

Fig. 8.1 Lester Young, pencil drawing by John Robert Brown

wanted to hear was that of Hawkins, Lester Young's alternative outlook provided a new option for tenor players, and eventually turned him into a guru for the bop movement and the cool movement. He did in fact coin the term 'cool', one of his many contributions from a language which was his own, at times surreal and certainly a veil to be used when convenient. Young's sound was one among many aspects of tenor performance which inspired players for many years. The sound itself initially concerned his colleagues – 'Why don't you play alto, man? You got an alto sound', he would be asked. The reply, tapping his forehead: 'There are things going on up there, man. Some of you guys are all belly.'[2] Along with this lightness of sound, Young introduced a sophisticated conception of time, an apparent casual regard for the bar line and a tonal effect he had learnt from Jimmy Dorsey which was to resurface many years later – false fingerings.

Young toured the Midwest with various bands from 1928 before joining Count Basie in Kansas City in 1934 (briefly), and then again in 1936; he worked with Basie until 1940, and again in 1943–4. The Basie band gave him national exposure, and he was featured as a stylistic contrast to Hershel Evans, who played in the style of Coleman Hawkins. Lester Young was taken on by the Fletcher Henderson band in 1934 – he went because Henderson was offering more money than Basie. He was engaged as a replacement for Hawkins, but despite being of equal musical ability he was rejected because his playing was so different. He was given accommodation at the Henderson house, and the story goes that Henderson's wife Leora would wake him early and play him Hawkins's recordings; he relates that he wanted to play like himself, but listened politely.[3]

Young's lightness of tone coincided with his lightness of phrasing. He used silence as a structural device, and often ran his phrasing across bar lines and against the usual accepted phrase lengths (two, four, eight bars etc.). Subtle rhythmic anticipations or delays and occasional dissonant intervals added to the tension in the improvised line. He used short simple motifs to develop his solos, and produced phrases around correct and alternative fingerings for the same and adjacent notes, providing lines of colour. This latter device was much used by Michael Brecker in the 1980s. Rips up to a high note come as a surprise and serve to enhance the musical contrast. And the vibrato – shallower and less demonstrative than Hawkins's; Young has the vibrato in waiting for when it is required, but often he holds a clean note and then suggests vibrato for a split second before leaving the note. Many of his phrases, vibrato-less in themselves, end on a clipped note, giving the ear the impression of little use of the device.

The big band

Throughout the 1920s there were steps taken towards the formation of an ensemble we now know as the 'big band', with the saxophone section as one of the internal groupings, along with trumpets, trombones and a rhythm section. Duke Ellington and Fletcher Henderson experimented with the larger ensemble, having taken their cue from Paul Whiteman's experience.

Paul Whiteman and his arranger Ferde Grofé introduced what they called 'symphonic jazz' around 1919, and the self-styled 'King of Jazz' was enormously popular in the 1920s. This was really dance and light music, expertly scored and expertly performed. Whiteman employed the highest

Fig. 8.2 Benny Carter, pencil drawing by John Robert Brown

skilled musicians, in turn enabling the arranger to write virtually anything. Jazz leaders of the time could see the obvious popularity of this
music, and the logical step was to introduce similar sections into a jazz
ensemble, sections which would play off against each other, giving a
heightened level of ensemble creativity, and setting their soloists in different timbral contexts. So successful were they in synthesising these elements that in 1927 Whiteman himself raided one band to provide his own
quality jazz soloists (including Frankie Trumbauer).

The five-saxophone section as a unit first appeared in 1933 in the
Benny Carter band; Carter had been with Henderson as an alto player (an
outstanding soloist) and also as arranger, and the concept of first and
second altos, first and second tenors and baritone, as a balanced section,
was eventually to become the standard line-up.

Benny Goodman was the most successful band leader of the 1930s,
and the subsequent swing craze produced many others such as the Dorsey
Brothers, Artie Shaw, the Casa Loma Band, Bob Crosby and Charlie
Barnet. Following the existing Henderson and Ellington bands came Earl
Hines, Cab Calloway, Chick Webb, Jimmie Lunceford and Count Basie,

Bennie Moten, Jay McShann and Andy Kirk. It was from within these groups that the major saxophonists appeared during the swing era. We have already noted Coleman Hawkins as a featured soloist with Fletcher Henderson, Hodges with Ellington and Young with Basie – the big band was the workplace for the leading jazz performers of the day.

Along with Johnny Hodges, the two other great alto players in the 1920s and 1930s were Benny Carter (*b.* 1907) and Willie Smith (1910–67). Carter was a versatile and influential musician – as well as his saxophone and arranging skills, he was also a fine trumpeter and trombonist. As with Hawkins–Young, Carter was Hodges's opposite, preferring a lighter approach to Hodges's sultry sound, and being recognised as one of the finest melodic improvisers. Willie Smith was a featured soloist with the Jimmie Lunceford band, and his style was marked by broken-chords, with occasional daring forays into 'outside' harmonies.

There was no one to match the superiority of Sidney Bechet on the soprano saxophone for many years, although players like Hodges did double occasionally. The soprano was not a complete unknown – many early jazz ensemble photographs show a section of three saxophonists complete with doubling instruments (often including three or four sopranos).[4] The tenor instrument, however, was a different matter. From the time of Coleman Hawkins's first recordings, the tenor suddenly became desirable, and Hawkins had shown the way. Some of the most important players who followed in his footsteps were Chu Berry, Arnett Cobb, Hershel Evans, Ben Webster, Illinois Jacquet, Buddy Tate and Don Byas. Chu Berry was the man in demand in the US during Hawkins's stay in Europe. Hershel Evans played the opposite tenor role to Lester Young in the Basie band, and Cobb and Tate were known as the 'Texas Tenormen' who played in a relatively wild blues-influenced style. Illinois Jacquet (*b.* 1922) is one of the most exciting disciples of Coleman Hawkins. Again, the Texas blues influence is very strong, in particular as featured on his performances of *Flying Home* with the Lionel Hampton Band. He used the upper (harmonic) register to great effect, and his influence spreads from the jump bands and rock and roll through to today's soul and funk players. Ben Webster (1909–73) is perhaps the most influential of the Hawkins school, combining sensuous ballad playing with a deep resonant tone effective at all speeds. His use of subtone (see 'Jazz and rock techniques' in the present volume) demonstrated a technique which has become synonymous with jazz tenor playing. He was Duke Ellington's featured tenor briefly in the mid-1930s, and then again from 1940 to 1943. He used a pronounced vibrato for effect, combined with sudden changes of timbre – one of his most celebrated recordings with Ellington is *Cottontail* (1940).

Another Ellington sideman, this time a long-stay member, was Harry Carney (1910–74), who defined the baritone model in the same way that Hodges had the alto. He joined the orchestra in 1927 at the age of sixteen, and remained for forty-seven years, outliving the Duke by only a few months. Carney's is one of the voices that immediately identifies the Ellington reed section, a rich sound full of character, yet pliable enough to blend into a texture. Ellington was renowned for writing for individuals rather than instruments and sections, and he exploited Carney's contribution to the full, often placing the baritone voice in unexpected areas of its range. His tonal focus and sustaining power anchored the section, and in later years he was one of the first jazz performers to develop circular breathing.[5] Carney reigned supreme on the instrument for many years.

The bebop revolution

The bebop period was a significant turning point in the history of jazz, and one of its two leading figures was an alto saxophonist. Charlie Parker (1920–55), along with his trumpeter colleague Dizzy Gillespie, achieved in his short lifetime a virtually complete overhaul of jazz style; harmony, rhythm, melody, ensemble and aesthetics were all put to the test, and a new set of values issued.

As with most revolutions, this was not an overnight event, but in musical terms it was pretty quick. Parker himself had been influenced in his teen years in Kansas City by Lester Young's style in its occasional asymmetrical phrasing and fragmented line. He was also a great blues player, never losing his feel for that idiom. After a well-documented disastrous start to his career (at the age of sixteen),[6] Parker invested time in serious technical and harmonic study, pondering all the while how he was going to play what he could hear. Eventually he realised that by using higher intervals of chord structures[7] in his melody line he would be getting near. By combining this with his eventual prodigious technical skills and rhythmic awareness, Parker had discovered what he was looking for.

Bebop flourished in the mid- to late 1940s, and jazz in 1950 was unrecognisable from that of 1930. The essential features of the style are: fast/virtuosic melodic lines which are often angular and fragmented; speeding up of harmonic rhythm (more chords per bar); an explosion in harmonic vocabulary (extended and altered chords, chord substitutions, passing chords and cyclic turn-arounds[8]); the main rhythmic unit becomes the quaver. The bass plays four in the bar, using scale, passing and chromatic tones – the whole rhythmic impetus comes from this instrument. Drums play a steady ten-to-ten rhythm[9] on the ride cymbal, with the foot hi-hat on beats 2 and 4, and the bass drum and snare drum providing accent emphasis. The piano 'comps', outlining the harmonic progression in a rhythmic yet light and sparse manner.

Thus Parker played in and around Kansas City from 1935 to 1939, listening and studying, before visiting New York for the first time; it was here during many jam sessions that he began to formulate his style and language. Back in Kansas City he joined the Jay McShann band from 1940 to 1942, touring extensively, and his first recordings date from this period. McShann was a notable bandleader; he considered Parker to be the finest blues soloist he had ever heard. Parker moved into the Earl Hines band where he met Dizzy Gillespie, and the two of them joined the Billy Eckstine band in 1944 along with several other modernists from the Hines band. From 1945, Parker appeared as a small-group bandleader – one of the features of bebop was that it was originally small-group based (usually a quintet of saxophone, trumpet, piano, bass and drums), which apart from anything else was economically much more viable than big bands of eighteen members.

His most productive period was 1947–51, and once he had formed his style by 1945, it changed little. As well as with Dizzy Gillespie, he worked regularly with Miles Davis (who was nineteen on his first outing with Parker). He also toured Europe and late in his short life experimented with recordings with string sections, and was due to take up composition lessons with the composer Varèse. His life was plagued by illness due to drug abuse, which gave him only a relatively brief time to demonstrate his genius.

His style *was* bebop, and he towered over a period when no other alto player could match him for technique and creativity. The new music was not popular to start with because of its uncompromising nature, but has become accepted as mainstream jazz. Basing his improvisations on the chords rather than the melody, Parker employed little vibrato in his search for clean unencumbered lines – he would use formulaic phrases frequently,[10] but they were always appropriate to the harmony and melodic logic. He could play in any key and his displaced articulation[11] paved the way for a stylistic norm for generations. He made use of the diminished and diminished whole-tone scales amongst others, enlarging the available melodic vocabulary; double-time passages were executed at breathtaking speed, and there were artistically applied swoops and growls. The musical forms he used were quite limited, in contrast to his improvised lines – he used the twelve-bar blues and the thirty-two bar AABA song format (*I Got Rhythm* in many guises, and several other reworked standard chord sequences). Parker's legacy is remarkable, and all-pervading. Bassist Charles Mingus said: 'If Charlie Parker were alive, he would think he was in a house of mirrors'.[12]

The big bands retained their mass popularity through the early 1940s, with new ones arriving in the shape of Woody Herman and Glenn Miller. After the end of the war, however, they saw a rapid decline. Maintaining a large ensemble on the road became prohibitively expensive for most; many of the progressive players were attracted by the new bebop small-group style. Audiences were finding some of the more challenging arrangements difficult to dance to, and as new wealth improved the attractions of home life, the revolution of television transformed much social activity at this time. In late 1946, no less than eight of the top US bands folded, and apart from the institutions of Ellington and Basie, it was left to new sounds to pick up the pieces – Herman was one of these, along with Stan Kenton.

Woody Herman (1913–87) was a clarinettist and saxophonist (in the style of Johnny Hodges, a fact which led to interesting solo contrasts amongst a band of young modernists). He led bands for fifty years until his death. Initially basing his programmes on blues performances, Herman then turned to incorporating bebop players into his band. Known as 'Herman's Herd', each successive reincarnation was the First Herd, the Second Herd, Third Herd etc. The Second Herd in 1947 became known as the ground breaking 'Four Brothers' band, featuring the tenor saxophones of Zoot Sims, Herbie Steward and Stan Getz, and the baritone of Serge Chaloff. Steward was replaced by Al Cohn the following year, and later members included Gene Ammons and Jimmy Giuffre. The name 'Four Brothers' is the title of a piece written by Jimmy Giuffre for the Herman band and featuring this unique sound. The three tenors and baritone played complex lines in close harmony, with short solos played as a competitive 'cutting' session. The warm sound that resulted was one of the most influential in the next twenty years. Serge Chaloff (1923–57) was notable as the first great baritone instrumentalist since Harry Carney; his smooth lines and even tone indicated how the large instrument might cope with bebop and move beyond it.

Two weeks with Miles Davis

Hardly was the ink dry on the bebop script before the reaction had begun. Music which was to symbolise the 1950s and many a film score thereafter was created for a two-week residency in 1948. Three recording sessions over the next eighteen months committed the sounds to disc, and Miles Davis's *Birth of the Cool* album was ready. The instrumentation, returning to Ellington's adventurism but taking its cue from the scoring in Claude Thornhill's band, consisted of trumpet, trombone, French horn, tuba, alto saxophone, baritone saxophone, piano, bass and drums. At a stroke the sound moved away from *both* the extrovert and sometimes senti-mentalised conventional big-band charts and also the freneticism and potential instability of bebop. Arrangements were by Gil Evans and Gerry Mulligan, and the saxophonists were Lee Konitz on alto, and Mulligan on baritone. Gerry Mulligan (1927–96) became the most recognised bari-tone voice of modern jazz. He had an uncanny knack for beautifully created improvised lines incorporating attractive melody as well as compositional development. He could hear the most obvious lines through chord changes, which make the listener think it must have been part of the original melody itself. Lee Konitz (*b.* 1927) was the first alto player apart from Sonny Stitt to emerge from behind the enormous pres-ence of Charlie Parker. Undeniably influenced by Parker, he none the less immediately made his presence felt with a clear, vibratoless sound, full in the classical sense, yet with a lightness which seemed to ride on top of an ensemble, outlining gentle contours. The complexity was there, but he was out to please and delight, rather than tease and provoke – he was Matisse to Parker's Picasso (Matisse – 'art should be like a comfortable armchair'). Thus the band that began the cool. The band itself was only together for two weeks as a live performing unit; Miles was twenty-one years old, Konitz and Mulligan both twenty.

From cool to the edge

In the 1950s the main alto influences were those of Parker and Konitz. Art Pepper (1925–82) was a significant voice in the Parker mould; he used his bop lines to express a range of emotions, and he was one of the best narra-tive improvisers. Paul Desmond (1924–77) found fame with the Dave Brubeck Quartet, a band which achieved popularity well beyond the norm for a modern jazz ensemble, and Desmond composed the hit number *Take Five* (1959). To have a jazz hit was one thing at this time, but one that was in $\frac{5}{4}$ time and swung was certainly a milestone; his sound was one of the lightest of all, one which hardly seemed to touch the ground. Other notable altoists at this time were Bud Shank and Herb Geller, both of whom were based on the West Coast along with Art Pepper.

The 1950s saw the emergence of Cannonball (Julian) Adderley (1928–75) as a possible successor to Parker. This was too much to ask of anyone, yet Adderley demonstrated both bop skills and his own individuality in his continuity of line and incorporation of chromaticism.

He fronted groups with his brother Nat, a trumpeter, and significantly he was in the Miles Davis band from 1957 to 1959, recording, amongst others, *Kind of Blue*, the groundbreaking modal album. He had a passion for soul and gospel music, which the Adderley brothers played with great feel, whilst his improvisations are never far from the blues.

After his time with Woody Herman, Stan Getz (1927–91), who had begun his career with Stan Kenton and Benny Goodman, chose the small-group format to display his creative melodic skills. An outstanding technician, as well as a leading ballad interpreter, Getz took many of his playing elements from the swing period, notably from Lester Young, including little vibrato and a tenor sound that seems to have the harmonic constituents of an alto. He played a major role in introducing the bossa-nova to mainstream jazz in 1962; Getz was occasionally criticised for 'stealing' this groove, and it is worth noting that the bossa-nova itself is a hybrid of samba and cool jazz – Getz referred to it as 'borrowing back'. This was by no means the first use of Latin American elements in jazz, but the popularity of Getz's work in this field must surely have opened the door to a later fusion of jazz and rock/pop elements, in particular the pre-dominance of even quavers and ostinato rhythm patterns rather than swing feel. His colleagues from Woody Herman's ground-breaking Four Brothers band also maintained their own small-group careers, with Zoot Sims and Al Cohn leading an influential two-tenor band for many years.

History's pendulum of taste and popularity seems to operate under natural laws. Coleman Hawkins, who dominated the tenor scene for so long in the 1920s and 1930s, seemed to take a back seat to Lester Young in his influence on aspiring jazz tenor players. Young paved the way for bop in his approach to the line, and his sound can be heard in others through-out the cool years of the 1950s. The arrival of Sonny Rollins (*b.* 1930) on the scene as a major artist in the mid-1950s brought back a big sound and rough energy. This had never in fact disappeared, and could be heard in the playing of Dexter Gordon and Sonny Stitt (equally at home on tenor or alto). Rollins's quality and temperament propelled him into the lime-light, and his album title of 1956 (*Saxophone Colossus*) aptly summed up the way he would stride across the jazz scene for many years, delivering passionate and structurally outstanding solos well into the 1990s. His sound – enormous in volume and depth of lower harmonic content – combined with his bop facility, made him a figurehead for the hard-bop movement. His playing is supremely confident, often witty and satirical in its melodic treatment, and his choice of material is of significance, in that he would often use very corny tunes as themes, and also make use of his Caribbean ancestry in his writing and playing, including many calypsos (for example, *St Thomas*). He is capable of playing at high speeds and can

Fig. 8.3 Sonny Rollins, pencil drawing by John Robert Brown

interpolate rapid double-time sections at will. He frequently uses rhythm for its own sake as a developmental device, and was instrumental in popularising the ¾ metre as a jazz norm. In his Latin numbers he sometimes relies on extremely simple rhythms, using melodic decoration for musical impetus. His melodic lines are often fragmented as they develop, and he is not frightened of using triadic material. He uses a varied selection of articulations, and can change at will; harmonically he is happy to play without piano as he can outline the harmonies in his lines – equally he enjoys the freedom of playing over pedal points. He later became noted for extensive solo performances, without rhythm section.

Freedom time – Coleman and Coltrane

The extraordinary developments that took place in the jazz avant-garde at the end of the 1950s and up to the mid-1960s have not lost their impact. Similar in vein to the revolutions in European music at the beginning of the twentieth century, they are all embracing. Harmony, melody and rhythm were thought to rest on safe fundamental concepts after the upheaval of bebop, but re-examination was imminent. And this time, tone and pitch were not immune.

It fell to two saxophonists to question our preconceptions and develop suitable responses. They were very different players, yet occasionally sounded to have the same result. They were certainly iconoclastic. Ornette Coleman (*b.* 1930) came from Texas and, like many artists from the southern states, was heavily influenced by the blues. This aspect of his performance style was often overlooked by commentators in his early career, because the blues were seen as old and traditional, whereas Coleman was everything new. He played what became known as free jazz, and, like Coltrane, influenced many players and artists who were never likely to play in such an unrestrained setting. The results of his achievements can be heard in many different musical environments.

He had what might be described as a non-standard musical upbringing. His parents were too poor to afford lessons on the saxophone, and in his early years of independent instrumental study, no one told him that saxophone notation differed from sounding notation. His early work was in rhythm and blues bands, and even at this time he would experiment, a habit which lost him more than one job. He studied harmony and theory, again by himself, whilst undertaking non-musical work. In 1958 he recorded his first albums, and the following year was invited to attend a summer jazz course, where he was an instant sensation, and was given a residency in New York. His music divided the critics, some considering him the new Parker, others writing him off as an unmusical charlatan; his style was already developed, unlike Coltrane who went through discernible periods of development.

Ornette Coleman's melodic style was to allow the melody to roam freely. A line would develop without being bound by specific changes, or harmonic markers. This gave rise in turn to a completely free concept of harmony, where harmonic effect is only relevant to the melody as it moves along, and this generates a sense of rhythmic liberation. The rhythm is undoubtedly felt very strongly by the performer, although at times this may be of a 'spiritual' rather than 'corporeal' nature[13] – a feature of later jazz. A bar will be extended here or there if the headlong logic of a phrase demands it, metre will be disrupted at will to accommodate the improvisational flow of the melody. And what of the melody itself? Fragmented lines, blues licks, bop interjections, repetitions, cries and wails, use of both extremes of register as pure sound, but always a sense of forward movement, of narrative. In the end, this is not abstract, although there are many parallels with the visual arts at the beginning of the twentieth century.

His albums *The Shape of Jazz to Come, Change of the Century* and *Free Jazz* (1959–60) are landmarks in jazz recording. Coleman continued his career through periods of performance and composition, until his Prime Time band of the 1980s again propelled the artist to the forefront of the avant-garde. Combining free playing with funk, and using two (electric) rhythm sections simultaneously were a shock to many who thought they had heard everything. The result is loud, funky and still free. Coleman's alto sound retained its splendour – rich and full when required, clear and bright, and with a pitch control leaning strongly towards a non-Western system of tuning. Thus we hear a continuation of the blues tradition in the aperiodic phrase and section lengths of Coleman's 1960s recordings (early blues would often have eleven- or thirteen-bar choruses instead of the later standardised twelve), and also the pitch bends found in all blues singing.

If Ornette Coleman arrived already packaged in style, then John Coltrane (1926–67) worked through periods of his own discovery. Unlike Coleman he was an accomplished musician in the traditional sense, and unlike Coleman he became recognised initially as a first-rate jazz per-former within the accepted and known boundaries of the time. His first big break came in 1955 when he joined the Miles Davis Quintet, with whom he remained until 1960, with a short break to work with Thelonius Monk. He also led his own recording sessions, including *Blue Train* and *Giant Steps*, during this time. He began to develop a very rapid playing style, whereby the semiquaver became the normal unit. These 'sheets of sound' acted as colliding simultaneous musical events, played horizon-tally but with the effect of vertical chords, and were driven by multiple chord substitutions and superimpositions. Coltrane's time with Miles Davis coincided with modal experiments, where the musicians impro-vised on a scale for several bars rather than constant harmonic changes (*So What* on *Kind of Blue*, 1959). In fact this is sometimes deceptive as Coltrane was always looking for ways of reaching out beyond the scale in his developing lines, and it is fascinating to compare the solos of Miles Davis, Cannonball Adderley and Coltrane on *So What*. Coltrane's own 'modal' period often used pedal points or two-chord ostinati (*My Favourite Things*, 1960), where his nascent free style could be observed – thus, if the net effect of constant turn over of harmonic change was the sheets of sound, one could root the harmony to a hypnotic ostinato pattern, freeing the soloist to take the improvised line anywhere at all, and still provide an overall implied complexity of harmony.

Around this time, Coltrane's drummer Elvin Jones was experimenting with lifting the stated beat into a swirling percussive impression of the pulse. This was helped by the tenor player's semiquaver lines which con-tained many quintuplets and septuplets, breaking up the symmetry, but which was rooted to a pulse none the less. This is of course another way of arriving at 'spiritual' rhythm rather than 'corporeal' rhythm. And here we see the connections and contrasts between Coleman and Coltrane;

Coleman played like that all along, presenting the case from the inside, whilst Coltrane had to crack the nut from the outside, over time. What is also clear is that you can hear Coltrane solving problems within a piece as he plays, trying similar ideas out for chorus after chorus. Coltrane progressed then into his final experimental period, where rhythm became a backdrop of sound, melody was both tender and brutish but often non-developmental, and harmony was whatever the melodic combinations provided (*A Love Supreme*, 1964; *Ascension*, 1965). The instrumental make-up was traditional (saxophone, piano, bass, drums) but all the functions had been reviewed. The bass, for instance, was now a melodic instrument with a low tessitura, which may or may not provide roots and shapes from time to time. In his last years, Coltrane began to work with the drummer Rashied Ali, with whom he recorded duets, and Pharoah Sanders, another tenor voice who would push him to extremes.

John Coltrane's control of sound (a big sound) was complete – he could operate clearly and cleanly at the bottom of the instrument, with a resonant and smooth sound, his tone was strong and confident, and he developed the upper harmonic register in a way that no jazz player before him had (although John Gilmore of the Sun Ra Arkestra had shown the way). He made use of multiphonics[14] and also extended the use of alternate/false fingerings from Lester Young's suggestions. His melodic lines were astonishing *tours de force* of creative energy, veering from pentatonicism into atonality.[15] His contribution was of course not limited to the tenor instrument, and he was the first major soprano soloist since Sidney Bechet, although Steve Lacy had shown the potential of the instrument in contemporary work. His Indian *shanai* tone and passionate playing on the smaller instrument single-handedly engineered its return from obscurity. He played seemingly different lines on the soprano, making great use of repetitive figures and simple musical cells, emphasising the folk element he was searching for.

Some of his later music could indeed be described as genuinely abstract. All of it was influential, and between them, Coleman and Coltrane set the scene for many later artists, often surprising in their diversity of response, ranging from Evan Parker to David Liebman, Michael Brecker to Kenny Gee.

And then what?

The freedom suggested and demonstrated by Ornette Coleman and John Coltrane, and its consequences, mirrored in many ways the historical development of Western art (classical) music in the twentieth century, and also the visual arts. Also the Russian experience of 1917 – after freedom, then what?

The options were as follows: continue the Rollins bop line; continue the free jazz line; return to mainstream; reassess the freedom parameters. Despite the enormous presence of the two free jazz protagonists mentioned above, which continued for many years, the one (at the time) surprising yet influential option appeared very soon after Coltrane's death: the return of tonality. This will be discussed below.

Amongst the band for Coltrane's *Ascension* album were the tenor players Pharoah Sanders and Archie Shepp. Along with Albert Ayler, these three tenor saxophonists drove the expansion of technique and tonal development forward, consolidating the use of upper-register playing along with the use of multiphonics. All three were exciting improvisers, and their extensive use of the upper register as a normal tessitura was to become a yardstick for later performers. This expansion of the saxophone range in jazz (despite its acceptance in classical repertoire) was initially used as an extreme of expression, and also as an abstract sound or pure noise. The constant pitch variants available via lip pressure in that register add to its comparison with the human voice, more often than not in a wailing capacity. Pharoah Sanders (*b.* 1940) often played with the Coltrane quartet in its last years up to 1967, where he seems to be used as a second-tenor alternative which pushes Coltrane to extremes even he had not considered. Sanders did not require any warm-ups in the normal register – he would often play at this time exclusively in the extended range. He would also balance multiphonics, split tones and runs based in the normal register with high excursions, while the lines themselves were sometimes fragmentary series of explosions. Archie Shepp (*b.* 1937) saw his free jazz work as political expression, whereas Albert Ayler (1936–70) seemed driven by religion and philosophy. Coltrane himself included pantheistic texts as an integral part of his music in his last years, and it seems quite natural for such extremely emotional music to have external references or driving forces such as these. Ayler died tragically young, but Shepp and Sanders continued to develop their styles, opening out into a wide range of influences and musical backgrounds. Joe Henderson (*b.* 1937) followed the Rollins style of playing, but was also greatly inspired by the work of Ornette Coleman.

Of the alto saxophonists in this free jazz period, undoubtedly one of the most exciting was Eric Dolphy (1928–64). Another musician struck down in his prime, he produced lines of breathtaking creativity – in their speed, development of material and choice of interval. It is this last aspect which clearly identifies a Dolphy solo, along with a masterly use of the altissimo register as a *normal* region in which to operate. He played flute

Fig. 8.4 Eric Dolphy, pencil drawing by John Robert Brown

as well, and was largely responsible for presenting the bass clarinet as a serious jazz instrument. He worked with Chico Hamilton, Charles Mingus and John Coltrane. Also with Coltrane, on the *Ascension* album were Marion Brown and John Tchicai. Arthur Blythe (*b.* 1940) produced work of a witty, almost surreal nature, moving at great speeds, and where Dolphy jumps register unexpectedly, Blythe would jump tempo. Dudu Pukwana (1938–90) successfully combined South African township music with the free flight of Ornette Coleman's melodic drive. Much later, the work of John Zorn (*b.* 1953) demonstrated the line of freedom into pure sound, without disregarding jazz history.

In 1965, the AACM (Association for the Advancement of Creative Musicians) became established in Chicago, featuring saxophonists Joseph Jarman, Roscoe Mitchell and, later, Anthony Braxton. Jarman and Mitchell are both musicians of diverse interest and eclectic awareness; they double on all members of the saxophone, clarinet and flute families. These two were founder members of the Art Ensemble of Chicago, formed when the AACM decamped to Paris in 1969. Their outrageous solo and group improvisations featured the performers playing not just their own instruments, but also many percussion instruments as well. Anthony Braxton (*b.* 1945) specialises in alto saxophone and contrabass clarinet, and has become an influential composer as well as performer and band leader. His music (and titles) often contain quirky humour, and much of his work exists in the fields of both avant-garde jazz and avant-garde classical music. Henry Threadgill (*b.* 1944) joined the AACM late in the 1960s, and formed the group Air in 1975, after earlier incarnations, playing saxophones and flute. This group was noted for its equal voicing in ensemble texture. All of these players emerging from the AACM shared a passion for free jazz, and also for live jazz history. Their groups were among the first to incorporate apparently incongruous pastiche elements into their performances, including swing, blues, New Orleans, ragtime, street marches and popular song. In particular the concerts given by the Art Ensemble of Chicago were veritable pageants of sound, colour and history; part of their motto is 'Great Black Music – Ancient to the Future'. It is worth noting here that AACM and other arts collectives were established to provide support and nurture within a community (the avant-garde art world) which by its very nature was devoid of general public acceptance. This is an artistic culture worlds apart from the swing craze of the 1930s.

From a similar community in St Louis, the Black Artists Group, came the World Saxophone Quartet in 1976. The first all-saxophone band in jazz had been formed in Britain in 1973 by Alan Skidmore, Mike Osborne and John Surman, and following the success of the WSQ in establishing the medium, many other ensembles appeared throughout the world in the next few years. Despite the fifty-year existence of the classical saxophone quartet, the notion of a jazz quartet (without rhythm section) was quite new. The members of the WSQ – Oliver Lake (alto), Julius Hemphill (alto), David Murray (tenor) and Hamiet Bluiett (baritone) – were all outstanding soloists in their own right; the group gave them an opportunity to add creativity within ensemble textures. Responsibility for musical impetus fell to the baritone, taking on the role of an absent rhythm section, but in the process it *became* that rhythm section, and absorbed the role as well as taking a full part in upper melodic and solo activity. Bluiett and later Jim Hartog of the 29th Street Saxophone Quartet showed the way with their drive, pure energy, and positive, barn-door tonal qualities. The WSQ immerse themselves in the avant-garde world of extremes of range as a rule, although their Ellington album displays extensive use of tonality (*WSQ plays Duke Ellington*, 1976); the 29th Street band draws on a wide range of influences and utilises strong riff-based ensemble passages for propulsion. The 29th Street colour is dictated in part by the free-flowing cheerful melodic lines of leader Bobby Watson. In Europe, the British band Itchy Fingers has had commercial success, offering a mixture of technical *tours de force* (Dolphy-esque), swing, funk, choreography and slapstick routines. Many of their numbers were written by their prolific tenor player Mike Mower. Listening to the individual sounds and blends of these ensembles, the influence of Ornette Coleman is all pervading in the use of pitch control as a tone colour.

In the meantime

Whilst the avant-garde was ploughing its often lonely furrow, main-stream jazz was continuing to produce a long list of outstanding saxo-phone soloists. Two of the most influential have been tenor player Dexter Gordon (1923–90) and altoist Phil Woods (*b*. 1931). Gordon's impor-tance spans many decades: he was one of the few great tenor bop players in the 1940s and a man whom Coltrane acknowledged as one of his major influences; like many musicians he went through periods when he was in and out of favour, yet his enormous sound (powerful but covered with velvet) and invention kept him as a 'name'; he acted and performed in the acclaimed feature film *Round Midnight* (1986).

Phil Woods has become recognised as the finest post-Parker bop alto player. His lines are often based on Parker models and shapes, yet he extends them into smoother developments, in a way not dissimilar to Cannonball Adderley. He possesses a very facile technique, a beautiful 'natural' tone production, encompassing a wide variety of colorations – in particular an effortless growl available in all registers and at any intensity. Woods himself says that his influences were 'Benny Carter, Johnny Hodges and Charlie Parker, in that order',[16] a fact which would account for much of his meticulous attention to tonal control. His tonal control, combined with quotations, a willingness to break solo and ensemble sections into smaller instrumentation without losing any musical impetus, and his later forays into Latin and funk, makes him one of the most complete jazz artists. In Europe, Peter King (*b*. 1940) inhabits a similar stylistic world; he plays effortlessly at breakneck speed yet with passion.

Towards the end of the century, the tenor playing of Scott Hamilton (*b*. 1954) and Joshua Redman (*b*. 1969) proved that traditional skills do not disappear, but can be recycled into challenging and exciting music. Redman is one of the most accomplished performers on the instrument. Joe Lovano (*b*. 1952) and Branford Marsalis (*b*. 1960) have both contrib-uted greatly to the bebop tradition.

The return of tonality

After the dash for freedom in the early 1960s and its consequent revolution in jazz thinking, the (at the time) surprising move for some came hard on its heels, much as cool had soon followed bop. Strangely enough, the same artist performed the role of catalyst. Miles Davis had taken his style from modal pieces to a certain kind of 'no-chord' freedom in the mid-1960s, and had begun experimenting with long and short repeated patterns as melodic thematic material. This almost minimalist melodic approach was then joined by an apparently simplistic rhythmic feel driven by (again) minimalist bass patterns. The predominant use of even, as opposed to swing, quavers within this style indicated that jazz-rock was about to appear. In 1969, Davis released *In a Silent Way* and *Bitches Brew*, both albums featuring Wayne Shorter. From 1965, Shorter (*b*. 1933) had produced tenor improvisations with rapid chromatic and altered scale movements as a foil to the ensemble ostinati – in the 1969 albums he moved on to soprano, creating space as well as coruscating runs against a rich tapestry of accompaniment, and where the distinction between solo and accompaniment became deliberately blurred. The use of (up to three) electric pianos and guitar with effects paved the way for standardisation of these instruments, along with electric bass and synthesizer, and bands led by Herbie Hancock, Chick Corea (with Joe Farrell, tenor) and Joe Zawinul were to follow this trend. One of the most successful was Weather Report, featuring Zawinul and Shorter, as well as bass phenomenon Jaco Pastorius.

This was, then, the return of tonal control in the shape of minimalism and rock influences, without the traditional cadence points of jazz harmony. From now on jazz was able to float in and out of the rock and commercial pop world, taking due note of soul, funk, reggae, punk, heavy metal, hip-hop, world music, electronic sequencing and studio recording techniques.

Michael Brecker (*b*. 1949) is one of the most influential saxophonists of the 1980s and 1990s. Working first with his brother Randy (on trumpet) as the Brecker Brothers, Michael formed Steps Ahead with vibraphonist Mike Mainieri in 1979, eventually reforming the Brecker Brothers in the 1990s. He has worked for many years as a session musician in New York, and began to front his own bands as soloist from the late 1980s. His technique on the tenor saxophone is a yardstick for players of this era. He cites Coltrane, Rollins, Joe Henderson, Shorter and Stanley Turrentine as his main influences, although his style is his own. He is equally at home in the bop environment – where his dazzling technical skills meet with the finest articulation control – and funk and

Fig. 8.5 Michael Brecker, pencil drawing by John Robert Brown

electric music – where his knowledge and application of sophisticated studio treatments enhance his feel for the idiom. From Coltrane, Brecker has developed the use of the higher register combined with false fingerings, often setting up breathtaking polyrhythmic textures. He shares with very few people in jazz history an ability to develop a narrative through his solo lines, based as usual on tension and release, which in his hands is capable of great musical and emotional heights. Therefore what sets Michael Brecker apart is his unusual combination of technical *and* emotional artistic genius. Some of the greatest artists display one or the other, but rarely both to the same degree. Following an illness, Brecker turned to the EWI (see 'Midi wind instruments' in the present volume), and again he assimilated the technique into the height of cultured style and musical expression (*In a Sentimental Mood* from the Steps Ahead *Magnetic* album of 1986). On the tenor instrument, other fine players in the jazz-rock mould have included Ernie Watts, Bob Mintzer, Bob Berg, Gato Barbieri and Grover Washington. Watts (*b.* 1945) has a very facile technique; Mintzer (*b.* 1953) possesses an ear for multi-layered development of material and a great skill for big band writing; whilst Berg (*b.* 1951) demonstrates a Dexter Gordon sound of a later generation.

Fig. 8.6 David Sanborn, pencil drawing by John Robert Brown

Where tenor players listen to Michael Brecker, the jazz-rock guru on the alto in the 1980s was David Sanborn (*b.* 1945). His style, like Parker's and Adderley's, is rooted in the blues. In Sanborn's case he is also influenced by gospel music, and the vocal style of singers such as Stevie Wonder (with whom he worked early in his career). He has had great commercial success and, despite confining his musical output to a relatively narrow area, has influenced many players. He is capable of setting up (like Brecker) complex polyrhythmic activity against a simple groove, in his case as a lick rather than as an integral part of a lengthy narrative. His powerful 'cry', an upper-register note, often distorted by splitting, became one of his trade marks. He is followed in this style by Nelson Rangell (*b.* 1961) and Eric Marienthal (*b.* 1958). Rangell is a highly accomplished funk altoist, with a beautiful clean sound, capable of distortion at will. Rapid bluesy lines cross registers with ease. Marienthal encompasses the jazz-rock idiom, yet reaches beyond, particularly in his work with Chick Corea, and was one of the most individual alto voices of the 1990s when all around seemed to be taking Sanborn's characteristics and honing them. Marienthal is more of a thematic and developmental player, with an unmistakable pitch language. Because of the nature of much rock music, which is generally based on Western tuning/equal temperament, the Ornette Coleman variable approach can clash too often over standard rhythm sections. Marienthal delves further back to Johnny Hodges in his use of altered pitch *relative* to the 'true' note, but produces his own style of frequent pitch bends at speed, not unlike the concept of Lyle Mays in his use of synthesizer pitch-bend wheel. Marc Russo, who preceded Bob Mintzer in the Yellowjackets band, is a high-note specialist, playing melodically in areas where others scream.

The European dimension

Whilst the progress of jazz history through the twentieth century was largely the story of one nation's culture, the last three decades of the century brought variety and genuine stylistic alternatives. From the 1960s, the aesthetics of free jazz encouraged a new sense of creativity amongst European musicians, influenced in part by the fact that the free jazz revolution had now encompassed much of what the classical avant-garde were investigating. Although the jazz story appears to be largely USA-based, we should not forget that most of the original cultural ingredients in the New Orleans melting pot in 1900 were from Africa and Europe. So the end of the century sees a kind of return.

There are three European saxophonists who should be mentioned here. They are of enormous stature in their fields, and have made a major influential impact: Evan Parker (*b*. 1944), John Surman (*b*. 1944) and Jan Garbarek (*b*. 1947). Parker is a British tenor and soprano player, who has chosen the often lonely path of extending the free concepts of John Coltrane's later work (others are Peter Brötzmann of Germany and Willem Breuker of Holland). Whereas most artists took a look at what Coltrane was doing and either withdrew from the brink or amalgamated his style into broader pictures, Parker more than any other saxophonist took on the implications of those great works of art. Comparison might be made here between Coltrane and the late quartets of Beethoven, which were so far ahead of their time as to be almost artistically divorced from the rest of his output.

Working within small groups, as a member of the London Jazz Composers' Orchestra and also as a soloist, Parker began to evolve, quite early in his career, a style which combined all the excessive expressionism of free jazz tenor playing, along with a disciplined method of note production and melodic/linear generation. This latter aspect has developed over many years' study to a point where Parker displays a completely individual style, often imitated in part, but so committed in its rigour that his playing has become an institution in itself. The above comment about a lonely path is not to suggest that Parker has worked on his own throughout his life (he has worked with many close colleagues) but that to concentrate one's work as an avant-garde artist is economically and artistically very challenging, and to specialise to the extent that he has done puts him in a very narrow field of communication indeed. It is worth mentioning here that, in common with many British jazz musicians, he has spent much time working in continental Europe, a fact which reflects very badly on the historic funding of jazz performance within the UK.

Evan Parker's stylistic development has been an interesting mix of both musical and instrumental technique leading each other. In exploring the torrents of notes in late Coltrane, it soon became apparent that if one could apply circular breathing, the lines could be unbroken for much longer periods of time. Once established, this technique enabled Parker to play without stopping the flow for as much as twenty minutes at a time (i.e. a whole piece). Also, once established, the continuous nature of the musical production meant, paradoxically, that the material could move in contrasted sections, and become more reflective. Parker's concept of note generation has taken on board Coltrane's scalic and multiphonic contribution, and he has moved into even higher registers, and also, by the use of false fingerings and completely new (non-Western) fingering patterns, learnt how to generate kaleidoscopes of subtly altering sounds. The word 'sound' rather than 'note' is chosen here, as often his work is a series of tone colours as much as pitches (cf. Debussy, Berio). There is also a conscious or unconscious use of classical minimalist technique in the way patterns are repeated before gradually being transformed, in vertical rather than linear thought. His work on the soprano follows a similar path to that on tenor, but makes much more use of pieces based on circular breathing, and effective interplay of pedal notes and multiphonics (where continuous patterns occasionally clear for upper or lower pedal notes to be reiterated). Often the effect is of several players, such is the speed of execution and balance of extreme registers. Many of these solo excursions are performances of great beauty – relaxing and meditative rather than frenetic. The fingers move quickly, but the underlying harmonic flow takes shape slowly and clearly (cf. Elvin Jones).

John Surman, another British artist who spent many years based in Europe, is a baritone, soprano and bass clarinet specialist. He is among the few genuine great players of the baritone instrument, following Harry Carney, Serge Chaloff, Gerry Mulligan and the bop artist Pepper Adams.

Beginning in the 1960s as a member of the Ronnie Scott band, he became known for his baritone and soprano playing. He took the low instrument to unheard of heights, playing cleanly in octaves above the standard range. His group S.O.S. (with tenor Alan Skidmore and alto Mike Osborne) explored saxophone ensemble textures following the free jazz lead. Eventually he turned to technology, and produced several albums where he would play solo lines above synthesizer ostinati – he then broadened this to provide acoustic ostinati by the use of multi-tracking. In his choice of material, particularly for the soprano instrument, he has often made great use of English folk tunes and derivatives, and along with Jan Garbarek he has made a major contribution to a tonal European jazz concept, incorporating as much European heritage as American. He has used his band 'Brass Project' as a stage for his compositions. His often mournful soprano sound, with its characteristic lilting style, is quite distinctive.

From Norway, and based there, Jan Garbarek has achieved enormous success as a player and composer. His playing style sets him apart, and this is driven both by his saxophone technique and his compositional directions. From his early days as a Coltrane enthusiast and as a member of the George Russell band, Garbarek began to develop a distinctive style of playing – within the jazz tradition yet influenced more and more by contemporary classical as well as Scandinavian folk elements. His compositions are frequently large-scale structures, and often take their inspiration from the literary arts (for example, *It's OK to Listen to the Gray Voice*, 1985, to the poetry of Tomas Tranströmer). As a tenor player he projects an enormous sound, full bodied and with as much 'presence' as any player; this quality of sound is similar to classical control and production, whereby subtle nuances are available at any dynamic, and he is a master of the high register, playing cleanly with a very refined tone. His tenor has a straight crook, whilst he favours the curved instrument for soprano. Again, precision marks his soprano playing, with a beautifully centred tone and clarity of light articulation. The centred tone he achieves should not be confused with his pitching; he often holds a note just under true pitch for effect, sometimes not resolving the bend. This aspect of his style allies him as much to early blues singers as to earlier saxophonists. His music is often sparse and abstract, and he uses tone colour on single notes for musical statements (his low tenor register is a sound unique in its harmonic make-up). One of his major (and most commercially successful) ventures in the 1990s was a collaboration with the Hilliard Ensemble, where he provided obbligato lines to medieval sacred and secular songs (*Officium*, 1994). He has made extensive use over the years of electronic devices to transform his saxophone sound to great

Fig. 8.7 Jan Garbarek, pencil drawing by John Robert Brown

effect. Paradoxically, when on tour with the Hilliard Ensemble, he exploited the cathedral acoustics in each venue, with no amplification whatsoever.

In the 1990s a new crop of saxophone leaders arose in Britain. Andy Sheppard (*b.* 1957) works with a small group in an eclectic style. His creative work is very inventive, making use of thematic development and group interplay. Courtney Pine (*b.* 1964) has amalgamated his effortless solo flights with hip-hop, and then reggae and then dance music. Tommy Smith (*b.* 1967) has produced thoughtful compositions displaying his prodigious tenor technique, whilst Iain Ballamy (*b.* 1964) and Julian Arguelles (*b.* 1966) are two saxophonists who graduated from the Loose Tubes band – a rollercoaster ensemble with an infectious amalgam of freedom and precision, but mainly groove. Tim Garland (*b.* 1966) uses folksong and dance from Britain and Europe to shape sinuous lines and textures of powerful impact. His use of world music is authentic, in that he borrows elements but develops them organically rather than preserving them as museum exhibits.

The story of jazz in the twentieth century is therefore very much allied to the development of saxophone progress within that art form. Jazz undoubtedly gave the instrument its high profile in the century, whilst in return the saxophone lent its expressive nature to the progress of the form at almost every turn. What can be seen and heard is that there is a natural thread connecting the earliest artists with those who take jazz into the twenty-first century. That thread works its way through an astonishing exhibition of sound, and technical and creative diversity.

9 Rock and the saxophone

RICHARD INGHAM AND JOHN HELLIWELL

In the vocally dominated genres of rock and pop, the saxophone has made its own special contribution, using its unique vocal attributes with conflicting personalities of sweetness and anguish. From the jump style of Louis Jordan to Courtney Pine's hip-hop, and from Junior Walker through the *Baker Street* phenomenon to Branford Marsalis and Kenny Gee, saxophone soloists and sections have played a crucial role. But is it rock or pop, is it rock and roll, rhythm and blues, soul, dance or funk? The transient nature of much popular music makes historical accounts sometimes vague, often conjecture, and always selective, but this short chapter will attempt to identify the general trends and most significant exponents.

The big bands of the 1930s and 1940s featured and relied on major soloists, and an important precursor of rock saxophone was to be found in the 'Texas' tenor sound of Arnett Cobb, Illinois Jacquet, Buddy Tate and the alto of Eddie Vinson. Stars of the Lionel Hampton and Count Basie bands in the main, their playing was renowned for its excitement and energy and was steeped in the blues. Cries and wails coloured their solos as well as riff developments; a trademark was the use of the extended upper register. Illinois Jacquet's solos with the Hampton band in *Flying Home* (original 1942) became legendary. 'Cleanhead' Vinson concentrated his career on blues playing and singing, although he was also a fine bop player, and employed the young John Coltrane in his band in 1948.

Simultaneously with the Texas sound came 'Jump', with its principal exponent Louis Jordan (vocal and alto). This style flourished from 1937 through the 1940s, and was titled because of its infectious dance rhythms. Big band versions were the well-known *One o' Clock Jump* and *Jumpin' at the Woodside* by Count Basie, but Louis Jordan and his Tympany Five established a small band set-up of trumpet, alto, tenor and rhythm section. The music was in swing style with much use of riffs, entertaining street-wise lyrics and perhaps above all a great sense of showmanship. Effective solos were not lengthy and cerebral, but in the groove, melodic and powerful. As a major part of the jazz-influenced blues at this time, Jordan was also significant in the development of rhythm and blues, leading the way to rock and roll. The popularity of this genre, with its first white stars of Elvis Presley and Bill Haley, followed by black stars Chuck

Berry, Fats Domino and Ray Charles, was the beginning of modern popular and youth culture in many respects. Despite the heritage of black music, it took white stars to force the white recording establishments to place black artists in a high profile national (US) context. This was profit driven, naturally, but opened up much potential cross-fertilisation of styles. Chuck Berry said that he identified with Jordan more than with anyone else; Bill Haley's Comets imitated the Louis Jordan rhythm – their producer would sing Jordan riffs for the Comets to pick up.

Another popular saxophonist at this time was Earl Bostic, an alto player with a big sound, omnipresent growl and melodic flair. His hits *Flamingo* and *Sleep* (1951) influenced countless instrumentalists. This was also one of John Coltrane's early bands (1952–3) – Bostic is reputed to have taught Coltrane upper-register playing. Saxophone solos in the Bill Haley band were taken by tenor player Rudy Pompelli (*Shake, Rattle and Roll*, 1954), and despite the growing domination of the (electric) guitar, the saxophone was relied on to push the excitement factor in many bands. Lee Allen featured with Little Richard and Fats Domino, King Curtis was the soloist on the Coasters' *Yakety Yak* (1958) and *Charlie Brown* (1959), and Ray Charles used Hank Crawford for many years. Others with their own hits included Red Prysock, Sam 'The Man' Taylor, Sil Austin and Jimmy Forrest. In Britain Red Price was the tenor player with Lord Rockingham's Eleven, to be followed in the 1960s by the Graham Bond Organisation, whose saxophonist Dick Heckstall-Smith appeared on many 1960s sessions.

The early 1960s produced two 'novelty' numbers which were none the less influential in their own way, Boots Randolph's *Yakkety Sax* (1963) and Henry Mancini's classic *Pink Panther*, recorded by Plas Johnson in 1964. The decade as a whole produced the great solo artistry of King Curtis and Junior Walker on the one hand, and the soul horn sections of James Brown and the Motown groups on the other. Junior Walker and King Curtis, both tenor players, were enormously influential and enjoyed great commercial success. They defined the rock tenor sound of the 1960s, with extraordinary control of high tones, flutter-tonguing, growls, shakes and, above all, sensitive phrasing. Curtis backed many artists as a session musician, as well as releasing his own numbers such as *Soul Twist* (1962) and *Soul Serenade* (1964), whilst Walker was a singer as well as a saxophonist – his hits included *Shotgun* (1965) and *How Sweet It Is* (1966) (see Ex. 9.1).

The horn section developed in this decade into a regular feature, particularly with the Motown vocal groups, where 'brass' came to mean trumpet, trombone and saxophones (various combinations but often alto, tenor and baritone). The horns were a vital part of the James Brown sound, from *Out of Sight* (1964), the beginnings of funk, through *Cold*

Ex. 9.1 Junior Walker, tenor saxophone introduction to *How Sweet It Is* (© Jobete Music UK Ltd).

Sweat (1967) and into the 1970s. The emerging funk style relied heavily on the horn section for punctuation and drive, and Pee Wee Ellis, Brown's tenor man, was largely responsible for writing *Cold Sweat*. This had a heavy brass riff on beats 2 and 3, in addition to alternate bass figures on the baritone highlighting beat 1 with a pick-up. Sections built up of extensive repetition without harmonic change were a feature of this style. Ellis, Maceo Parker and St Clair Pinckney formed the sax section at around this time, and Parker was to follow bassist Bootsy Collins into George Clinton's Parliament band. This was funk plus rock plus psychedelic anarchy plus spaceships. This outstanding band of the 1970s featured the 'Horny Horns' led by Maceo Parker, and included the Brecker Brothers amongst others.

The end of the 1960s saw jazz embracing rock in the work of Miles Davis and others; in the band Blood, Sweat and Tears, the reverse process occurred simultaneously. Known as a rock 'big band', one of its most notable recordings was *Spinning Wheel*, with Fred Lipsius (alto). The successful band Chicago included Walter Parazaider on saxophone. These groundbreaking ventures also seemed to give legitimacy to the idea of jazz artists being used as session players for rock and pop recordings. One of the best-known collaborations in the 1970s was Phil Woods's solo in the Billy Joel song *Just the Way You Are* (1977); Paul Simon's album *Still Crazy After All These Years* (1975) features Michael Brecker on the title track, and Phil Woods contributes a surreal coda to *Have a Good Time*. This same album contains *Some Folks' Lives Roll Easy* where the saxophone section plays occasional semibreves. This particular saxophone section, comprising David Sanborn, Eddie Daniels and Michael Brecker, could probably claim to have played the most expensive long notes in history. The Simon/Brecker relationship was revived years later for the Graceland tour in 1990.

The saxophone's role in rock and pop music was thus richly varied in the 1970s, with featured sections and also soloists. Some bands made a success out of integrating the saxophonist into the band (as opposed to a hired session player) as performer and writer. Andy Mackay took a major role with Roxy Music, John Helliwell in Supertramp, and Clarence Clemons with Bruce Springsteen. Mackay's saxophone skills as well as his electronics expertise combined well with the specialist knowledge and creativity of Brian Eno, also in the band. Early hits were *Virginia Plain* (1972) and *Do the Strand* (1973). Mackay's hard-rock licks, individual lines, and electronic treatment were an essential part of the Roxy Music sound. Ian Dury and the Blockheads enjoyed a brief time at the top of the music business, producing memorable numbers such as *Hit Me With Your Rhythm Stick* (1978), including Davey Payne's outrageous double saxophone solo. To be outrageous in the punk era was quite something.

The year 1978 saw the appearance of what can only be described as the *Baker Street* phenomenon. An attractive but seemingly innocuous rock ballad, a hit for singer/composer Gerry Rafferty, was decorated by a handful of notes turned into an eight-bar phrase at the beginning and between verses. No one really knows why, but following the success (and consequent air-play) of this number, it seemed that every self-respecting band had to include a saxophone. Soon after that an enormous percentage of TV advertisements had a sultry tenor or wailing alto taking prominence, and in the mid-1980s the saxophone became the most popular instrument for youngsters starting out. Rafael Ravenscroft, the player in question, can thus be said to have initiated the biggest boom in saxophone sales since the craze of the 1920s. This is testimony to the power of the mass media, as well as music itself, and follows in a direct line from Acker Bilk, whose *Stranger on the Shore* was responsible for a generation of clarinet players, and later James Galway with *Annie's Song*, similarly providing for flute players. It seemed that *Baker Street* legitimised the saxophone in mainstream pop, instead of being an extra instrument on loan from jazz. Almost the best part of this whole story is the fact that, like many inventions, it appeared quite by chance. The band were recording the number, and Rafael Ravenscroft was booked to do a session on soprano (heard briefly in the introduction). Having completed this, they were still waiting for the guitarist to arrive, who was due to record the now famous opening phrases. Time passed and Ravenscroft mentioned that he had an alto in the car if that would do as a substitute for the guitar. It was found to be satisfactory.

The Logical Song (1979), by Supertramp, continued the enhanced profile of the saxophone. John Helliwell's high-energy soulful alto contributions neatly combined his rhythm and blues heritage with the requirements of modern pop. Their album, *Breakfast in America*, was a huge hit internationally (the best-selling album in the world during 1979) – the saxophone image was there on the air waves and there in the lengthy stadium tours, with Helliwell as saxophonist and occasional keyboard player.

Other bands who featured saxophone in the 1970s were the Average White Band – Roger Ball and Malcolm 'Molly' Duncan (*Pick up the Pieces*, 1975) – and the exciting funk sectional playing of Earth, Wind and Fire on *Got to Get You into My Life* (1978) and *In the Stone* (1979). Deliberately less commercial but none the less successful were Tower of Power with saxophonists Skip Mesquite, Lenny Pickett, Richard Elliot, Emilio Castillo and Stephen 'Doc' Kupka, whose solid funk grooves backed often extended solos. Lou Marini was the tenor soloist with the Blues Brothers and Wilton Felder's unmistakable tenor sound was a vital part of the Crusaders, who began as a jazz group in the late 1950s, later incorporating rock and soul influences and finding commercial success with numbers such as *Street Life* (1979). The strongly jazz-influenced Steely Dan had a regular throughput of top session players. Phil Woods recorded *Dr Wu* with them in 1975, while Pete Christlieb played tenor on *Deacon Blues* (1977) – other notables included Tom Scott and Wayne Shorter. Even the more symphonic Pink Floyd used Dick Parry's atmospheric baritone and tenor on their *Wish You Were Here* album in 1975, and most notably his tenor on the track *Money* (*Dark Side of the Moon* of 1973). And then there was Sonny Rollins's appearance with the Rolling Stones in 1981 on *Waiting on a Friend*. 'Famous amateurs' Van Morrison, David Bowie and Joe Jackson provided some of their own horn lines.

Many soloists also recorded their own predominantly instrumental albums, among the best known being Grover Washington, whose light-toned mixture of jazz and soul can be heard on *Mr Magic* (1974) and *Winelight* (1980). Tom Scott, one of the finest saxophone and Lyricon session players, released *Blow it Out* (1977) and *Desire* (1982). Jay Beckenstein led Spyrogyra to commercial success with *Morning Dance* (1979) and *Catching the Sun* (1980). Ernie Watts, David Sanborn and Michael Brecker crossed easily from jazz into rock and pop, Sanborn in particular releasing many solo albums since the 1970s; Brecker, surprisingly, released his debut solo album in 1987 but he had much success with trumpet playing brother Randy in the Brecker Brothers Band. Tenor player Gato Barbieri encompassed everything from folk tunes to the avant-garde, and when working in commercial areas he brought a strong

Latin influence from his Argentinian roots, and made extensive use of the growl like Earl Bostic before him. Frequently used at points of no tension, this timbral shift is very similar to subtle guitar distortion.

Often session players would team up to record an album; one such band was Dr Strut, with David Woodford on saxophone, who released *Struttin'* in 1980, an outstanding blend of rhythm and blues, funk and jazz. The title track was used as a signature tune for Alexis Korner's cult rhythm and blues radio show in the UK. Another one-off success of the 1980s was the baritone solo by Ronnie Ross on Matt Bianco's *Get out of your Lazy Bed* (1983). Others who featured with this band were Phil Todd, Jamie Talbot and Ed Calle. Hue and Cry were to use Lenny Pickett, Lou Marini, Dave Tofani and Roger Rosenberg in their horn section for *Remote* (1988) – subsequently the section was led by Tommy Smith, who also contributed several horn arrangements. It is interesting that 'live' horn sections were being used at this later period, which was the beginning of accessible midi technology – many bands used synthesiser brass pads for fills and stabs, which was perfectly adequate as long as you weren't listening too closely.

The 1980s saw the continuation of Sanborn, Brecker and Scott playing for major artists (for example Tom Scott on Whitney Houston's *Saving all My Love for You* in 1985). One of Brecker's most breathtaking solos is *The Dry Cleaner from Des Moines* on the 1979 Joni Mitchell album *Shadows and Light*. Commercial funk was catered for by the likes of the Icelandic band Mezzoforte, which included Kristinn Svavarsson on saxophone along with session players Chris Hunter, Martin Dobson, Phil Todd and Dave O'Higgins – they released their debut album *Surprise Surprise* in 1982. Instrumental albums by Grover Washington, David Sanborn and Tom Scott are numerous, but for mainstream popular appeal (and coinciding with the terrific rise in popularity of the instrument), Kenny Gee and Candy Dulfer lead the field. Gee has a very attractive fluid sound and technique to match. Some of his music is similar in groove to that of David Sanborn; the emphasis is always on melody and production, with busy improvisations; a significant number of his tunes are of the soothing ballad variety. His 1987 album *Duotones*, including the hit single *Songbird*, was an international success. Candy Dulfer plays an exciting brand of raw funk on albums such as *Saxuality* (1990) and *Sax-a-go-go* (1992), where the powerful themes are matched by the solos.

One of the most significant bands of the 1980s was the band Sting formed for the *Dream of the Blue Turtles* album in 1985, in which Branford Marsalis (tenor and soprano) played a major role. Marsalis, whose previous employment had been with Miles Davis, returned to the band in 1987 for *Nothing Like the Sun*; many of the songs on these two albums became

Ex. 9.2 Branford Marsalis, soprano saxophone solo on *Little Wing* (© Intersong Music UK Ltd).

classics, including *Fortress Around Your Heart*, *Consider Me Gone* and *Englishman in New York*. A film of the band's 1985 tour including the title track, Police number *Bring on the Night*, won many awards. As well as very fine playing, the film includes several insights into rehearsal techniques and business reality. The nature of the music allowed Marsalis to reveal his skills as a performer of the highest calibre – his fills always catch the mood, his riffs are never less than exciting, and the solos are finely honed works of art. One of his finest is the short chorus on *Little Wing*, from *Nothing But the Sun*; this Jimi Hendrix song contains a guitar solo by Hiram Bullock, paying homage to the composer – Marsalis picks up from the end of the guitar line on a deceptive high long note, and successfully turns the music round from the guitar wails to the ensuing relaxed vocal entry (see Ex. 9.2).

There was much debate at the time of Paul Simon's 1986 *Graceland* album concerning the use of world music. In this instance Simon collaborated with South African performers and composers in the project, as well as with American musicians. The question was: was he using First World technology and marketing to project Third World music into a position where it could reap its just rewards, or was he exploiting these musicians for his own ends? From the musical content and from the obvious expansion of influence of many forms of African music, the answer would seem to be the former. From the USA, he used saxophonists Lenny Pickett, Alex Foster, Ronnie Cuber, Johnny Hoyt (of Rockin' Dopsie and the Twisters) and Steve Berlin (of Los Lobos). From South Africa he used Barney

Rachabane, Mike Machalemele and Teaspoon Ndlela. Senegalese singer Youssou N'Dour uses a similar mixture on his 1989 album *The Lion*, with David Sanborn, Phil Todd and Jimmy Mvondo Mvele on saxophones.

Courtney Pine, like Branford Marsalis, comes from a jazz performing background: his work in the rock field is radically different, and as much a contribution to the 1990s as Marsalis's was to the 1980s. Similarly to many players of his generation and younger, he was actually brought up listening to pop and rock music, learning jazz at a later stage. He has made many forays into soul, reggae, hip-hop and dance (rave) music. As a featured soloist on *Soul II Soul Volume II* on the track *Courtney Blows*, released in 1990, he creates a haunting soprano sound, which is probably quite original, typically for hip-hop the saxophone is down in the mix (both melody and solo). The whole concept is innovative, and Pine developed this further in subsequent albums. His classic track *In the Garden of Eden* from *Modern Day Jazz Stories* (1997) exposes a long soprano melody of great simplicity and restraint in the most solid of grooves, with solo episodes occasionally hinting at Garbarek and Evan Parker but really outlining his own style in an authoritative manner.

Style and fashion change rapidly in the world of pop and rock, but good songs remain essential. One of the major bands of the 1990s, Simply Red, use the technical bravura and creative improvising of Ian Kirkham, whilst the distinctive cry of Snake Davis on soprano and tenor is a vital component of songs like *Search for the Hero* (M-People, 1995). The studio player will adapt to requirements, having been booked for his/her playing qualities in the first place. The essence of a good rock solo is perhaps best summed up by Sting discussing Marsalis: 'In jazz, [he] is allowed three or four verses to warm up his solo, so he makes this organic curve and he's allowed to wander around, and find this avenue, and jettison that, and go somewhere else. In rock music you have to burn from the first bar.'[1]

10 The saxophone today

The contemporary saxophone

CLAUDE DELANGLE AND JEAN-DENIS MICHAT
(TRANSLATED BY PETER NICHOLS)

In praise of saxophonists

With so-called traditional instruments, the gradual emergence of major works and an evolution of repertoire have, over time, contributed to the steady development of a particular school, usually with consistent and well-defined concepts of writing, phrasing, tone and stylistic parameters – in other words, a clear notion of what represents 'good' playing.

Saxophonists themselves have long faced the thorny problem of repertoire, both in terms of quality and quantity. Although orphaned for the sins of its youth, the saxophone is currently enjoying one of its most fruitful phases, with the emergence of a stability not dissimilar to that being experienced by contemporary composers.

The fifty years since the Second World War have seen both iconoclastic and purely exploratory adventures: the blind alley of total serialism and the experimental electronic ideas of the 1980s. Today's young composers see themselves as educated but not 'academic', knowledgeable but still inquisitive, displaying both brilliance and perception. The same applies to saxophonists. Free from any musical 'establishment', they have a ferocious appetite for new music and an acute sense of responsibility which will undoubtedly benefit the generations of the twenty-first century. Very rarely tied to one style, method or particular practice, their cultural base, while not actually larger than that of other instrumentalists, is often much more receptive to the most stimulating of influences. Coming from a state of 'No Fixed Repertory' the saxophonist can often end up trying everything, as much a polymath as his instrument is a polymorph. He plays all the instruments of the family, teaches and fits easily into the most diverse 'socio-musical classes'. The development of a student reflects this: basic technique (Boehm system) is based on the concept of 'everything is playable'. As nineteenth-century saxophone music is virtually non-existent, the student has hardly known the type of repertoire in which the fingers trust the ear. Instead, he is brought up from the start in an atonal, often extremely chromatic, language. Melodically tortuous lines sustained by unstable harmonies in fast tempi can over-exaggerate the importance of technical dexterity. Once the study repertoire of the flute, oboe and clarinet (Marcel Moyse, Marcel Mule) has been absorbed (usually rapidly) the next step, apart from the specific studies for the instrument, is to tackle violin music (with Paganini *Caprices* at the top of the list!).

All improvised music (jazz, ethnic etc.) is an integral part of the modern saxophonist's culture. Even if this is not played regularly, the cord which binds the classical performer to the notes has been irrevocably severed, along with the phrasing and all the formal 'limitations' which can characterise the concert in its inherited nineteenth-century form.

The nature of the saxophone family has given rise to a large number of transcriptions, so creating as broad a repertoire as possible: oboe, violin, flute on the soprano saxophone; clarinet, viola, French horn on the alto saxophone; viola da gamba, French horn on the tenor saxophone; bassoon, cello on the baritone saxophone.

With all this wide experience, the saxophonist can sympathise with the dilemma of the contemporary composer – how to build on quasi-virgin territory? All saxophonists today are interested in the creative process, although obviously each one has their own stylistic preferences. New works are often the result of artist–composer relationships and can reflect the personality of the dedicatee.

In America, John Sampen has been responsible for works by Shrude, Beerman, Francesconi, Mabry, Subotnick, Martino, Glass, Harbison, Furman, Babbitt, Cage, Tower, Noda, Stockhausen and Mays. Kenneth Radnofsky collaborates with many of the above as well as with Bell, Theofanidis, Schüller, Sims and Korde; he is also the inspiration behind the World Wide Concurrent Premières and Commissioning Fund, Inc., a world association of saxophonists promoting new music; William H. Street, Paul Bro, Kenneth Fischer, the Chicago Saxophone Quartet and many others are constantly generating new repertoire.

In France, Jean-Marie Londeix has worked extensively with composers, notably a young generation taught by Fusté Lambezat in Bordeaux (Lauba, Rossé and Havel). His successor Marie Bernadette Charrier has also inspired many works (Havel, Lauba, Melle and Rossé). Daniel Kientzy has turned towards electro-acoustic music in collaboration with the Groupe de Recherche Musicale; and Teruggi with Romanian composers Anatole Vieru, Stefan Niculescu, Myriam Marbé and Costin Miereanu. A number of saxophone quartets commission composers: Xasax (Barry Guy, Alex Buess, Alvaro Carlevaro, Bernardo Kuczer and Denis Levaillant); the Diastema Quartet work with Dubedout, Martin, Level and Burgan. Serge Bertocchi, outside of his work with Xasax and Ars Gallica, is developing an important repertoire for the baritone saxophone: De Clerck, Bruno Giner (*Yod*), Henry Kergomar (*Vianässa*) and Marie Helene Fournier (*Hyppogriffe*).

In Italy, Federico Mondelci, a composer and performer, Alberto Domizi and the Academia Saxophone Quartet promote their country's composers (Scogna, Rossi Re, Tesei and Sbordoni). In Germany, Johannes Ernst works with well-known composers (Kyburz, Staude, Mundry and Zimmermann). The American saxophonist John Edward Kelly and the Rascher Quartet are also responsible for a lot of creative activity in Germany; *Rasch* by Franco Donatoni, written for them, is heavily influenced by Latin poetry and displays astonishing rhythmic vitality in its classical writing. In Russia, Alexander Volkov; in the Netherlands, Arno Bornkamp and Henry Bok; in Belgium, Hans de Jong (also a composer); in England, John Harle (with composers Muldowney and Birtwistle); and in Cuba, the saxophonist Villafruela. In Scandinavia, the New Danish Saxophone Quartet are building a substantial Danish repertoire (Lorentzen, Norholm, Hentze and Roikjer).

In Croatia the Zagreb Quartet perform music by Papandopulo, Ruzdjak, Bjelinski and Detoni, combining the Croatian folk tradition with twelve-tone or post-classical principles. Manuel Mijan and Francisco Martinez Garcia work closely with the Spanish composers (Tomas Marco, Rojo, Angulo, Alis, Seco and Louis De Pablo). In Finland, the saxophonist Pekka Savijoki has commissioned a number of talented composers, among them Magnus Lindberg and Esa-Pekka Salonen, to produce concertos, solo works and chamber music. In Austria, the Vienna Quartet are putting together an interesting and high quality repertoire (Engebretson, Urbanner and Wagner). In Switzerland, Marcus Weiss, the successor to Iwan Roth, has inspired the creation of a substantial solo repertoire (Sotelo, Haubenstock-Ramati and Walter Zimmermann) and works for the Acantus Trio (saxophones, piano and percussion). In Japan, the Quatre Roseaux Quartet and soloist Nobuya Sugawa have premièred many new works; the saxophonist composer Ryo Noda has developed an important repertoire for his instrument, principally for solo saxophone.

The vocal saxophone

Invented by Adolphe Sax around 1840, the saxophone was intended to be an outdoor instrument combining the phrasing and tone of stringed instruments with the power of brass instruments. The result was undoubtedly a success, except, far from being an instrument of compromise, it actually accumulated the respective qualities: the powers of expression, attack and graininess of the strings come naturally to it, as do the breadth, volume and roundness of the brass. Its dynamic palette is enlarged further by the intrinsic qualities of a single-reed instrument which endow it with the extremely soft dynamics of its clarinet cousin. It lacks only words as the sound is, with its flexibility and expressiveness, the closest to the human voice (not for nothing is it the 'voice of jazz'). With a concentration of harmonics at around 2000 Hz (the optimal zone of acute hearing) it is very similar to the human voice.

It is significant that the saxophone was introduced into vocal music in such a natural way. One of the first notable examples is the use of the alto saxophone to unite, sustain and guide the children's choir in Puccini's *Turandot*. The timbre obtained is highly effective, the flexibility of the instrument being so close to the purity of the children's voices that the ensemble produces an intriguing and hitherto unprecedented texture. It is also interesting to observe that a great number of composers attracted to the human voice have instinctively adopted the instrument, even using it exclusively for characters in their dramatic works. Indeed, the credit for introducing the saxophone into the orchestra should go to opera, and not to any symphonic tradition.

The Italians lead the way in employing the saxophone to good effect: Berio with *Air Aus* (tenor), *Traces* (three saxophones), *Un Re In Ascolto* (alto), *La Vera Storia* (two altos) and *Outis*, performed in Milan in 1996 with full quartet (SATB). When doubling the choir strictly it thickens the texture, and when underscoring it helps the voice and also gives discreet intonation support. Dallapiccola's music is a natural home for the instrument – *Il prigionero* (tenor, alto), *Ulysse* (two altos), *Canti di liberazione* (two saxophones) – as is Maderna's: *Don Perlimplin* (five saxophones). If it seems to be a second skin in vocal music, it is an equally indispensable tool of orchestration with its capacity to integrate with, and forge an active link between, all instrumental groupings. Consider its place in the dramatic works of the Second Viennese School: Berg's *Lulu* (alto), Schoenberg's *Von Heute auf Morgen* (soprano/alto, tenor/bass) and Webern's *Das Augenlicht,* Op. 26. Its strong tonal identity is required here, an identity that can even make social statements as in Stockhausen's *Licht,* Zimmermann's *Die Soldaten* or Henze's *Das Floss der 'Medusa'.*

In intimate settings the saxophone blends supremely, its considerable dynamic range (from *pppp* to *fff* in Berio), its ease of glissando (to the sixth harmonic in the top register), and its palette of colours and timbres make it a popular chamber music partner. Take for example *Plupart du temps II* by Jolas for tenor saxophone, tenor voice and cello; Raskatov's *Pas de deux* for tenor and soprano saxophones and soprano voice; Scelsi's *Yamaon* for bass voice, alto and baritone saxophones, contrabassoon, double-bass and percussion; and Berio's *Prière* for voice and eight instruments. Perhaps the saxophone is even beginning to supplant the clarinet in its role as the instrumental double of the voice. When not actively replacing it, it can function as a textural and dynamic extension: *Schlimann* by Jolas (clarinet and tenor sax), Berio's *Canticum Novissimi Testamenti* for eight voices, four saxophones and four clarinets. Any analysis of the saxophone–voice relationship would be incomplete without mentioning the dramatic effect of the instrument in Pousseur's *Votre Faust*. In France, Georges Aperghis, a composer of Greek origin, has written *Simplexis* (two altos, two tenors, baritone) and *Signaux* for four instruments of the same range. The latter, a strangely hypnotic work, is based on three tirelessly reproduced series of eight quarter-tones and has parallels with the work of John Cage. The composer Alain Louvier in *Le Jeu des sept musiques* sets several styles against each other with a particularly attractive scenario in which rock music triumphs! Similar in philosophy to John Cage, the Dutchman Eric De Clerck displays an interesting use of space in his solo baritone piece *Why?* In Kagel's *Zwei Akte* for alto saxophone and harp the instrumentalists do not actually move but dramatic action takes place within the music. This natural extroversion, the principal reason behind suspicion of the instrument from some quarters, is but one facet of the saxophone's personality, its polymorphic nature having led it naturally towards solo performance.

Certain works require the simultaneous playing of two saxophones. If the use of four or more saxophones in the course of a piece achieved a certain success in the 1980s (Jolas, Marbé, De Pablo and Donatoni), composers today seem to have gone back to using one or two. This latter solution employed by Raskatov (*Pas de Deux*: soprano and tenor) and Jolas (*Lumor*: soprano and tenor) seems to be an interesting middle course allowing the development of the soloist without turning him/her into a furniture-mover or musical freak-show!

The origins of contemporary technique

When Adolphe Sax was displaying his saxophones, creating a repertoire, playing or teaching, his priority was to demonstrate the revolutionary acoustical qualities of his invention. Beautiful lyrical melodies and 'showy' variations from the early works illustrate the essential qualities of all the family. The repertoire built by Elise Hall at the turn of the century reveals the expressive potential of the instrument in much greater depth through its phrasing, projection and dynamic variety.

The classical schools subsequently began to develop a high level of virtuosity; in Berlin, Bumcke analysed the fundamentals of technique and introduced the concept of altissimo (*Saxophon Schule*, Edition Benjamin, 1926), and Schoenberg used bass and tenor saxophones with altissimo as early as 1930 in the orchestra of *Von Heute auf Morgen*. Thereafter, the altissimo was widely developed by Sigurd Rascher, based on the natural harmonics of the low register.

Under the influence of Rascher, composers such as Frank Martin, Jacques Ibert, Karel Husa and Henry Cowell made use of a four-octave saxophone. The American school carried on this tradition: Ted Nash (*High Harmonics*, 1946), Rosemary Lang (*Altissimo Register*) and Eugene Rousseau (*Saxophone High Tones*). In this respect, France did not make up its lost ground until the 1970s: Denisov (*Sonata 1970* written for Londeix) and Constant (*Concertante*, 1978). Until then Marcel Mule, the founder of the French school, had little interest in this aspect. Instead, through his teaching, his didactic works and his transcriptions (Mule–Leduc) he contributed greatly to widespread improvements in sound, dynamics, tonal homogeneity, virtuosity of articulation and velocity. Originally a violinist (as was his successor at the Paris Conservatoire, Daniel Deffayet), he began with an analysis of the violin and brought to the saxophone aspects of string style. The origins of saxophone vibrato can also be traced back to this.

Through their analyses of acoustic phenomena, approaches to technical improvement and their graded studies, early performers and teachers paved the way for an explosion of techniques seen in today's repertoire. Working with composers creates a repertoire ever closer to the true acoustical nature of the instrument, although the reverse can be true – difficulties encountered in a work can inspire an objective analysis of the problems and lead to the creation of appropriate exercises. Certain artists are notable for their work in codifying techniques: Larry Teal (in *The Art of Saxophone Playing*) tackles all the main points of technique, including the more advanced aspects (such as altissimo and double-tonguing). Donald Sinta has produced a video in which techniques are demonstrated with great virtuosity. In Japan, Sakaguchi has laid the foundations for solid technical training, producing players of the calibre of Omuro, Sugawa and Muto. In the USA, Eugene Rousseau and Frederick Hemke have contributed to the development of an American repertoire by composers such as Muczynski, Creston, Stein, Heiden and Karlins. In France, Jean-Marie Londeix has written numerous works: *Hello! Mr Sax* and *Paramètres du Saxophone* (Leduc) deal with different parameters of sound (pitch, timbre, duration, volume and attack), with corresponding charts.

Fig. 10.1 Nobuya Sugawa,
Fourth British Saxophone
Congress, 1996

Star quality

The instrument has been a success in jazz where, as previously mentioned, the hybrid nature of its tone is underlined. For jazz musicians the saxophone is a member of the brass family, whereas for classical players it is a woodwind. A saxophonist is recognised to a greater extent than any other instrumentalist by personal sound quality. For so-called 'academic' composers, the history of jazz and its saxophonists has long been a unique reference point when writing for the instrument. It is clear that the baggage of the modern saxophonist is the legacy and accumulation, as much as the synthesis, of all the modes of playing, of sounds and of styles developed by Charlie Parker, John Coltrane, Ornette Coleman, Dave Liebman etc. Of all the jazz techniques, only subtone (Ben Webster, Lester Young, Coleman Hawkins) seems to have originated in jazz itself. Jazz saxophone has virtually developed in parallel with the contemporary saxophone: the young generation make great use of multiphonics (Michael Brecker), slap-tonguing, circular breathing (James Carter) and double- and triple-tonguing (Louis Sclavis).

These parallels are sometimes openly acknowledged as composers attempt to capture on paper an improvised style. For example, *Opcit* by Hurel for tenor saxophone, where the manipulation of sound is a key factor (harmonics, growling etc.); *Hard* by Lauba for tenor saxophone which uses multiphonic rhythms as an analogy to the layered sounds of heavy rock; Denisov's *Sonata* for alto and piano, a 'classic' of the repertoire with a finale influenced very firmly by post-bop and perfectly written for the instrument. The fact that a Ben Webster, a Sonny Rollins or a Michael Brecker can draw from the same 'tool' such disparate sounds demonstrates the extraordinary tonal resources of the instrument, and above all its flexibility. This propensity for metamorphosis has given rise to a number of works with tape, for example Cavanna's *Goutte d'or blues* (soprano, sopranino and tape) and Zbar's *Jazzy Night in Yellow* (tenor and tape).

Some jazz saxophonists have written for the instrument themselves: Phil Woods gives a personal touch to be-bop with repetitive figures and irregular accents (*Sonata, Three Improvisations for Quartet*); François Jeanneau writes in a way which preserves the spontaneity of improvisation (*Suite for Quartet, Une Anche Passe*); David Liebmann fits together complex rhythms and silences in an unpredictable way (*A Moody Time*); tonal freedom, thematic fragmentation and textural juxtapositions are characteristic of Martial Solal (*Une Pièce pour Quatre*); the sense of pulse is a determining factor in the quartet *Attractions* by Denis Levaillant.

In his concerto *For Stan Getz*, Richard Rodney Bennett combines jazz harmonies with free twelve-tone technique: he mixes the genres without a trace of compromise. The blues feature in concertos by Stanley Myers and the Flemish composers René Pieper and Kees Schoonebeek; whilst Michael Torke writes short, memorable themes, not unlike advertising jingles, in an attempt to make his music accessible. Martijn Padding mixes be-bop and classical styles within a more abstract form (*Quatuor Rotorno*); Tristan Keuris (*Music for Saxophone*) is not afraid of tonal references even if he sometimes uses harsh and strident sounds as a reaction against the lyrical style of the classical saxophone quartet. Geert Van Keulen uses four saxophones as a big band, and the distorted sounds of free jazz – use of the voice, shouts, coarse flutter-tonguing, playing with the teeth on the reed – form the basis of the compositional language of the Swiss composer Alex Buess (*Hyper Baton*). Unusual jazz improvisation sequences and untempered notes are the hallmark of Paul Méfano in *Périples* (1978), which takes the natural tone of the tenor as its starting point, whereas jazz-rock is the central theme of *Anu Anvil* and *Parachutes de Dror Feiler*.

Some other works reflect not so much the jazz identity of the saxophone but rather the ethnic connotations of its improvisatory character: *Aulodie* by Mâche (soprano and tape) is originally for oboe da caccia, but is more convincing on the soprano. The popular roots of the instrument and its appropriation of the most diverse traditions – Indian music, Balkan music, South American music etc. – have influenced many composers. Based in Berlin since 1982, the Filipino composer Conrado Del Rosario, a member of a gamelan ensemble, wrote *Ringkaran* in 1990, the title inspired by South Philippine religious chants. Christian Lauba synthesises Western music with North African music – the music of his childhood – and Japanese music. *Les Sept Isles* for saxophone ensemble is a true meeting of cultures out of which the composer produces a sophisticated mosaic; his violent and extrovert solo saxophone work *Hard* is influenced by rock music while *Steady Study on the Boogie* (1993) reveals its roots in the title. The American composer William Albright introduces elements of popular American music in the *Scherzo* of his post-classical Sonata (1984). A chaconne variation shows the influence of Baroque music.

Japanese composers refer to their traditional music in different ways: descriptions of nature are to be found by Takashi Yoshimatsu in *Fuzzy Bird Sonata* and *Cyber Bird Concerto*; references to Japanese instrumental techniques in Ryo Noda (*Maï, Improvisations I, II, and III, Gen Concerto*), Joji Yuasa (*Not I but the Wind*) and Natsuda (*West*); references to the theatrical concepts of time and space in Yoshihisa Taïra (*Pénombres VI*), Toshio Hosokawa (*Verticale Time Study II*) and Toru Takemitsu (*Distance*, originally written for oboe, with optional sho [a Japanese mouth-organ] accompaniment). Takemitsu's conception of time is very pertinent: 'Whereas the modern Western concept of time is by nature linear, that is to say its duration always keeps the same state, in Japan, time is seen as an entity which continually repeats itself'.[1]

The Romanian composer Stefan Niculescu uses a Byzantine melody as the basis of his Symphonie Concertante No. 3 'Cantos', as well as elements of Gregorian and non-European music; in his Concerto, Myriam Marbé makes use of popular songs. John Harbison's *San Antonio Sonata*, although of a classical structure, is based on popular Mexican music, funk and be-bop.

As it gradually frees itself from jazz and popular influences, and asserts its independence, the modern saxophone, far from disowning its roots, will increasingly exploit its unique duality: aggressive or tender, refined or vulgar. Ever since composers learned how to quantify and exploit the uncertainties of 'real-time' creation, the modern classical saxophone school has produced artists able to master even the most transcendent of works.

There is a great deal of repertoire for solo saxophone, and as with other instruments, the great names stand out. Berio's two *Sequenze IXb* (alto, originally for clarinet) and *VIIb* (soprano, originally for oboe): apart from the intrinsic interest of these two pieces, it is revealing to compare the originals with the new versions and to identify their respective characteristics – the uniqueness of the clarinet legato and the alto saxophone cantabile; the even tone of the soprano and the inimitable sound of the oboe. They are not 'saxophone versions', but two idiomatic and autonomous masterpieces. Similarly with Stockhausen's *In Freundshaft* (alto or soprano, originally for clarinet but transcribed for all instruments by the composer) where the compositional process is continued by gestural evolution (the work is played from memory). *Anubis-Nout* by Grisey demonstrates the tonal richness of the bass saxophone, its capacity to isolate harmonics (a ghostly effect) and also the remarkable nature of a family whose deeper instruments have a flexibility and speed that almost equal those of its higher members. Because of the progressive transformations and the subtly varied sequences employed, it is a demonstration of development through tiny transitions rather than through contrasts.

This love of tonal metamorphosis is exemplified in the work of Giacinto Scelsi, who displays the harmonic power of saxophone timbre not through different modes of playing but by the examination of sound in an expanded temporal space in *Tre Pezzi* (soprano or tenor), *Maknogan* (baritone) and *Ixor* (soprano). The influence of Tibetan and Indian music is discernible, particularly in the modal nature of the works. All of Scelsi's attention is centred on the properties of sound, energy and life itself. Very often his music is built on the struggle between rest and movement, with repeated long notes set against rapidly moving neighbours.

The expressiveness and agility of the instrument, the spirit and charisma of its advocates, as well as its symbolic 'seul contre tous' image, have made the saxophone so attractive and yet so difficult for composers: Jolas' *Fourth Episode* (tenor), De Pablo's *Oculto* (baritone or alto), Takemitsu's *Distance* (soprano), Campana's *Acting In* (alto and tenor), Glass's *Gradus* (soprano), Wildberger's *Portrait* (alto), Méfano's *Tige* (alto), Ballif's *Solfegietto 8* (alto) and Fournier's *Horoscope* (alto). As concerto-type pieces become increasingly common, perhaps Adolphe Sax's brilliant invention will enter the orchestra via the front door, the soloist's entrance. It is true that its hybrid character, its capacity to drown out, fade away or blend, to disappear then return transformed or, indeed, in an unrecognisable form, allows the realisation of any number of compositional fantasies: a saxophonist never says no! All permutations are viable: full orchestra, for instance Denisov's *Concerto* (alto and orchestra), Constant's *Concertante* (alto and orchestra), Jolas' *Lumor* (tenor, soprano and orchestra) and De Pablo's *1 Couleur*; string orchestra, for instance Rossé's *Triangle pour un souffle* (alto and twelve strings); and various combinations, for example Jarrell's *Résurgences* (alto/soprano and eight instruments) and *Points d'Or* by Betsy Jolas for one saxophonist playing SATB, and fifteen instruments.

The saxophone and electronics

The harmonic-rich sound of the saxophone lends itself well to endless transformations. Furthermore, the range of the instrumental family allows the retention of each register's principal properties and reduces the need for sampling which could distort the signal. A varied repertoire, which is still little known, expanded rapidly in the 1980s, in particular Decoust's *Olos* (tenor and electro-acoustic diffusion), Kurtag's *Interrogation* (tenor, bass, real-time Electronic IRCAM and tape) and Radulescu's *Astray* (saxophones, prepared piano and tape). Tape replaces the piano in a sonata combination very effectively, thereby sparing it the frequent unbalanced duels and unhappy marriages, despite the undoubted successes of the Denisov *Sonata* (alto and piano), Rossé's *La Main dans le souffle* (alto and piano), Hurel's *Bacasax* (alto and piano), Savouret's *A flanc de Bozat* (soprano/tenor and piano), Nodaira's *Arabesque 3*, Taira's *Pénombres 6* and the numerous works of Tisné, Gastinel, Gotkovsky and Robert.

Music for saxophone and tape

One particular scenario is common in compositions for instrument and tape: the instrument played live with its own projection on tape – for instance Isabel Mundry's *Composition 1992* – often with the tape part varying and breaking up the saxophone material, as in François Bernard Mâche's *Aulodie* and *Ensemble Invisible* by Aurelio Samori.

Milton Babbitt, one of the fathers of electronic music in the United States, has written a number of works for pure electronics or for instrument and tape. *Images* (1979) explores the various relationships possible between an instrument (here alto, soprano and sopranino) and tape. In *Voilements* and *Saxatile*, Jean Claude Risset expands the parameters of conventional listening – it is a shrewd person who can separate the saxophone from its treatment by the computer. A galactic world, atoms, particles and infinitely small domains await us in *Exultitudes*, composed in the studios of the Groupe de Recherches Musicales de l'INA (Radio France) by Gilles Racot. Other substantial works stand out: by Burton Beerman (*Concerto One* for saxophone and tape), Bernard Cavanna (*Goutte d'Or Blues*), Costin Miereanu (*Do- Mi- Si- La- Do- Ré-, Variants-Invariants*), Steve Reich (*Vermont Counterpoint*) and Michel Zbar (*Jazzy Night in Yellow*).

Real-time transformations

This is sometimes a question of using space or creating resonance. Joji Yuasa uses two microphones in *Not I but the Wind*, one to spatialise the instrument and the other linked to an echo chamber. Mention can also be made of *Métaksax* by Anatol Vieru for saxophone and envelope transformer.

Some composers use far more sophisticated computerised systems. Following a preordained program, the computer reacts to and transforms the instrumentalist's sounds in real time. Reference points can be directly recognised by the machine in the course of the performance or when the player himself controls the program via a pedal: for most of the time an assistant technician/musician is required to balance the sound, oversee the smooth running of the changes or indeed 'play' the changes live. Although fascinating, such systems are cumbersome and last-minute breakdowns happen without warning. In France, the Groupe de Recherches Musicales de l'INA has introduced a real-time audio-digital 'SYTER' system, a programmable and interactive sound processor. Wholly digital, this system combines the recording, processing and control elements necessary for such high-quality work. It has been responsible for several saxophone works, including *Xatys* by Daniel Teruggi.

Morton Subotnick, a leader and pioneer of new musical technology, maintains the duality between the traditional instrument and machine in his concerto *In Two Worlds* (optional version with orchestra), in which the saxophonist controls the electronic and computer-transformed sounds with a pedal. In *Music for Saxophone and Electronics* by Pablo Furman, a wide variety of sounds serves as the basis for the electronic part. Other substantial electronic works include *Olos* by Michel Decoust, *Solo* and *Spiral* by Karlheinz Stockhausen and *S* by Maurisio Bisati. Some composers have juxtaposed video, tape and musical text as in *The Stillness* by the American Reynold Wiedenaar. Sometimes the electronic part is played live on a synthesizer with acoustic instruments remaining untreated, as in *Linker Augentanz* by Stockhausen and *Moments Rituels* by Ton That Tiet.

Chamber music

The use of the saxophone in chamber music has long been a strict family affair. The 'classical' quartet (soprano, alto, tenor, baritone) has all the qualities of a perfect ensemble, but few great composers have found it a source of inspiration. If the tonal homogeneity of the quartet was an attraction for classical composers, our contemporaries have often seen it as a handicap, a strong and inviolable identity. The best is yet to come, with the exceptions of *Xas* by Xenakis, *Vue sur les jardins interdits* by Henri Pousseur, *Four⁵* by John Cage, *Le Jeu des Sept Musiques* by Alain Louvier and the quartets of Dufourt, Dubedout and Nodaïra.

The saxophone ensemble (often three sopranos, one doubling on sopranino, three or four altos, three tenors, two baritones and a bass) is in effect a three-dimensional quartet. Here the tonal inertia is actually a plus point, the sheer numbers allowing great textural variety with the colours changing in the manner of an organ. The many permutations of instruments, dynamics and numbers allow for rewarding orchestrations. Several first-rate works are beginning to appear: Stockhausen's *Linker Augentanz* (ensemble, synthesizer and percussion), Tisné's *Messe pour notre Temps* (ensemble), Tiet's *Moments Rituels II* (ensemble), Eloy's *Quattrocento* (ensemble), Escaich's *Le chant des Ténèbres* (solo soprano and ensemble), Lauba's *Mutation-Couleurs IV* (ensemble) and Mantovani's *La fuite et son Ombre* (solo soprano and ensemble).

For contemporary saxophonists the route to total integration, acceptance and recognition without classical connotations depends increasingly on chamber music with other instruments. Due to its new-found stability, composers can easily imagine the instrument as a part of their music. It is no longer an experimental, exotic curiosity but is gradually being recognised for its intrinsic qualities. There are some excellent precedents: Webern's *Quartett*, Op. 22 (clarinet, tenor sax, violin and piano), Denisov's *Sonata* (alto and cello) and *Concerto Piccolo* (alto and six percussion), Jolas' *Plupart du Temps II* (tenor, tenor voice and cello), Leroux's *Phonie Douce* (alto, oboe and cello), Lindberg's *Linea d'Ombrea* (alto, flute, guitar and percussion), Tiet's *Moments Rituels I* (tenor, percussion and synthesizer) and Gilbert Amy's *Le Temps du Souffle* (violin, tenor and trombone). The mixture with 'les autres' – winds, strings or percussion – gives the 'sound painter' one extra primary colour on the palette. The twenty-first century will undoubtedly see the blossoming of a new 'traditional' instrument.

Current techniques: control of dynamics

Dynamic control is obviously not a new technique. Composers have always appreciated the saxophone's wide range of dynamic possibilities. As a result, the mastery of extreme contrasts, subtle intermediate shades and the softest dynamics has become obligatory for today's performer.

Changes of timbre

The classical school has taken finger dexterity to a virtuosic degree (for example, in the music of Ibert and Desenclos) and developed an awareness of sound from established sources, principally the Romantic violin and bel canto (Tomasi, Glazunov). Today, without losing this precious heritage, saxophonists are expanding the notion of the 'beau son' considerably by developing a sort of 'tonal virtuosity' adapted to the language of each composer.

Vibrato

Classical repertoire is distinguished by a generalised use of vibrato, but in contemporary music the use of this tonal ornament is less systematic. Many composers require a particular sound: at the opening of *Sequenza IXb* Berio writes 'senza vibrato'. Alain Louvier (*Cinq Ephémères*), Ryo Noda (*Improvisations, Maï*) and Stockhausen (*In Freundshaft*) note precisely what must be vibrated, the speed or amplitude, and the nature of the undulation, pitch vibrato (obtained by jaw movement) or intensity vibrato (variation of the air-speed). This usage is similar to ornamental Baroque vibrato which was considered to be separate from sonority.

Flutter-tonguing

A classic contemporary technique, flutter-tonguing is obtained by rolling the tongue against the palate. With the tongue forward it is clear and smooth, particularly in *piano/pianissimo* passages; with the throat it is coarser, but can be used delicately for soft dynamics and extreme registers.

Microtonal trills

Microtonal trills (bisbigliando) create different colourings of the sound without unduly affecting intonation. They are generally soft and subtle and can be very fast, for instance in Yoshihisa Taïra's *Pénombres 6* and Ichiro Nodaïra's *Arabesque 3*. Berio constructs his *Sequenza VIIb* (soprano version) around a B which sounds gently throughout the piece as if emanating from another instrument or a synthesizer. Variations of timbre, multiphonics, different articulations and subtle dynamics create an electro-acoustic effect. The second part of Grisey's *Anubis* for solo bass saxophone is punctuated by timbral melodies that echo the pitched melodies. The different fingerings of each pitch are precisely notated. Francis Cournet's *Thésaurus du Saxophoniste* (published by Billaudot) gives a comprehensive list of fingerings.

Subtone

A surprisingly soft sound can be obtained in the low register with the use of subtone; lower-jaw pressure is replaced by the tongue under the lip, or the tongue lightly touching the reed (as if pronouncing the word 'the'). Alternatively, the embouchure can be moved towards the end of the mouthpiece, holding it only with the lips and without pressure from the teeth. In each case the reed is partially prevented from vibrating and the upper partials are subdued: for use of this technique, see Paul Méfano's *Périple*, Jolas' *Fourth Episode* and Nodaïra's *Arabesque 3*.

Breath noise

As on the flute, the breath of the performer can mix with or replace the sound. In *Acting In* for solo tenor, the Argentine composer José Luis Campana notes precisely the quantity and proportion of the real sound and the breath: breath only/breath and sound/normal sound. François Rossé uses similar methods in his solo alto work *Le Frêne Egaré*. Sometimes the amount of breath and sound is left to the player. In *Not I but the Wind*, Joji Yuasa gives indications such as 'airy sound' or 'like a shakuhachi sound' or 'pure sound', invoking the tone colours of the Japanese wind instrument. Breath, either alone or mixed with the tone, is audible from *pp* to *mp*, but beyond that the tone will mask its sound unless one blows on the edge of the mouthpiece without touching it, as in Toshio Hosokawa's *Elemental Study 2*.

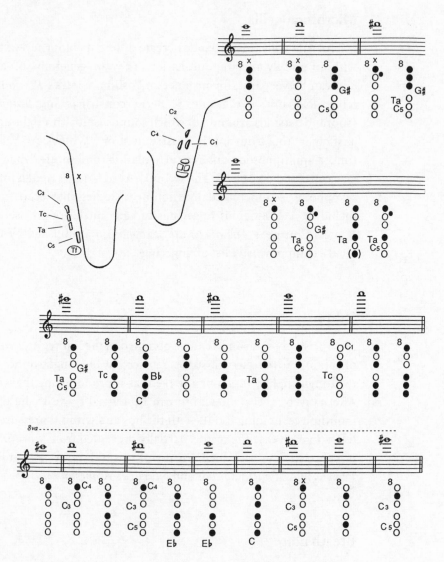

Fig. 10.2 Altissimo register fingering chart, alto saxophone (Claude Delangle)

Overblowing

By changing the shape of the oral cavity, altering the lower-jaw pressure and forming a variety of vowel shapes, different colours and harmonics can be produced. This technique also allows the separation of the upper partials, and it is the basis of Sigurd Rascher's work on the altissimo register.

The altissimo register

Although this register will always be difficult (in terms of intonation, extreme dynamics, legato and running passages), it is now standard practice.[2]

Today, even without including the works dedicated to Rascher or the Rascher Quartet, there are many pieces which use this register. It permits microtones (mastering intonation is difficult), glissandi, bends and microtonal trills (and often provides some of the notes of multiphonics), although conversely a large number of other contemporary techniques are not possible here (flutter-tonguing, breath noise, circular breathing etc.). Apart from works for soloists, composers are advised to use the altissimo in moderation. Harmonic tones should not be confused with altissimo. A composer will indicate 'o' to signify the use of a colour (similar to a violin's harmonic) in the high register or during extremely quiet passages. *Xas*, the quartet by Iannis Xenakis, explores the transformation from order to chaos, using a dual texture of sweeping lines which fragment into an ever-expanding range, up to the limit of the altissimo register.

Micro-intervals, glissandi and portamenti

At a moderate tempo all the quarter-tones from $c\sharp^1$ are playable, although the intonation of the quarter-tone above G (written) is approximate.

Many quarter-tone trills are fairly easy and, in this respect, the tables in the book *Hello! Mr Sax* (Leduc) by Jean-Marie Londeix are very useful. Intervals less than a quarter-tone (third-tone, fifth-tone) are not all possible. Michaël Jarrell uses them very skilfully in *Résurgences* for saxophone and small ensemble. The sextet for violin, viola, cello, saxophone, horn and clarinet by Ezra Sims, a microtonal work based on a 72-note chromatic scale (!), includes quarter-tones, sixth-tones and twelfth-tones. In *Périples* (Paul Méfano) and *Le Frêne Egaré* (François Rossé) the micro-intervallic writing creates a detempered scale where the composers do not require absolute intonation. In *Four*[5], John Cage does not indicate any micro-intervals as such but specifies that 'intonation must be specific to each musician: a unison is therefore to be understood as a unison of differences'.

With the exception of the low register, glissando is fairly straightforward for small intervals (seconds and thirds) although beyond that portamento, as used by singers, tends to be adopted, as, for example, in Betsy Jolas' *Fourth Episode* and *Points d'Or*. A glissando can be produced either

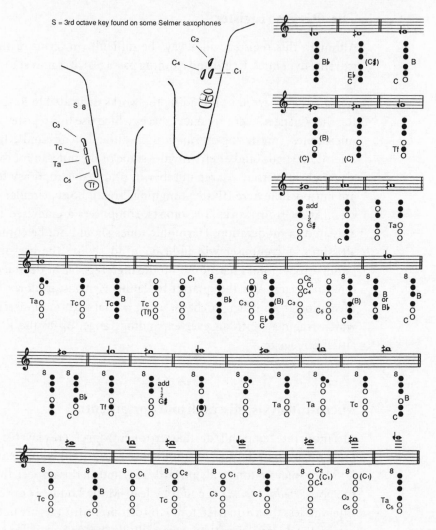

Fig. 10.3 Quarter-tone fingering chart (Claude Delangle)

with the lips and oral cavity or by gradual movement of the keys. It can be wide in the high register (up to the sixth harmonic) but is restricted in the lower register where it is less than a semitone. It is difficult to change registers when producing a glissando by key movement.

Circular breathing

An old folk-music technique common to many countries, this consists of breathing in through the nose while continuing to play with the air collected in the cheeks. With a little practice, a player can do this discreetly so that it does not detract from the music. Certain pieces make this technique essential: Betsy Jolas' *Fourth Episode*, Christian Lauba's *Etudes* and Drake Mabry's *Ceremony I*.

Articulation

Today saxophonists have learnt to master different types of articulation in the manner of the consonants to be found in human language. Composers sometimes demand silent production (clarinet attack) or conversely extremely percussive attacks, including slap-tonguing. The latter is a very dry attack produced by pressing the reed against the mouthpiece, thus creating a vacuum before the tongue is quickly withdrawn. The reed comes away from the mouthpiece violently and hits it hard, as in Alain Louvier's *Le Jeu des sept musiques*. The sound is prolonged by continuous breath in Denisov's *Sonata*. The speed of slap-tongue repetition is not very high and can be compared with 'Bartók pizzicato' on stringed instruments. For open slap-tonguing the mouth is opened thus changing the pitch (a tube open at both ends), as in *Du Sonore* by José Louis Campana. Between these two extremes, all types of attack are possible: less precise, more precise, dry, coloured by the breath, tongue noise, or even an imitation of double-reed instruments, strings or percussion.

Double- and triple-tonguing

For very rapid tonguing, the single 'tu' is not sufficient. Saxophonists use double-tonguing ('tu-ku-tu-ku', etc.) for binary rhythms and triple-tonguing ('tu-ku-tu tu-ku-tu' or 'tu-tu-ku tu-tu-ku') for ternary rhythms. In *Arabesque 3*, Ichiro Nodaïra uses this technique for timbral variation.

Playing and singing

Well known in jazz, the 'growl' consists of singing in a random manner when playing fairly loudly. This technique is employed in several works, although it can be improved by pitching the voice exactly, so producing precise intervals with the saxophone sound. The latter technique works very well at dynamics below *mp* – as in Taïra's *Pénombres 6* (alto and piano) and Hurel's *Opcit* (tenor) – and is particularly interesting when combined with subtone. In Hosokawa's *Elemental Study 2* the instrumentalist has to sing almost permanently, creating a luminosity of sound not unlike flutter-tonguing.

Multiphonics

Using certain fingerings, several sounds can be produced simultaneously. Some of these are consonant sounds, although the majority are dissonant with the intervals of a seventh and ninth causing the clashes. *Les Sons multiples aux saxophones* (published by Salabert) by Daniel Kientzy and *Multiphonics* by Ken Dorn contain comprehensive fingering charts, although it is important for composers to collaborate directly with the instrumentalist.

Various techniques

Trumpet sounds: the mouthpiece is removed and the lips, which are placed directly on the crook, vibrate like those of a trumpeter (Christian Lauba, *Les Sept Iles*).

Playing two saxophones simultaneously: this impressive technique was used in the 1980s by Daniel Kientzy. Only the left-hand keys are employed, ideally only on the higher saxophones (Jolas' *Points d'Or*, Savouret's *A flanc de Bozat*).

Ram-tonguing: this very abrupt sound, also employed by flautists, is produced by tonguing strongly into the crook itself (Franco Donatoni's *Hot*, Jean Claude Risset's *Voilements*).

Key noise: a percussive effect obtained by slapping down the pads without blowing, producing a sort of articulation. By slapping the notes (with one or more fingers) from written bb^2 to c^2, the instrument can be resonated at *p* or *pp*, and if the mouthpiece is in the mouth the normal playing pitch can be obtained. Sometimes hitting the keys can give the impression of filtering the sound. The tone is so diminished that only the key noise seems to be left. The 'skeleton' of the sound remains but the texture is lost (Christian Lauba's *Etudes*, Nodaïra's *Arabesque 3*).

The many ways of finishing a note must also be mastered – echoes, whispered sounds, dampened or brutally interrupted notes. Reversed sound (imitating a recorded sound played backwards) is a startling example; played without attack, the sound grows until suddenly stopped by the tongue. The works of Daniel Kientzy (*L'art du saxophone* – Nova Musica CD and booklet) and Jean-Marie Londeix (*Hello! Mr Sax* – Leduc) attempt a comprehensive list of types of attack.

Contemporary saxophone teaching

Despite an unprecedented development of repertoire and technical diversification, teaching of contemporary styles and techniques has not progressed accordingly. There are, however, some works which adopt a progressive approach to techniques. The *Quinze Mosaïques* by Hubert Prati put an emphasis on changes of timbre, micro-intervals and multiphonics, and are clearly notated. In *Aphorismes* (pieces of seventy to eighty seconds), the saxophonist composer Etienne Rolin introduces young players to a variety of styles: jazz, non-European music and electro-acoustic-related techniques. He shows how multiphonics can be adapted for different uses: broken tone, tonal transformations, moving the sound from one register to another, harmonic swoops, polyphonic effects. The *Douze Etudes Complètes pour les Jeunes Saxophonistes du XXIème Siècle* by Nicolas Prost display an interesting approach to time signatures that are unusual at a junior level (⅝, ⅞, ¹²⁄₈), proportional notation, different types of attack, and a thoughtful guide to multiphonics and microtonal trills.

In the United States, Ronald L. Caravan's *Preliminary Exercises and Etudes in Contemporary Techniques for Saxophone (Introductory Material for the Study of Multiphonics, Quarter Tones and Timbre Variation)* (Dorn Publications) is a major educational work. The exercises are straightforward but give a substantial introduction to the techniques. The same author has written a book of relatively simple concert studies entitled *Paradigms I*, which help young saxophonists to become familiar with different techniques including proportional notation and graphic improvisation. These ten short pieces contain references to modal music and blues.

The Bordeaux composer Christian Lauba has produced a major work for Leduc with his *Neuf Etudes,* divided into four books (soprano, alto, tenor and baritone). Each étude builds up to extreme virtuosity in an instrumental parameter: continuous breathing, resonance-free tone, multiphonics, slap-tonguing etc. In an essentially idiomatic language, the work gives great importance to dynamics, timbres, attacks and rhythms. According to the composer 'the noises of keys and breath, simultaneous sounds and subtones reveal a different aspect of the instrument, or rather its true character'.[3] Mention must also be made of the *Douze Etudes*

Fig. 10.4 Extract from *Bat* for baritone saxophone (1996) by Christian Lauba

Modernes by Pierre Max Dubois, *Les Douze Esquisses* of Guy Lacour, *Connexions 1* by Laureau, Lejet, Rolin and Rossé (published by Billaudot); the *Sept Jeux Musicaux* of Jean-Pierre Baraglioli and Yves Queyroux introduce improvisational concepts.

As educational works *per se* are thin on the ground, an educationally structured repertoire is vital.

Rhythmic freedom
Alain Louvier, *Hydre à Cinq Têtes* (second year); Graciane Finzi, *De l'un à l'Autre* (third year); Edith Lejet, *Trois Préludes* (fourth year); Christophe Havel, *Trois Rides sur l'Horizon* (fifth year); Alain Louvier, *Cinq Ephémères* (sixth year).

Microtonal trills and micro-intervals
Edith Lejet, *Trois Préludes* (fourth year); Thérèse Brenet, *Phoinix* (fifth year); Alain Louvier, *Cinq Ephémères* (sixth year).

Multiphonics
Christophe Havel, *Trois Gestes*; Thérèse Brenet, *Phoinix*; Ryo Noda, *Requiem*; Patrick Choquet, *Aires*.

Flutter-tonguing
Marie-Hélène Fournier, *Quatre Duos*; Edith Lejet, *Jade for Alto Saxophone and Percussion*.

Subtone
Marie-Hélène Fournier, *Hemlock*.

Glissandi and portamenti
Marie-Hélène Fournier, *Sétiocétime*; Ryo Noda, *Improvisations*.

Slap-tonguing
José-Luis Campana, *Pezzo Per Claudio*; François Rossé, *Lobuk Constrictor*.

Double-tonguing, growling, singing/playing, harmonics
Javier De La Vega, *Mosaïcos para saxofono contemporaneo*; Serge Bertocchi, *Techniques du Saxophone*.

In his book *Les Etudes contemporaines pour le saxophone et les nouvelles techniques*, Vincent David assesses the study books and educational repertoire that make use of contemporary techniques, as well as analysing in detail the works of Lauba, Grisey, Stockhausen and Berio. There is also a series of eight studies giving an introduction to microtonality by Bruno Mantovani.

Midi wind instruments

RICHARD INGHAM

The treatment of sound externally to the saxophone follows a natural course, beginning with the pure acoustic developments of the instrument – conical tube design, mouthpiece chamber matching and reed choice. Before the advent of amplification, the musician would be concerned with note and tone production as the instrument produced them. When sound amplification is available for those who choose to use it, a new realm of possibilities emerges (although it should be remembered that room acoustics have always been taken into account by musicians as an external influencing factor on the sound as it is perceived by the listener).

From the basic reverberation effect (as used by Charlie Parker with Slim Gaillard in the 1940s, and Earl Bostic in the 1950s), further developments were minimal until the acceptance of electronic sound creation and transformation. In the 1970s, when sound synthesis became generally available, suggesting new timbral concepts, more elaborate treatment devices began to be used in rock, jazz-rock and contemporary classical music – for example delay, ring modulation and pitch shifting (octivider). It was at this point that saxophonists began to experiment with sound transformation, and players such as Andy Mackay, Michael Brecker, Jan Garbarek and Sal Gallina were looking for new textures and timbres.

Eventually, much of this experimentation culminated in the invention of the Lyricon, an electronic instrument which retains the essential fingering system of the saxophone, yet acts as a controller serving a synthesiser unit. The Lyricon was devised and first produced by Bill Bernardi and Roger Noble in the USA in 1974, and operates using a transducer system to convert wind pressure into synthesizer control information. It was used by Tom Scott, Wayne Shorter, Kenny Gee, John Walters and David Roach amongst others. At the same time, Nyle Steiner was developing his Electronic Valve Instrument (EVI), which was later followed by the Electronic Wind Instrument (EWI).

After the initial commercial success of the Yamaha DX7 keyboard synthesizer from 1983, a breath controller was produced as a means of gaining more expressive quality from the synthesizer; the keyboard player holds a note or chord, and by means of breath pressure alters the volume of the sound. Whilst quite rudimentary, the potential of this was not lost on the Yamaha company, who produced their WX7 midi wind controller in 1987 (MIDI = Musical Instrument Digital Interface). At almost exactly the same time, the Akai company, who had taken over Nyle Steiner's operations, released the EWI/EVI as commercial products. Both these instruments, although very different, can be played by saxophonists, and both make use of breath control and woodwind articulation for expressive performance of synthesized sounds. The introduction of midi enabled the performer to use a range of electronic equipment, rather than being limited to, and governed by, one sound source.

The WX7 is a controlling device, which will work in conjunction with any midi receiving module. The instrument transmits on two midi channels, and offers pitch choice through a range of over six octaves based on slightly adapted saxophone/recorder fingering. This is naturally the woodwind equivalent of depressing the keys on a keyboard. The wind and lip sensors, however, convert (via transducers) breath and lip alterations into midi messages, enabling the performer to use typical wind performance techniques with similar responses to acoustic instruments (for example an increase of air gives higher volume; adjustment of lip pressure produces pitch alteration for bends and vibrato). An incidental use of these facilities is that wind and lip control can easily be assigned by midi to operate any parameter – thus air increase may produce pitch change instead of volume change. Control by the tongue is crucial, not only in differentiating between a successful and a tasteless performance, but also in grading the resultant tone colour very finely. The tongue attack (equivalent of 'keyboard velocity') can produce a very subtle opening to a note (or can ruin it) and, like an acoustic instrument, can produce anything from a very light to a very heavy attack, the reasons for which will be dependent on style and context. The stock-in-trade techniques taken for granted by wind players as part of their natural training now become of enormous importance in emphasising the expressive function within electronic performance.

Other features of the WX7 midi wind controller and later models WX11 and WX5 include program change keys, a pitch wheel and a drone facility (whereby one note may be held while a separate line is played simultaneously). The mouthpiece is designed to be similar to saxophone and clarinet mouthpieces, although no sophisticated embouchure is necessary (due to the 'reed' not vibrating acoustically) and options are available to the player when setting the air resistance (whether the player wishes to feel the air passing through the instrument when blowing, as with recorder and flute, or feel resistance in the mouthpiece, as with the clarinet). The wind and lip sensors are set by the individual player to correspond to their particular breath and lip strength and sensitivity.

The EWI is a completely different looking beast to the WX7, but produces a broadly similar result, inasmuch as the two can be interchangeable as controllers. The EWI has been described as a 'chair-leg' design, but the almost deliberate non-chic appearance belies its sophistication. Whereas the WX7 is designed to feel like a saxophone as far as the mouthpiece and fingers are concerned, the EWI has a flattened teat for a mouthpiece, and touch sensors for a fingering system. Vibrato is achieved by squeezing the mouthpiece, which is relatively straightforward for a wind player, but finger control requires delicate co-ordination. The system works very well, once the player has learnt not to touch the sensors unless required – an accidental slight finger movement will trigger a different note (unlike the WX7 which requires key depression). Left-thumb rollers at the back of the instrument operate octave changes, and a glide plate for the right thumb allows portamento. Whereas the WX7 controls a midi tone generator directly, the EWI requires its own sound module, incorporating features such as transposition and chord production. This module can be used in conjunction with any midi receiving device, thus the available sounds are largely the same on both instruments – limited only by the tone generator and creativity of the programmer.

When the instruments were launched in 1987, each company had an outstanding exponent of the instrument to ease over the uncertainty of new technology. Yamaha presented a series of remarkable demonstrations given by Sal Gallina, whose concept of orchestral sound from a synthesizer was matched by his inventive flair. His programmed sounds were largely imitative of orchestral, jazz and rock instruments and sections. By clever use of the drone feature, he was able to create many layers of sound and texture. His finale was a heavy metal guitar feature. It should be noted here that Gallina's impact was possible due to the expressive nature of the wind controller. The enormous range of sensitivity and tonal control available to the wind player could now be used to control synthesized sound in a way not heard before. This was a notable step forward, not just for wind instrument technology, but also for synthesized sound, its use and perception.

Michael Brecker's *Magnetic* album with Steps Ahead (1986) introduced the 'Steiner EWI' on several tracks. This is the instrument which Akai manufactured the following year, and Brecker's version of Ellington's *In a Sentimental Mood* on this album became a classic. The sounds he employed were not extensive in number (they were largely 'created' – non-imitative), but his artistic use of them was as breathtaking as his saxophone playing. He was able to exploit the eight-octave range and new fingering system to point to dramatic new possibilities for the wind player. By controlling the Oberheim Xpander synthesizer via the EWI he could operate filter changes through breath control, giving a very exciting yet subtle shading to his playing. On *Michael Brecker* (his first solo album), released in 1987, he used chordal playing to great effect in *Original Rays*. The following year *Itsbynne Reel* on the album *Don't Try This at Home* was an excellent example of his use of layered voicings, in this case a string/flute sound. Through the work of Gallina and Brecker, saxophonists were able to hear the full range of potential at the highest standard of performance – both the range of imitative sound possibilities with Gallina, and the solo excursions of Brecker.

Initial response to the instruments was varied – some players embraced the new technology and incorporated it into their work, others rushed to invest in the latest thing and wondered what they might do with it; some found themselves unwilling to cross the technology barrier, and others did not see it as any relation to the acoustic instrument at all. One of the initial marketing problems was that the instruments were sold in stores designed to sell keyboards, because of the equipment required, yet those most likely to buy them were woodwind players who needed the long term-expertise and back-up of specialist woodwind suppliers. The instruments did sell in their numbers, however, and despite its youth and the requirement for rethinking, the midi wind controller has already been involved in and been responsible for much genuine artistic creativity.

Concert works were written as early as 1988, including the *Concerto for Electronic Wind Instrument and String Orchestra*, premièred by Frederick Hemke at the 9th World Saxophone Congress in Tokyo/Yokohama. John Sampen was the soloist for *In Two Worlds* by Morton Subotnick, where the soloist moves between wind controller and saxophone; as well as driving sounds, live electronics are controlled by the wind controller via computer during the performance. The 10th World Saxophone Congress in Pesaro, Italy (1992), contained two WX7 recitals, by Bruce Ronkin and Richard Ingham, featuring *Future Echoes from the Ancient* by William Moylan, *Whale* by Terry Davies, *Junctions* by Allan Greenwood and *Still Life* by Richard Ingham. Debra Richtmeyer gave performances of *Proper Behavior* by Steven Everett in the USA and Europe in 1994; this work requires the soloist to play WX7, saxophone and to speak – all the material is combined to produce a very fine example of interactive electronics.

The early concert items, the album session work by Sal Gallina and the solo output by Michael Brecker all demonstrate the breadth of use of this electronic instrument. David Roach, using the Akai EWI and latterly the Yamaha WX11, has inspired several composers at the Royal National Theatre in London to write for the instrument, notably Dominic Muldowney (*The Pied Piper* and *Under Milkwood*) and Paddy Cunneen (*Millennium* and *Perestroika*). Roach was one of the few in the UK to own a Lyricon, and his marvellous programming skills followed him on to the

Fig. 10.5 Debra Richtmeyer with Steven Everett (composer of *Proper Behavior*), Third British Saxophone Congress, 1994

EWI–Oberheim Xpander combination, later adding the WX11 controller–VL1m virtual acoustic tone generator to his list. Each sound he created, along with customised effects, was a demonstration of possibilities, as well as being integral to the drama. Perhaps it is in the theatre that this frightening instrument can best display its potential, with a full range of imitative and created voices. Other theatrical midi events in Britain have included Terry Davies's music for *Whale* at Sheffield Crucible, and his *Kes* at Bolton Octagon.

In summing up the potential and the problems, we return to one of the inventors of the Lyricon, Bill Bernardi:

> A synthesizer's ability to replace or surpass conventional musical instruments as art forms will rely heavily on how well they are able to translate, in natural fashion, the player's expression into sound ... an acoustic instrument is basically a highly sensitive and articulate control system coupled to a human player who is capable of transmitting highly subtle degrees of control into the acoustic sound generating system. The awesome complexity lies with the ability of the instrument to interface and relate to the player.[1]

11 Teaching the saxophone

KYLE HORCH

Saxophone teaching and learning comprise a diverse field. Every student is an individual, as is every teacher; study can be at any level from elementary to conservatoire or university; it can take place in one-to-one or group situations; and of course there are many different musical idioms to explore using the saxophone. It is difficult to imagine a 'complete' guide to teaching and learning the saxophone. However, I shall try to offer at least a personal view of what I consider to be some of the essential factors, common threads running through good teaching and learning at all levels.

Although there are a very few exceptional saxophonists who are truly self-taught, learning usually occurs through a process of interaction between students, teachers and institutions. The goals of this learning process are: the awakening and refining of the latent talent and musical imagination which is there to a greater or lesser extent in all saxophone students; the equipping of the student with the skills, techniques, judgement and experiences to draw upon in giving the imagination a voice, making communicative and accurate performances. These performances may be made by playing from written music, from memory or by ear, in as many of the different styles of music available to saxophonists as possible or desired.

Music is a complicated subject. It has physical, emotional and intellectual components, which all need to be addressed. There is a long continuum of levels of achievement; through the learning process the effort of the student, guided by the teacher possibly in the environment of an institution, is directed towards gradually improving the communicative range and technical standard of their playing. Incremental improvement, focused through realistic goals, is, in my view, a key to successful learning at all levels, from absolute beginner to doctoral candidate. For example, some students may be only moderately committed to music, viewing it as an amateur pastime or as one of many competing interests. While they may not aspire to a professional standard of playing, as long as there is a sense of motivation towards discovery and at least small improvements, their encounter with music and the saxophone is likely to be a positive one. Likewise, I observe that even the finest players continually seek to monitor and improve their playing, and remain curious and open-minded in their attitude to playing long after they have ceased formal study with a teacher. In this sense, the student–teacher relationship is really, for the serious student, a launch-pad for a lifetime of self-motivated learning.

Instrumental learning can take place in groups, particularly in early stages; however, it is usual at some point that, for any student whose interest is beyond the minimum, a one-to-one student–teacher situation will form a substantial part of the learning process. Both student and teacher may be thought of as having clear roles in the learning process. The student's role, first and foremost, is to be interested, curious and motivated to learn at least partly from within themselves. Successful students are willing to do daily practice, take initiative in their work and see the teacher as a guide rather than as a substitute for their own work. It is hoped that their initial interest will spring from an enjoyment of listening to music as much as playing it, and the student will seek to make connections between the two activities as improvements are made. No teacher, no matter how gifted, can play an instrument on behalf of a student. Ultimately, the responsibility for learning lies with the student. Those with an early understanding of this are inevitably the ones who improve the most. The teacher, meanwhile, has a role as an explainer, awakener, sharer, encourager, demonstrator, inspirer and co-explorer. It is up to the teacher to channel the student's talent and motivation through a disciplined and progressive approach, setting sensible yet challenging standards on an individual basis, appropriate for the level of each student.

A good teacher is honest with the student in assessing work, offering praise where deserved, constructive criticism and occasional censure if required. I have seen good teachers of many different personality types; some are outgoing, some are reserved, some informal, some formal and so on. What they all share is a commitment to playing a positive role – whether in a one-off lesson/masterclass or in a long relationship – in using lesson time to help the student's musical personality bloom, passing on their interpretative and technical knowledge to enable the learning player to improve their communication of musical ideas. This provides a basis upon which the student can build in individual practice.

Institutions provide a wider musical environment. An institution which is committed to music provides a community of interest, an atmosphere both of support and healthy competition, and creates opportunities for students to use their skills in group playing. Often, they provide instruction in the academic sides of music – theory, history, composition, arranging – either as a support to instrumental study or, in advanced courses, as ends in themselves. Keyboard study, aural training, study on other woodwind instruments and specialist work on jazz improvisation may be obtainable as well. These are all invaluable opportunities, which, at elementary level, add to the fun of playing (especially group playing) and, as higher levels are reached, enable the student to gain a wide variety of performing/learning experiences aside from solitary practice, and enter into a broader musical world. A single saxophone teacher may not be able to provide all of these experiences in one-to-one lessons, but can and should encourage students to take advantage of as many opportunities to learn as are possible or appropriate.

Overcoming technical difficulties: approaches, examples

During the course of any student–teacher relationship, long or short, the teacher will be faced with problems in the student's playing which must be overcome. The teacher's role is rather like that of a doctor: teachers must correctly diagnose the causes of problems and then take action to correct them. In diagnosing problems, teachers will listen, observe and sometimes ask questions about how the student is carrying out actions. Fixing problems is the task most generally associated with teaching, and it is a complex area requiring thought and sensitivity. With problems in technique, sometimes straightforward explanations of how physical actions should be performed are enough to put students on the right track. At other times, teachers may draw upon a repertoire of analogies and models, verbal or physical, to help the student along. I believe that the use of such models and analogies are of great assistance in teaching. They reduce complicated physical interactions to an easily understandable level and because they simplify complex tasks in students' minds, aid in creating good habits and confidence in playing. And, of course, as the technically adept performer tries to minimise actions and effort, so the adept teacher will seek to find succinct formulae for getting concepts across so students can quickly understand them and succeed in achieving them in reality.

Here are some examples of how I might approach certain general and specific problems.

(1) I use the syllabic method outlined in Chapter 6 to teach and practise reading rhythms, articulations and in creating tone-colour models. I sing or 'say' musical examples a lot in demonstration to my own students, at all levels, and I encourage them to do the same in practice. Even if the pitches of a melody are sung incorrectly, it is an excellent way to solidify musical shapes in the imagination and to get an instinctive sense that playing is a realisation of sounds which begin in our minds (whether the student is intellectually aware of this or not). It also prepares the tongue, in

particular, for the actions it will need to carry out in actual playing. Likewise, in teaching phrasing, singing is of great use, because it models the musical shape without the use of the fingers, which are often a distraction when phrasing is of concern. With young students new to the concept of phrasing, singing words to match the phrases is of assistance in understanding the commonly used analogy between musical phrases and speech.

(2) When helping a beginning pupil form an embouchure and get a first sound, rather than wasting too many words on embouchure and potentially confusing the pupil, I simply demonstrate a model of the embouchure using my index finger in my mouth instead of the mouthpiece; the pupil imitates this, using a mirror if necessary. Then we transfer the 'practice' embouchure to the instrument itself, perhaps using the reed/mouthpiece set-up alone as an intermediate step. It only takes a couple of minutes, yet it gives the student a valuable point of reference and a meaningful, physical paradigm for the shape his or her mouth needs to take.

(3) In starting a vibrato, I return to the embouchure on the finger and ask the student to hold the finger in the 'practice' embouchure while saying the syllables YUYUYUYUYUYUY . . . or WAWAWAWAWAWA . . . thus causing the jaw to undulate slightly. While the tongue is partially involved in saying these syllables in a way in which it will not be in actual playing, as long as the student's attention is focused on the jaw movement, this 'practice' vibrato can quickly be transferred to the mouthpiece/instrument. Again, having a physical paradigm to which to relate the actions involved in vibrato is invaluable in making a fairly easy and painless beginning in this often troublesome technique.

(4) Many students at one time or another face the problem of having a constricted sound caused by an embouchure which is too tight. Even once aware of this problem intellectually, it can be a difficult habit to break. To force the pupil to loosen all excess pressure on the mouthpiece/reed I might ask them to blow plenty of air through the instrument – but without allowing the reed to buzz and create a tone. Once used to this new looseness in the jaw and facial muscles, the tone may be attempted again, usually with better results.

(5) The diaphragm can be a difficult muscle to identify in one's own body. It is worth getting students to recognise its uses in everyday life, or in feeling its movement during laughter. Once identified through such analogous activities, the diaphragm and its function become much more apparent to the saxophone student.

(6) Beginning students tend to think one note at a time, often therefore creating interrupted, distorted or uneven phrases. When trying to teach even breath support across fingering exchanges, particularly in slurs, one effective technique is for the teacher to stand close behind the student and reach around the student's body, working the keys of the saxophone while the student concentrates on blowing consistently. This is particularly useful for breaking the habit of adjusting support as the resistance of the saxophone changes between differing fingerings, for example when moving across the break:

(7) In working towards reducing finger movement away from the keys, it can be useful to put some double-sided tape on the keys. This will not prevent the fingers from leaving the keys, but will certainly make the pupil physically aware of what is happening in a way that simply watching in a mirror (another way of dealing with this problem) may not. When used in conjunction with simple scale-based exercises, slow and fast, a pupil can usually break long-ingrained habits of poor finger and hand position.

(8) Squeaking is a problem which virtually all saxophonists face at least occasionally when learning. It can happen for a number of reasons: poor or incorrectly assembled reed/mouthpiece, instrument problems, embouchure problems, tonguing problems or poor support. Harmonic noises are sometimes mistaken for squeaks and these can also be caused by many of the above reasons as well as by poor fingering co-ordination. Although the teacher will have to observe the playing carefully in order to determine the cause, as an instinctive first response it is often a good idea to suggest that the student takes less of the mouthpiece into the mouth. Or, they might imagine the mouth in the shape of an 'overbite', i.e. tuck the lower teeth/lip back further under the upper teeth, closer to the tip of the reed. This allows the reed to be more under the control of the lip and, if tightness is a problem, forces the player to relax the embouchure to get a sound. Once the immediate squeaking is solved, the student's confidence will return and the underlying problem can be addressed.

By no means do I suggest that the techniques of teaching I have outlined above are the only way of teaching, nor are they particularly original; most are commonly used by many experienced teachers. However, it is worth remembering that these methods are widely used because they are successful – and they are successful because they relate the actions used in playing the saxophone to models that every student can comprehend and relate to without excessive physical or intellectual effort. They are logical and engender confidence by persuading the student that they already know how to accomplish a task. The student is enabled to get a physical 'feel' for the techniques of playing almost immediately, and this is of great value even if a full intellectual understanding comes only much later. This general approach can be used through all educational levels, whether teaching concepts to a young player for the first time, or making fine adjustments to an advanced player's technique. When used in conjunction with clear explanations and an encouraging attitude, the teacher can usually lay a sound technical foundation upon which the student can build.

Issues of broader musicianship

In addition to helping to overcome problems in the mechanics of playing the saxophone, a teacher must also oversee the wider musical development of the pupil. In my view, two issues are of paramount importance. First, it is essential that saxophonists, who have such a diverse repertoire (including standard works, transcriptions, avant-garde contemporary works, light music, jazz, rock and pop; roles ranging from concerto soloist, chamber music, orchestral instrument, big band section, jazz combo, rock group, to name just a few), develop a strong sense of historical and stylistic context. Second, students should gradually be encouraged to take a creative role in music making, eventually finding a personal way of expressing themselves – a possibly unique voice on the instrument. These aims may seem paradoxical. The key from the teacher's point of view is to set parameters and encourage creativity within them.

Taking the first point, in building an understanding of context it is obviously valuable to have a sense of variety in a teaching regime: lessons may include work on long notes, scales and arpeggios, exercises, studies, pieces played by the student, duets, pieces played with piano if the teacher has this skill, and improvisation. Of course, with a beginner, it takes time to work up to all of these things. But in my own teaching, as early as I can, I try to have a beginning student play at least one scale from memory and a mix of solo, duet and accompanied pieces in both classical and popular styles. Time may not permit each bit of material to be examined each lesson, but I try to make an assignment each week of a small body of work which typically includes, at different times, at least some of the following items: some material to be played without music, some material to be played using printed music, some work containing progressively graded technical challenges and some which are pieces for fun or review, some work to be played alone, some to be played together, some pieces the student may already know and some which require them to decipher a new tune. Occasional sight-reading in lessons is a useful discipline.

As a student progresses beyond the beginning stages they may be allowed to set more of the agenda, pursuing interests that they may have, but the teacher should generally try to make sure that students do not close themselves off from any one style of music prematurely. Even at the college level, I find it of value to have a wide range of technical work, studies, repertoire of all types, duets, orchestral excerpts and so on. Of course, different college programmes will place more emphasis on classical music or on jazz/popular music. But even at this level, why not keep encouraging students to develop a multiplicity of skills? Those on classical courses, in my opinion, should be encouraged to develop at least a minimum proficiency in improvisation, and likewise those on jazz courses could benefit from at least a limited encounter with what is now a rich repertoire of concert music for the instrument.[1] Similarly, all advanced student saxophonists should be familiar with all members of the saxophone family and can benefit from some study of other woodwind instruments. All of these experiences aid musical development, offer new perspectives on music and techniques, encourage confidence by discouraging fear of the unknown, and obviously add to the range of skills which can be drawn upon in the working musical world. Within the environment of a school, university or conservatoire, it is usually possible to create the necessary opportunities for these studies if they are not all available within the weekly study with a single saxophone teacher. At any rate, versatility is a key to understanding and appreciating context and idiom and is in my view something that teachers should continually encourage in their students. It is true that eventually most saxophonists seem to specialise in certain broad areas to a greater or lesser extent – but it is to be hoped that this occurs naturally through instinct, being drawn to certain music and by having enough work to choose between, rather than as the result of a limited education.

In working more specifically with interpretation and in trying to develop a sense of personal expression, the Socratic method – that is, teaching by asking questions – is an effective technique. Asking a student what form a piece is in, what mood it has, what characters they are trying to make as it develops, how does the music make them feel – all of these questions require the student to listen to what they are doing, engender a personal involvement with the music and help to crystallise ideas in the student's mind much more clearly than if the teacher simply says, 'this is how it should be done'. Even if the student comes up with what the teacher regards as crazy ideas, it can be the beginning of a dialogue which allows the student a creative input.

Occasional memory playing and improvisation are, again, useful disciplines in getting beyond the concerns of technique and note-reading. In interpretation, as with technique, judicious demonstration by the teacher is often helpful, as is playing together with the student (duets or even on the same melodic line) – for example, to get the feel for rubato over particular phrases. To modify the well-known saying, an aural picture is worth a thousand words. Taking part in larger groups (bands, orchestras, jazz and pop ensembles) is absolutely essential for learning, as well as being fun. This sort of work is a powerful motivating force and reinforces the work being done one-to-one with interpretation and, especially for young students, rhythm. Involvement in a chamber-sized group, such as a saxophone quartet or a small jazz group, is particularly useful, because in rehearsals students learn to converse and collaborate in interpretation rather than always awaiting instruction from teachers and conductors.

Learning needs to be directed towards goals, so that the practice has a purpose which helps the student remain motivated. The goals are performances, which can come in all shapes and sizes and can play a role right through the learning process. For the beginning player, the weekly lesson is in itself a performance of sorts. As time goes on, performance goals of varying degrees of pressure might include playing in band or other ensemble concerts; playing to family; entering for examinations such as the British Associated Board exams or American solo and ensemble 'contest'; taking part in masterclasses or workshops; playing a piece at a school concert; auditioning for youth groups, courses and colleges; or taking part in an international solo competition. All of these goals are appropriate for different students, at different times.

A sensitive teacher will try to guide students individually through a progression of increasingly challenging goals, which the student will enjoy as well as deriving educational benefit. Learning music without these performance goals, no matter how elementary, is rather like learning French but never using the language to converse. Music is a communicative art and the saxophone is a vehicle for this communication; saxophone teachers should never lose sight of this idea amidst all of their technical teaching.

In conclusion, a couple of points can be made. First, the most successful saxophone students are those who want to learn, practise daily, listen to music, and use their imaginations as they address musical and technical challenges. Without these basic elements, even an excellent teacher will fail to make much of an impact. Second, the best teachers I know, the ones most able to inspire and guide these attitudes in their students, are those who lead by example; they are still curious to learn new things, hear new ideas and increase the communicative range in their own playing. Where both the student and teacher are motivated, the learning process can be an immensely rewarding experience, particularly as the saxophone provides such an unusually diverse world to explore together. While the saxophone was once thought of as a 'limited' or 'extra' instrument, during the past century it has developed beyond all recognition, capturing the public imagination and gaining an enviable, perhaps uniquely wide, repertoire. The future of the instrument certainly seems bright. The saxophone is now one of the most popular instruments to learn and qualified teachers are widely available. With the saxophone as a vehicle, the sky is the limit as to what musical results may be achieved.

Notes

1 Invention and development

1 Wally Horwood, *Adolphe Sax 1814–1894 : His Life and Legacy* (Baldock, 1983), p. 20.
2 Quoted in Frederick Hemke, *The Early History of the Saxophone*, Ph.D. diss., University of Wisconsin (1975), p.16.
3 Horwood, *Adolphe Sax*, p. 24.
4 Quoted in Kenneth Deans, 'A Comprehensive Performance Project in Saxophone Literature with an Essay Consisting of Translated Source Readings in the Life and Work of Adolphe Sax', Ph.D. diss., University of Iowa (1980), pp. 92–3.
5 *Ibid.*, p. 96.
6 Horwood, *Adolphe Sax*, pp. 47–8.
7 Unless used within a quotation, all pitches are notated using the conventional Helmholtz system.
8 Malou Haine, *Adolphe Sax (1814–1894): Sa vie, son œuvre, ses instruments de musique* (Brussells, 1980), pp. 179–80.
9 Malou Haine and Ignace De Keyser, 'Les estampilles des instruments Sax', *Brass Bulletin*, 30 (1980), p. 45.
10 Horwood, *Adolphe Sax*, p. 142.
11 *Ibid.*, p. 144.
12 Deans, 'A Comprehensive Performance Project', pp. 141, 171–9.
13 Léon Kochnitzky, *Adolphe Sax and his Saxophone* (New York, 1949; rpt. 1985), pp. 32–3.
14 Nicholas Bessaraboff, *Ancient European Musical Instruments: an Organological Study of the Leslie Lindsey Mason Collection at the Museum of Fine Arts, Boston* (New York, 1941), p. 80, plate III, no. 91.
15 Adam Carse, *Musical Wind Instruments* (London, 1939; rpt. New York, 1965), p. 176.
16 Bessaraboff, *Ancient European Musical Instruments*, plate III, no. 121.
17 Francis G. Rendall, *The Clarinet: Some Notes upon its History and Construction* (New York, 1954), p. 149.
18 Horwood, *Adolphe Sax*, p. 86.
19 Carse, *Musical Wind Instruments*, p. 174.
20 Anthony Baines, *European and American Musical Instruments* (New York, 1966), plate 651.
21 *Ibid.*, plate 655.
22 Carse, *Musical Wind Instruments*, p.180.
23 Hemke, *The Early History of the Saxophone*, pp. 8–9.
24 *Ibid.*, p. 13.
25 *Ibid.*, p. 10.

26 Jean-Marie Londeix, *150 Years of Music for Saxophone* (Cherry Hill, 1994), p. 177.
27 Hemke, *The Early History of the Saxophone*, p. 357.
28 Harry R. Gee, *Saxophone Soloists and their Music, 1844–1985* (Bloomington, 1986), p. 13.
29 Hemke, *The Early History of the Saxophone*, p. 333.
30 Gee, *Saxophone Soloists*, p. 14.
31 Quoted in Hemke, *The Early History of the Saxophone*, pp. 345–6.
32 Quoted in Deans, 'A Comprehensive Performance Project', p. 35.
33 Excellent photographs of original Sax saxophones are found in Ventzke's *Saxophonisches Seit 1842* and in *Die Saxophone* by Ventzke and Raumberger (see the bibliography for full details). An alto saxophone dating from 1867 at the Museum of Music in Paris may be viewed at: http://www.cite-musique.fr/anglais/Le_musee/ Les-collections/2_Ez0_collections.htm.
   A quartet of saxophones (soprano, alto, tenor and baritone) by Sax is to be found at the Shrine to Music Museum in South Dakota and may be viewed at: http://www.usd.edu/smm/cutler6.html.
34 Noted in Hemke, *The Early History of the Saxophone*, pp. 41–2.
35 *Ibid.*, p. 31.
36 Hector, Berlioz, *A Treatise upon Modern Instrumentation and Orchestration* (Paris, 1848), trans. by Mary Cowden Clarke (London, 1958), pp. 233–4.
37 Hemke, *The Early History of the Saxophone*, pp. 258–9.
38 Bruce Ronkin, 'The Music for Saxophone and Piano Published by Adolphe Sax', Ph.D. diss., University of Maryland (1987), pp. 61–2.
39 Hemke, *The Early History of the Saxophone*, p. 72.
40 *Ibid.*, pp. 82–3.
41 *Ibid.*, p. 86.
42 Quoted *ibid.*, pp. 19, 20.
43 Kochnitzky, *Adolphe Sax*, p. 11.
44 Quoted in Deans, 'A Comprehensive Performance Project', p. 95.
45 Quoted in Hemke, *The Early History of the Saxophone*, pp. 35, 36.
46 *Ibid.*, p. 293.
47 *Ibid.*, p. 296.
48 Carse, *Musical Wind Instruments*, pp. 151–2.

49 *Ibid.*, pp. 220, 224.

50 Bruce Ronkin and Robert Frascotti, *The Orchestral Saxophonist,* vols. I and II (Cherry Hill, 1978–84).

51 Leonard Feather, *The Book of Jazz* (New York, 1959), p. 92.

52 Gunther Schuller, *Early Jazz: its Roots and Musical Development* (New York, 1968), p. 243.

53 Hemke, *The Early History of the Saxophone,* p. 373.

54 *Ibid.*, p. 239.

55 *Ibid.*, pp. 395–404.

56. Michael Hester, 'A Study of the Saxophone Soloists Performing with the John Philip Sousa Band: 1893–1930', Ph.D. diss., University of Arizona (1995), p. 21.

57. *Ibid.*, p. 35.

3 Influential soloists

1 The author is aware that no article of this nature can be exhaustive and will date itself immediately upon publication. Apologies are extended to all those performers who ought to have been included and who have been overlooked, or whose hugely important contributions have not been detailed fully due to space restrictions.

2 Wally Horwood, *Adolphe Sax 1814–1894: his Life and Legacy* (Baldock, 1983).

3 An excellent source of further information on the early history of the saxophone, its development, repertory and performers, is Frederick Hemke *The Early History of the Saxophone* Ph.D. dissertation, University of Wisconsin [1975], available from University Microfilms International, Ann Arbor, Michigan. For information on saxophone performers from the time of Adolphe Sax almost to the present day, and the works dedicated to or commissioned by them, there is no better source than Harry R. Gee's *Saxophone Soloists and their Music, 1844–1985* (Bloomington, 1986). This author is greatly indebted to both the above writers. This chapter could not have been produced without their scholarship and dedication.

4 Hemke, *The Early History of the Saxophone,* p. 333.

5 Larry Teal, *The Art of Saxophone Playing* (Evanston, 1963)

6 Sigurd Rascher, *Top Tones for the Saxophone* (New York, 1941 and 1977).

7 Eugene Rousseau, *Marcel Mule: his Life and the Saxophone* (Shell Lake, 1982), p. 30. A fine source for information on Mule and his saxophone classes at the CNSM.

4 The repertory heritage

1 Jean-Marie Londeix, *150 Years of Music for Saxophone* (Cherry Hill, 1994), p. vi.

2 'Clarinet', *New Grove Dictionary of Music and Musicians,* ed. Stanley Sadie (London, 1980).

3 Bruce Ronkin, 'The Music for Saxophone and Piano Published by Adolphe Sax', Ph.D. diss., University of Maryland (1987), pp. 108–9.

4 Harry R. Gee, *Saxophone Soloists and Their Music, 1844–1985* (Bloomington, 1986), p. 21. See Frederick Hemke, *The Early History of the Saxophone,* Ph.D. diss., University of Wisconsin (1975), pp. 429–47, for a more complete discussion.

5 Hans and Rosaleen Moldenhauer, *Anton von Webern: a Chronicle of his Life and Work* (New York, 1979), pp. 422–5.

6 Sigfrid Karg-Elert, *25 Capricen und Sonate* (Frankfurt am Main, 1965), p. 3. Two other composers for the saxophone who became acquainted with the instrument because of military service during World War I were Henry Cowell and Percy Grainger.

7 Eugene Rousseau, unpublished class notes of 10 March 1980.

8 Eugene Rousseau, *Marcel Mule: His Life and the Saxophone* (Shell Lake, 1982), p. 108.

9 Sigurd Rascher, 'A Master Lesson on the Ibert *Concertino da Camera*', *Instrumentalist,* 22 (April 1968), p. 36.

10 Thomas Liley, 'A Teacher's Guide to the Performance of Selected Music for Saxophone', Ph.D. diss., Indiana University (1988). Robert Sibbing, 'An Analytical Study of the Published Sonatas for Saxophone by American Composers', Ph.D. diss., University of Illinois (1969).

11 For example, Ronald Caravan, 'Structural Aspects of Paul Creston's Sonata for Alto Saxophone, Op. 19', *Saxophone Symposium,* 1/3 (Summer 1976), pp. 7–15; idem, 'Bernhard Heiden's Sonata for Saxophone: Some Observations on its Form and Content', *Saxophone Symposium,* 10/4 (Fall 1985), pp. 10–16; Marlene Langosch, 'The Instrumental Chamber Music of Bernhard Heiden', Ph.D. diss., Indiana University (1973).

12 David DeBoor Canfield, 'An Interview with Bernhard Heiden', *Saxophone Symposium,* 10/4 (Fall 1985), pp. 7–9; Cecil Leeson, 'Remembering Paul Creston', *Saxophone Journal,* 10/1 (Summer 1986), pp. 25, 34–9; Rascher, 'A Master Lesson'; idem, 'Alexander Glazounov *Concerto pour Saxophone Alto avec l'orchestre de cordes*', *Saxophone Symposium,* 13/2 (Spring 1988), pp. 16–19; Rascher, 'Ibert's *Concertino da Camera*: Comments and Clarifications', *Saxophone Symposium,* 7/2 (Spring 1982), p. 10; Donald Venturini, *Alexander Glazounov: his Life and Works* (Delphos, 1992), pp. 45–6, 48.

13 Rousseau, *Marcel Mule,* p. 108. But see also

the notes to Londeix's recording Golden Crest RE 7066, which state that Mule gave the first performance of *Scaramouche* on 28 February 1936 and give additional information concerning the version for two pianos.

14 Rousseau, *Marcel Mule*, p. 109.

15 Willi Apel, 'Arrangement', *Harvard Dictionary of Music* (London, 1944 and 1969).

16 Léon Kochnitzky, *Adolphe Sax and his Saxophone* (New York, 1949; rpt. 1985), pp. 16–17.

17 Hemke, *The Early History of the Saxophone*, pp. 392–4.

18 Paul Creston, 'The Saxophone in Concert', *World Saxophone Congress Newsletter* (October 1970), p. 9.

19 Paul Cohen, 'The Saxophone Concerto of Ingolf Dahl: Masterpiece or Compromise?', unpublished performance lecture, 26 June 1985, p. 4.

20 Rousseau, *Marcel Mule*, p. 103.

21 *Ibid.*, p. 105.

22 Eugene Rousseau unpublished class notes, 16 June 1982.

23 Private communication with Karel Husa, 18 March 1982.

24 Lawrence Hartzell, 'Karel Husa: the Man and his Music', *Music Quarterly*, 62 (January 1976), p. 91.

25 Private communication with Karel Husa, 18 March 1982. See also David Ezell, 'Karel Husa's Concerto for Alto Saxophone and Concert Band: its Importance in the Saxophone Repertory', Lecture recital at Ithaca NY College, 1979; Donald McLaurin, 'The Life and Works of Karel Husa: with Emphasis on the Significance of his Contribution to the Wind Band', Ph.D. diss., Florida State University (1985).

26 John Sampen, 'Saxophone Masterworks of Late 20th Century America', *Saxophone Symposium*, 18/3 (Summer 1993), pp. 20–2. The article also contains information about works by Walter Mays, Gunther Schuller, John Anthony Lennon and Donald Martino.

27 Other worthwhile chamber works involving saxophone include those written by Jørgen Bentzon, Marc Eychenne, Walter S. Hartley, Bernhard Heiden, Leon Stein, Henri Tomasi and Heitor Villa-Lobos.

28 Christopher Kelton, 'Meet Eugene Rousseau: Saxophone Performer and Professor', *Instrumentalist*, 38/2 (September 1983), p. 16.

29 Londeix, *150 Years of Music for Saxophone*, p. vii.

5 The saxophone quartet

1 Other contemporary quartets in Britain include the Adelphi, Delta, Ebony, Phoenix, Quartz, Saxology and Saxploitation.

2 Saxophone ensembles, with formation dates where known: Ensemble de Saxofóns de Barcelona (Spain); Mi-Bémol Saxophone Ensemble Osaka, director Masahiro Maeda (Japan, 1984); Sax & Co, big band, director Philippe Geiss (Italy, 1989); Sax Chorus, director Alberto Domizi (Italy, 1990); Saxofon Ensemble Francisco Salime (Italy, 1992); Saxophone Baroque Osaka (Japan, 1996); Saxophone Orchestra, director Federico Mondelci (Italy, 1985); Saxophone Sinfonia, director David Bilger (USA); Saxophon-Projekt Wien, director Oto Vrhovnik (Austria, 1992); World Saxophone Orchestra, director Ed Bogaard (Holland).

Conservatoire and university saxophone ensembles: Bowling Green State University (USA); California State University, Long Beach (USA); Colchester Institute (UK); Ecole Lyonnaise (France); Grand Ensemble de Saxophones du CNM Paris (France); Guildhall School of Music and Drama, London; Royal Northern College of Music, Manchester; University of Colorado (USA).

7 The professional player: the saxophone in the orchestra

1 Jean-Marie Londeix, Bulletins of the Association des Saxophonistes de France nos. 22 and 24 (April 1983 and April 1984).

2 H. Berlioz, 'Instruments de musique de Monsieur Sax', *Journal des débats*, 12 June 1842: 'I do not know any instrument actually in use … which may be compared to it [the saxophone]. It is full, mellow, resonant, tremendously powerful but capable of sweetness … composers will owe much to Monsieur Sax, when his instruments are in general use …'. Earlier in the same article, Berlioz had written: 'Monsieur Sax's new bass clarinet retains nothing of the old but its name'. This is the instrument which is used today, with modern refinements. It caught on more quickly than did the saxophone at the outset, perhaps because it was an improved instrument rather than a complete novelty.

3 Adolphe Sax, letter to Ambroise Thomas, 30 July 1883, French National Archives, quoted in Malou Haine, *Adolphe Sax, sa vie, son œuvre, ses instruments de musique* (Brussels, 1980).

4 Wally Horwood, *Adolphe Sax 1814–1894: his Life and Legacy* (Baldock, 1983).

5 Norman del Mar, *Richard Strauss: a Critical Commentary on his Life and Work* (London, 1963), I, p. 183n.

6 Horwood, *Adolphe Sax*, p. 181.

7 *Ibid.*

8 Eric Blom, 'Gershwin', *Grove*, 5th edn (London, 1954), III, p. 607.

9 Norman del Mar, *Anatomy of the Orchestra* (London, 1981), p. 206.

8 Jazz and the saxophone
1 Bechet is also credited with one of the few recorded sarrusophone solos (*Mandy, Make Up your Mind*, with Clarence Williams's Blue Five in 1924). The sarrusophone was a brass instrument of conical bore, played with a double reed.

The Swiss conductor Ernest Ansermet said on hearing Bechet in 1919: 'an extraordinary clarinet virtuoso . . . an artist of genius'. This coincides with much jazz-influenced clarinet writing in classical music at exactly that time.
2 Joachim Berendt, *The Jazz Book* (Frankfurt, 1953–89; rev. G. Huesmann, 1992), p. 242.
3 *Ibid.*, p. 84.
4 Orrin Keepnews and Bill Grauer, Jr., *A Pictorial History of Jazz* (New York, 1955 and 1966), pp. 36 and 37.
5 Circular breathing is a skill known to many folk musicians throughout the world, and is a method of producing a continuous flow of air without any apparent pause for breathing. The player uses a small amount of stored air from the cheeks to maintain the flow whilst replenishing the supply through the nose. Multi-instrumentalist Roland Kirk (1936–77) made great use of the technique.
6 Parker attempted a solo line that was beyond him and was given an appropriate reception from the rest of the band he was sitting in with. He disappeared for weeks in order to work on his technique.
7 Ninths, elevenths and thirteenths.
8 Use of substitute chords based on the cycle of keys.
9  in swing rhythm (sounding 'ten ten-to ten ten-to . . .').
10 Lines derived from short 'formula' phrases or 'licks', which are skilfully integrated into the flowing melodic material.
11 Offbeat tonguing, for example,

12 Quoted in D. Baker, *Charlie Parker, Alto Saxophone* (New York, 1978), p. 9.
13 Corporeal: a stated rhythm; spiritual: an implied rhythm, felt but not heard as a pulse (see W. Mellers, *Music in a New Found Land* [London, 1964], p. 347, and *Caliban Reborn* [London, 1967]).
14 Playing more than one note simultaneously, by using non-standard fingerings which

produce a false fundamental and simultaneous partials above.
15 Coltrane made great use of Nicholas Slonimsky's book *Thesaurus of Scales and Melodic Patterns* (New York, 1947) in his practising. The book shows how almost limitless atonal lines and octave divisions may be generated.
16 Liner notes to 'Another Time, Another Place' (Phil Woods and Benny Carter), quoted in the record review, *Saxophone Journal*, 21/5 (March/April 1997), pp. 74–5.

9 Rock and the saxophone
1 Sting, *Bring on the Night* (A & M Films, 1985).

10 The saxophone today: the contemporary saxophone
1 Quoted by F. Broman in the CD booklet accompanying Claude Delangle's 'Solitary Saxophone', CD B15 (1994).
2 Rascher's work on this was highly influential (*Top Tones for the Saxophone* [New York, 1941]) although there were many other saxophonists both before him (Gustav Bumcke, *Saxophone Schule* [Berlin, 1926]) and after him (Rosemary Lang, *Altissimo Register* [1971]; Jean-Marie Londeix, *Fingering Chart* [Paris, 1974]; Eugene Rousseau, *Saxophone High Tones* [Shell Lake, 1978]; Pedro Iturralde, *Los Armonicos En El Saxofon* [Madrid, 1987] and Francis Cournet, *Le Thésaurus du Saxophoniste*, vol. II [Paris, 1992]) who have contributed to the development of this technique.
3 Jean-Marie Londeix and Claude Delangle, interview with Christian Lamba, *Cahier du saxophone n° 1 / Association des Saxophonistes* (Paris, 1996).

10 Midi wind instruments
1 Quoted in John Walters, 'A History of Wind Synthesizers', *Sound on Sound*, 2/11 (September 1987), p. 36.

11 Teaching the saxophone
1 The importance of improvisation studies is to be found not only in the development of skills for those choosing the route of jazz and popular music, but in the broadening of listening skills and interpretation options for musicians working within a classical context. Free, intuitive improvisation, as in free jazz or in *From the Seven Days* by Stockhausen, is a very valuable experience, aspects of which can be introduced at any level. For pure development of analytical improvising skills, however, restricting tuition to accepted jazz and popular styles is recommended as an introduction.

Improvising on pentatonic blues scales, using simple note cells over a static harmony and then over a blues progression, and in question and answer format within a group, can be very effective and endlessly variable. The pentatonic scale leads neatly to the Dorian scale which, when combined with the Mixolydian and major scales, forms the basis of the II–V–I harmonic progression, of fundamental importance in jazz structures. This stage of development can be achieved quite quickly by a responsive student, and provides access to the skill of improvising on standard thirty-two-bar chord progressions. Beyond this, a lifetime's study beckons for the specialist, but the beauty of basic improvisation studies is a quite clear expansion of musical listening and response, along with a creative confidence which may be utilised in any idiom.

Appendices

Appendix 1 Works attributed to Elise Hall's patronage

Caplet, André	*Impression d'automne*	*c.* 1905
	Légende	1903
Combelle, François	*Fantaisie Mauresque*	1920
Debussy, Claude	*Rhapsodie*	1903
Dupin, Paul	*Chant pour saxophone*	1910
Gaubert, Philippe	*Poème Elégiaque*	1911
Gilson, Paul	*Premier Concerto*	1902
Grovlez, Gabriel	*Suite*	1915
Huré, Jean	*Andante*	1915
	Concertstück	after 1915
Indy, Vincent d'	*Choral Varié*	1903
Loeffler, Charles M.	*Ballade Carnavalesque*	1903
	Divertissement Espagnol	1900
	Rhapsodie	—
Longy, Georges	*Impression (Pièce)*	1902
	Rhapsodie (Lento)	1904
Moreau, Léon	*Pastorale*	—
Mouquet, Jules	*Rhapsodie*, Op. 26	1907
Schmitt, Florent	*Légende*, Op. 66	1918
Sporck, Georges	*Légende*	1905
Woollett, Henry	*Octuor No. 1*	1909
	Siberia, Poème Symphonique	1909–10

This list was kindly provided by William H. Street of the University of Alberta, Edmonton, and is extracted from his thesis: 'Elise Boyer Hall, America's First Female Concert Saxophonist: Her Life as Performing Artist, Pioneer of Concert Repertory for Saxophone and Patroness of the Arts', Ph.D. diss., Northwestern University (1983).

Appendix 2 Contemporary repertoire

Composer	Title	Instrumentation	Publisher
Adams, John	*Postmark*	Ssx Pno	
Adler, S.	*Pensive Soliloquy*	Asx Pno	
Albright, William	*Pit Band*	Asx Pno ClBas	Schirmer
	Rustles of Spring	Asx Pno Fl Vln Vlc	
	Sonate	Asx Pno	Peters
	Postcard from Kansas	Asx Pno	
Amy, Gilbert	*Le temps du souffle*	Vl Asx/Tsx Tbn	Amphion
Babbitt, Milton	*Images*	3 Sx (Asx Ssx Snosx) Tape	
	Whirled Series	Asx Pno	Peters
	Recitative	Ssx Pno	
Bassett, L.	*Duo Concertante*	Asx Pno	Peters
	Music	Asx Pno	Peters
Bedford, David	*Backings*	Ssx and Tape	
Berio, Luciano	*Recit (Chemin VII)*	Asx Orch	Universal
	Sequenza IXb	Asx	Universal
	Sequenza VIIb	Ssx	Universal
Birtwistle, H.	*Panic*	Asx/Perc. solo & Orch (3.3.2. Bcl.4.4.3.1.perc.)	Boosey & Hawkes
Cage, John	*Four*⁵	Saxophone ensemble (4 parts)	Peters
Campana, J. L.	*Du Sonore*	Asx Perc	Lemoine
	Acting In	Asx Tsx	Salabert
	Pezzo Per Claudio	Asx	Lemoine
Caravan, Ronald L.	*Paradigms I*	Asx	Dorn
Carpenter, Gary	*Sonata*	Asx Pno	Camden
Carter, Elliott	*Canon for 3*	3 Sx	Amp
	Canonic Suite	4 Altos	A.m.b.
Cavanna, Bernard	*Goutte d'or blues*	Ssx (+Sino) Tape	Salabert
Charpentier, Jacques	*Gavambodi 2*	Asx Pno	Leduc
Chen, Qigang	*Feu d'ombres*	Ssx Orch 1111 2220 Perc Harp Bass	Billaudot
Cholerton, Andy	*Sonata*	Tsx Pno	
Constant, Marius	*Concertante*	Asx Orch	Ricordi
Cooper, David	*In Luminae Sapientiae*	Bsx Pno	
	Solipsism	Bsx	

Composer	Title	Instrumentation	Publisher
Davis, Tony	*Lament Habanera*	Ssx/Asx/Tsx and Tape	Ard
	Sonata	Tsx Pno	Ard
De Pablo, Luis	*1 Couleur*	6 Sx (Snosx Ssx Tsx Bsx Bssx Cbssx) Orch 3222 443 Harp Timp Perc Pno Cel Str	Zerboni
	Oculto	Bsx or Asx	Ricordi
Decoust, Michel	*Olos*	Tsx, Dea	Salabert
Del Rosario, Conrado	*Ringkaran I for Alto Saxophone*	Asx	Apoll edition
Denisov, Edison	*Concerto*	Asx Orch	Sikorski
	Sonate	Asx Cello	Billaudot
	Quintette	Ssx Asx Tsx Bsx Pno	Leduc
	Deux pièces	Asx Pno	Leduc
	Sonate	Asx Pno	Leduc
Donatoni, Franco	*Hot*	Snosx Tsx ClBas Cl Tpt Trb Perc Bass Pno	Ricordi
	Rasch 2	Sax quartet Perc Pno	Ricordi
Eisma, Will	*Non-lecture II*	Asx	Donemus
Endrich, Tom Archer	*Nomad*	Asx	
Finzi, Graciane	*De l'un à l'autre (initiation)*	Asx Pno	Leduc
	Cinq Séquences	Ssx Asx Tsx Bsx	Billaudot
Fournier, M. H.	*Oxydes*	2 Asx	Lemoine
	Regard sur l'île d'alcine (initiation)	Asx Perc	Lemoine
	Horoscope (initiation)	Asx	Combre
Francesconi, Luca	*Plot II*	Ens Ac Asx	Ricordi
Giner, Bruno	*Yod*	Bsx	Durand
Glass, Philip	*Aus Schmerz und Trauer*	Asx	Breitkopf
Gregory, Will	*Interference*	Ssx and Tape	
Harbison, John	*San Antonio*	Asx Pno	
Hurel, Philippe	*Opcit*	Tsx	Billaudot
	Bacasax	Asx Pno	Billaudot
Husa, Karel	*Two Moravian Songs*	Asx Pno	

Composer	Title	Instrumentation	Publisher
Jarrell, M.	*Resurgences*	Asx/Ssx Fl Cl Cor Trbn Pno Perc Vcl Cbs	Lemoine
Jolas, Betsy	*2ème Concerto*		
	Points d'Or	4 Sx (Ssx Asx Tsx Bsx) Orch	Ricordi
	Musique pour Xavier	Cl Tsx Vl	Billaudot
	Plupart du temps II	Tsx Tvoice Vlc	Leduc
	Episode 4e	Tsx	Leduc
Kagel, Mauricio	*Zwei Akte*	Sx, Harp	
	Atem	Asx	Universal
	Tanz-Schul	Tsx/Orch	Peters
Keuris, Tristan	*3 Novelettes*	Asx Orch	Novello
Kitazume, Michio	*Air*	Asx Pno	Lemoine
Kolb, Barbara	*Related Characters*	Asx Pno	Boosey & Hawkes
Kyburz, Hanspeter	*Cells*	Satb Orch (16)	Bote and Bock
Landini, Carlo Alessandro	*Incantation*	Asx	Leduc
Lauba, Christian	*Adria*	2 Asx	Fuzeau
	Hard	Tsx	Fuzeau
	Reflets	Ssx Asx Tsx Bsx	Fuzeau
	Chott II	Ssx	Fuzeau
	Steady Study On The Boogie	Sx solo	Billaudot
	Neuf études	Asx	Leduc
Lefanu, Nicola	*Ervallagh*	Asx	
Leibowitz, René	*Variations pour Quatuor de Saxophones*	Ssx Asx Tsx Bsx	Jobert
Lejet, Edith	*Cérémonie*	4 to 50 Sx	Lemoine
	Trois petits préludes	Asx Pno	Lemoine
	Aube Marine	Ssx Asx Tsx Bsx	Lemoine
	Jade	Asx Perc	Salabert
Lenners, Claude	*Monotaurus*	Asx	Lemoine
Lennon, John-Anthony	*Distances Within Me*	Asx Pno	Dorn
Leroux, Philippe	*Phonie douce*	Asx Ob Vlc	Billaudot
Liebman, David	*South Africa*	Ssx Vla	Liebstone Mus.
Lindberg, Magnus	*Linea d'ombra*	Fl Asx Guitar Perc	Hansen
Louvier, Alain	*Cinq portraits et une image*	Cl Ob Asx Bsn	Leduc
	Le jeu des 7 musiques	Ssx Asx Tsx Bsx	Leduc
	Cinq éphémères	Ssx Pno	Leduc

Composer	Title	Instrumentation	Publisher
	Hydre à 5 têtes	Asx Pno	Leduc
Mabry, Drake	*Ceremony I*	Ssx	Lemoine
Mache, François-Bernard	*Aulodie*	Asx Tape	Durand
Marbe, Myriam	*Concerto*	3 Sx (Bsx Asx Snosx) Orch	Editura Musicala
Martin, Frédérick	*Deux titres*	4 Sx (Asx Tsx Ssx Snosx)	Billaudot
Matsushita, Isao	*Atoll II*	Asx Pno	Ongaku No Tomo
Méfano, Paul	*Périples*	Asx	Salabert
	Tige	Asx au choix	Salabert

Merilainen, Usko	*Sonate*	Asx Pno	M (Centre de
			  Musique
			  Finlandaise)

Michat, J. D.	*Plume...*	Sx Pno	Lemoine
Miereanu, Costin	*Do Mi Si La Do Re*	Asx Tape	Salabert
	Variants–Invariants	Asx DEA	Salabert
	Aksax	Bsx	Salabert
	Ondes	Asx	Salabert
Morgan, Nigel	*Fragments*	Ssx Pno	
Morland, Stephen	*Parallels*	Tsx Pno	Broadbent and Dunn
	Recitatives	Solo ssx	Broadbent and Dunn
Morricone, Ennio	*Blitz*	Ssx, Asx, Tsx, Bsx	Suivini Zerboni
Muldowney, D.	*In a Hall of Mirrors*	Asx Pno	Universal

Niculescu, Stefan	*Cantos 3e*
	  Symphonie
	  Concertante
		4 Sx (Snosx Asx Tsx
		  Bsx) Orch 3433
		  Tub 3Perc Str
			Editura Musicala

	Chant-Son	2 sx (Asx Ssx)	Salabert

Nikiprowetsky, Tolia	*Tetraktys*	4 Sx (Ssx Asx Tsx
		  Bsx) 2Perc
		  Pno Str
			Jobert

Nilsson, Ivo	*Passad*	Ssx, Trb	
Nobuhara, Masao	*Obsession*	Asx Pno	
Noda, Ryo	*Murasaka No* *Fuchi 1*	2 Asx	Leduc
	Improvisation *1, 2, 3*	Asx	Leduc
	Mai	Asx	Leduc
	Phoenix	Asx	Leduc
	Pulse 72	Asx	Leduc
Nodaira, Ichiro	*Arabesque No. 3*	Asx Pno	Lemoine
	Quatuor	Ssx Asx Tsx Bsx	Lemoine
Oliveros, Pauline	*Mirrorim*	Ssx Pno	

Composer	Title	Instrumentation	Publisher
Pousseur, Henri	*Caprices de saxicare*	Asx Orch Perc	Suvini Zerboni
	Vue sur les jardins interdits	Ssx Asx Tsx Bsx	Suvini Zerboni
Raskatov, Alexandre	*Pas de deux*	1 Sx (Ssx/Tsx) Voice	
Redgate, Roger	*Graffiti*	Ssx	Lemoine
Reich, Steve	*Vermont Counterpoint*	Ssx Asx Tsx Bsx	Boosey & Hawkes
Rice, Hugh Collins	*St Godric's Dance*	Tsx Pno	
Ricker, Ramon	*Jazz Sonata*	Ssx or Tsx Pno	Advance Music
Riemer, Franz	*Reigen*	Asx Pno	Ries und Erler
Risset, J. C.	*Saxatile*	Tsx Tape	
	Voilements	Tsx Tape	Salabert
Robert, Lucie	*Cadenza*	Asx Pno	
Robinson, Martin	*Inter-Meta*	Asx & Tape	
Rogers, Rodney	*Lessons of the Sky*	Asx Pno	
Rolin, Etienne	*Tandems*	2 to 5 Sx	Lemoine
	Aphorismes VII	Asx	Lemoine
	Tréssage	Ssx Pno	Lemoine
Rossé, François	*Anchée*	Ob Cl Sx Bsn	
	Lombric	Asx Sx Pno	Lemoine
	Triangle pour un souffle	Asx 12 Strings	Billaudot
	Le Frêne Egaré	Asx	Billaudot
	Lobuk Constrictor	Asx	Billaudot
	La Main dans le souffle	Asx Pno	Billaudot
Rotaru, Doina	*Concerto*	Sx (SAB) Orch	
	Legend II	Ssx	
Salonen, Esa-Peka	*Concerto*	Asx Orch	Hansen
Sandroff, Howard	*Eulogy*	Asx	Lemoine
Sandstrom, S. D.	*Moments Musicaux*	Ssx Asx Tsx Bsx	Hansen
Scelsi, Giacinto	*3 Pezzi*	Ssx or Tsx	Salabert
	Ixor	Ssx	Salabert
	Maknongan	Bssx	Salabert
Schuller, Gunther	*Concerto*	Asx Orch	
Shrude, Marilyn	*Concerto*	Asx & Harp	
	Renewing the Myth	Asx & Pno	Am. Comp. All.
	Postscript	Asx Pno	
Solal, Martial	*Pièce de collection*	Asx	Misterioso
Souster, Tim	*Zorna*	Ssx Live Electronics 3 Perc	OdB
Steadman, Robert	*Puddle Jumping*	Tsx	Vanderbeek and Imrie
	When the Seagulls Follow the Trawler...	Tsx	Vanderbeek and Imrie

Composer	Title	Instrumentation	Publisher
Stewart, Ian	*Panaiya Point*	Ssx Vlc Pno	
	Who Would You Like to be Stranded on Es Vedra With?	Ssx & Tape	
Stockhausen, Karlheinz	*Knabenduett*	2 Ssx	Stockhausen
	Linker Augentanz	8 Sx Synth Perc	Stockhausen
	In Freundschaft	Asx	Stockhausen
	Tierkreis	Ssx Pno	Stockhausen (Salvi)
Takemitsu, Toru	*Distance*	Ssx (Ob) (and Sho)	Salabert
Tann, Hilary	*Windhover*	Ssx	OUP
Tisne, A.	*Espaces irradiés*	Asx Pno	Choudens
	Music for Stonehenge	Asx Pno	Choudens
	Alliages	Ssx Asx Tsx Bsx	Billaudot
Ton That, Tiet	*Moments Rituels*	Tsx Synth Perc Tape DX7	Jobert
	Moments Rituels II	12 Sx	Jobert
Torke, Michael	*Concerto*	Ssx Ch11cor A20–4OO11–perc 2vib2mar	Boosey & Hawkes
Tower, Joan	*Wings*	Solo Sx	Amp
Turnage, M. A.	*Concerto*	Sx Orch (Pno)	Schott
	Two Elegies Framing a Shout	Ssx Pno	Schott
Vieru, Anatol	*Metaksax*	Asx Suiveur d'enveloppe	Salabert
Villa, Rojo	*Eclipse*	Asx	Emec
Vivier, Claude	*Pulau Dewata*	Satb	
Wildberger, Jacques	*Prismes*	Asx	Gerig
	Portrait	Asx	Universal
Wilson, Ian	*Drive*	Ssx Pno	Camden
Wood, Nigel	*Cries of the Stentor*	Ssx Pno	Saxtet
Xenakis, Iannis	*XAS*	Ssx Asx Tsx Bsx	Salabert
Yuasa, Joji	*Not I but the Wind*	Asx Tape	Pronova/Sonoton
Zbar, Michel	*Cinq clairs-obscurs*	Asx	Misterioso

The above listing was made possible thanks to the research work of Claude Delangle and Jean-Denis Michat.

Appendix 3 Midi repertoire

Apfelstadt, Marc	*Industrial Orient* (WX7)
	Duo (two wind controllers)
Ball, Leonard V.	*and they spoke of things transfigured* (WX11)
Bauer, John	*Colors-O'Keefe* (wind controller and sequencer)
Beck, Stephen David	*Love's not Time's Fool* (WX7 and computer)
Beerman, Burton	*Fragments* (wind controller and delay)
Birkby, Peter	*Dance Suite* (WX7 and DX7)
Bizet, Georges	*Suite from Carmen,* arr. Ronkin (wind controller and piano)
Chapman, Nigel	*Dance Steps* (WX7 and DX7)
	Façade (WX7 and DX7)
Cooper, David	*Metamorphosis* (WX7)
Cox, Michael	*Improvisation Matrices I–VII* (wind controller and drums)
Davies, Terry	*Whale* (WX7 and DX7)
Durant, Douglas	*Skelter Memory* (wind controller)
Ehle, Robert	*Sonata* (wind controller and computer)
Endrich, Tom Archer	*Dewdrop* (WX7, DX7 and computer)
Everett, Steven	*Proper Behavior* (WX7 / alto saxophone / voice with interactive electronics)
Fish, Greg	*The Hammer and the Arrow* (wind controller and computer)
Freund, Donald	*Not Gentle* (wind controller and computer)
Greenwood, Allan	*Junctions (Waking in the Blue)* (WX7 and delay)
Hertzog, Christian	*Angry Candy* (wind controller)
Ingham, Richard	*Hopper 1,2,3* (WX7 and delay)
	Still Life (WX7 and delay)
	Rothko Soundings (WX7 and delay, DX7, computer)
Karpman, Laura	*Song Pictures* (WX7 and voice)
Kefala-Kerr, John	*Comics* (WX7)
Lennon, John and McCartney, Paul	*Yesterday* arr. Ronkin (wind controller and piano)
Leroux, Phillipe	*Image à Rameau* (WX11 controlling four SY99 synthesizers)
Mahin, Bruce	*Synapse* (wind controller and computer)
Mondelci, Federico	*Pan* (midi saxophone and tape)
Monnet, Marc	*L'Exercise de la bataille* (Two WX11s with chamber ensemble)
Moylan, William	*Future Echoes from the Ancient* (wind controller and piano)
Nelson, Gary Lee	*Refractions* (4 WX7s)
	Interactive works for Midihorn and computer
Ronkin, Bruce	*Transient States* (wind controller and piano)
	Twelve Moods: A Musical Setting of the Langston Hughes

	Poem 'Ask Your Mama – 12 Moods for Jazz' (two narrators, wind controller and brass and rhythm chamber ensemble)
Ruggiero, Charles	*Interplay* (WX7 and tape)
Sandroff, Howard	*Concerto for Electronic Wind Instrument and String Orchestra*
Shrude, Marylin	*Drifting over a Red Place* (WX7)
Smith, Howie	*A First Time for Everything* (4 wind controllers)
Steadman, Robert	*Whalesong* (WX7 and Concert Band)
Strauss, Richard	*Klavierstucke*, Op. 3, arr. Ronkin (wind controller and piano)
Subotnick, Morton	*In Two Worlds* (WX7 / alto saxophone and orchestra)
Trythall, Gil	*Rima's Song* (wind controller and computer)
Wyatt, Scott	*Vignettes* (wind controller and tape)
Young, Charles	*October in the Rain* (wind controller, horn, piano, synthesizer and percussion)

The above listing of works for midi wind controller was made possible thanks to the research work of Bruce Ronkin, Claude Delangle and Jean-Denis Michat.

Bibliography

Baines, A., *European and American Musical Instruments* (New York, 1966)
    Woodwind Instruments and their History (London, 1967)

Baker, D., *Jazz Monographs: Charlie Parker, Alto Saxophone* (New York, 1978)
    The Jazz Style of John Coltrane (Lebanon, 1980)
    The Jazz Style of Sonny Rollins (Hialeah, 1980)

Baker's Biographical Dictionary of Musicians, rev. Nicola Slonimsky (New York, 1992)

Berendt, J. E., *The Jazz Book* (Frankfurt, 1953–89; rev. edn 1992)

Bessaraboff, N., *Ancient European Musical Instruments: An Organological Study of the Leslie Lindsey Mason Collection at the Museum of Fine Arts, Boston* (New York, 1941)

Brown, J. R., *Pure David Sanborn* (Woodford Green, 1988)

Butler, H., *Cannonball Adderley – 20 Solos* (New York, 1990)

Caravan, R. L., *Preliminary Exercises and Etudes in Contemporary Techniques for Saxophone (Introductory Material for the Study of Multiphonics, Quarter Tones and Timbre Variation)* (Medfield, 1991)

Carr, I., D. Fairweather, and B. Priestley, *Jazz: The Rough Guide* (London, 1995)

Carse, A., *Musical Wind Instruments* (rpt., New York, 1965)

Clark, A., 'Rock 'N Roll Saxophone', *Saxophone Journal*, 20/3 (November/December 1995), pp. 57–62, 80

Coan, C., *Michael Brecker, Artist Transcriptions* (Milwaukee, 1995)

Cole, B., *John Coltrane* (New York, 1976)

Collier, G., *Jazz* (Cambridge, 1975)

Cournet, F., *Le Thésaurus du Saxophoniste* (Paris)

David, V., *Les Etudes Contemporaines pour le Saxophone et les Nouvelles Techniques* (unpublished, reference material in Conservatoire Médiathèque, CNSM, Paris)

Dawson, J., *Music for Saxophone by British Composers: An Annotated Bibliography* (Medfield, 1981)

Deans, K., 'A Comprehensive Performance Project in Saxophone Literature with an Essay Consisting of Translated Source Readings in the Life and Work of Adolphe Sax', Ph.D. diss., University of Iowa (1980)

Dorn, K., *Multiphonics* (Medfield)

Ellington, E. K., *Music is my Mistress* (London, 1974)

Feather, L., *The Book of Jazz* (New York, 1959)

Ferron, E., *Ma voix et un Saxophone* (Paris, 1996)

Gallina, S., *Expressive FM Applications* (New York, 1987)

Gallina, S., and N. Steiner, 'The Power of Wind' (interview with Nick Armington and Lars Lofas), *Music Technology*, 2/2 (December 1987)

Gee, H., *Saxophone Soloists and their Music, 1844–1985* (Bloomington, 1986)

Gelly, D., *Lester Young* (Tunbridge Wells, 1984)

Grigson, L., *A Charlie Parker Study Album* (London, 1989)

Haine, M., *Adolphe Sax (1814–1894): Sa vie, son œuvre et ses instruments de musique*
    (Brussels, 1980)
Harvey, P., *Saxophone* (London, 1995)
Hatch, D., and S. Millward, *From Blues to Rock* (Manchester, 1987)
Hemke, F. L., *The Early History of the Saxophone*, Ph.D. diss., University of
    Wisconsin (1975)
Hester, M., 'A Study of the Saxophone Soloists Performing with the John Philip
    Sousa Band: 1893–1930', Ph.D. diss., University of Arizona (1995)
Horricks, R., *Gerry Mulligan* (London, 1986)
Horwood, W., *Adolphe Sax 1814–1894: his Life and Legacy* (Baldock, 1983)
Keepnews, O., and B. Grauer Jr., *A Pictorial History of Jazz* (New York, 1955 and
    1966)
Kernfeld, B. (ed.), *New Grove Dictionary of Jazz* (London, 1988)
Kientzy, D., *Les Sons Multiples aux Saxophones* (Paris, 1982)
Kochnitzky, L., *Adolphe Sax and his Saxophone* (New York, 1949; rpt. 1985)
Kool, J., *Das Saxophon*, trans. L. Gwozdz (Baldock, 1987)
Kynaston, T., *Phil Woods Improvised Saxophone Solos* (Lebanon, 1981)
Liley, T., 'A Teacher's Guide to the Interpretation of Selected Music for Saxophone'
    Ph.D. diss., Indiana University (1988)
Londeix, J.-M., *150 Years of Music for Saxophone* (Cherry Hill, 1994)
    Hello! Mr Sax (Paris, 1989)
    Méthode pour Etudier le Saxophone (Paris, 1997)
Lyricon Owner's Manual (Elkhart, 1987)
Mellers, W., *Caliban Reborn* (London, 1967)
    Music in a New Found Land (London, 1964)
Miedema, H., *Jazz Styles and Analysis* (Chicago, 1975)
Nash, E., *High Harmonics* (New York, 1946)
Parker, C., *Charlie Parker Omnibook*, transcr. J. Aebersold and K. Slone (New York,
    1978)
Pepper, A. and L., *Straight Life* (New York, 1979)
Perrin, Marcel, *Le Saxophone* (Paris, 1955)
Price, T., *Hot Rock Sax* (Milwaukee, 1995)
Priestley, D., *John Coltrane* (London, 1987)
Rascher, S. M., *Top Tones for the Saxophone* (New York, 1941 and 1977)
Rees, R., and L. Crampton, *Guinness Book of Rock Stars* (London, 1989 and 1991)
Reisner, R. G., *Bird: the Legend of Charlie Parker* (London, 1974)
Rendall, F. G., *The Clarinet: Some Notes upon its History and Construction* (New
    York, 1954)
Ronkin, B., 'The Music for Saxophone and Piano Published by Adolphe Sax', Ph.D.
    diss., University of Maryland (1987)
    'Revisiting the Lyricon', *Saxophone Journal*, 18/6 (May/June 1994), p. 66
Ronkin, B., and R. Frascotti, *The Orchestral Saxophonist*, Volumes 1 and 2 (Cherry
    Hill, 1978)
Rousseau, E., *Marcel Mule: his Life and the Saxophone* (Shell Lake, 1982)
    Saxophone High Tones (Shell Lake, 1978)
Russell, R., *Bird Lives* (London, 1973)

Sadie, S. (ed.), *New Grove Dictionary of Music and Musicians* (London, 1980)

Saxophone Journal (Medfield)

Schleuter, S.L., *Saxophone Recital Music: A Discography* (Westport, 1993)

Schuller, G., *Early Jazz: its Roots and Musical Development* (New York, 1968)

Sibbing, R., 'An Analytical Study of the Published Sonatas for Saxophone by American Composers', Ph.D. diss., University of Illinois (1969)

Sickler, D., and B. Porcelli, *The Artistry of John Coltrane* (New York, 1978)

Simpkins, C. O., *Coltrane: a Biography* (Perth Amboy, 1975)

Slonimsky, N., *Thesaurus of Scales and Melodic Patterns* (New York, 1947)

Spellman, A. B., *Four Lives in the Bebop Business* (London, 1967)

Synthophone, the MIDI Sax (Operating Manual) (Switzerland, 1987–91)

Teal, L., *The Art of Saxophone Playing* (Evanston, 1963)

　The Saxophonist's Workbook (Ann Arbor, 1958 and 1988)

Tec, R., *Who's Who in Soul Music* (London, 1991)

Thomas, J. C., *Chasin' the Trane* (New York, 1975)

Venturini, D., *Alexander Glazounov: his Life and Works* (Delphos, 1992)

Ventzke, K., *Saxophonisches Seit 1842: Fruhzeit Instrumente und Dokumente aus der saxophonhistorischen* (Düren, 1981)

Ventzke, K., and C. Raumberger, *Die Saxophone: Beiträge zu Baucharakteristik und Geschichte einer Musikinstrumentenfamilie* (Frankfurt am Main, 1979)

Walters, J. L., 'A History of Wind Synthesizers', *Sound on Sound*, 2/11 (September 1987), pp. 36–40

　'A Breath of Fresh Air, the Yamaha WX7 and the Akai EWI', *Sound on Sound*, 3/2 (December 1987), pp. 18–22

　'Akai EWI, Yamaha WX7', *Making Music*, 19 (19 October 1987), pp. 40–1

Wilmer, V., *Jazz People* (London, 1970 and 1977)

WX7 Wind Midi Controller (Owner's Manual) (Hamamatsu, 1987)

Index